SIDERIS

AF854818

Oracle Database 11g R2: Grid Infrastructure & ASM

Oracle curriculum
Database Administrator section

ISBN: 978-1-936930-15-9

AUTHOR

Sideris is the world leader in information technology (IT) courseware and training books, optimized for instructor-led, self-paced, and virtual training, as well as eBook readers.

info@sideris.com

http://www.sideris.com

+1.617.965.9800

Introduction

Objectives

- ✓ About This Course
- ✓ About The Sample Database

About This Course

Course Objectives

This training course provides a step-by-step guide for configuring and using the Oracle Grid Infrastructure in a single server environment, and it forms the basis for expanding this infrastructure to a clustered server configuration. Advanced database and storage administration tasks are considered, including Oracle Restart and Automatic Storage Management (ASM). With this course you will learn about:

- Preparing a host system for the Grid Infrastructure and Oracle RDBMS installations and performing those installations.
- Preparing a host system for ASM storage management.
- Partitioning and configuration of storage devices for ASM storage on both Linux and MS Windows servers.
- Utilizing Oracle Restart for automatic sequencing and restarting of Oracle software components.
- Obtain an introduction to Oracle High-Availability Services including the Server Control and Clusterware Control utilities.
- Review the Oracle server stack architecture including operating system virtualization and storage subsystem virtualization layers.
- Using ASM for storage of some or all database files, thereby providing a database-centric and optimized storage and volume manager.
- Exploiting ASM storage from the Database Configuration Assistant (DBCA), Database Upgrade Assistant (DBUA) and the Enterprise Manager (EM) interface.
- Administration of an ASM instance and management of ASM disk groups.
- Implement advanced storage capabilities including Intelligent Data Placement, High-capacity disk drives and access control privileges.
- Manage storage systems using the ASM Configuration Assistant (ASMCA) and the ASM command-line interface (ASMCMD).
- Migrate a database from traditional file system storage to ASM storage.
- Monitoring performance and throughput of ASM devices.

Target Audience

The primary target audiences for this course are:

- Database administrators
- Web server administrators
- System administrators
- Implementation specialists
- Data center support engineers
- Senior application designers and developers

Course Prerequisites

Many students taking this course have familiarity with system administration and administration of other non-Oracle databases, and this is helpful though not mandatory. Specific course prerequisites for this course are these Sideris titles:

- *ORACLE DATABASE 11G: SQL FUNDAMENTALS – COMPLETE LIBRARY*
- *ORACLE DATABASE 11G: PL/SQL FUNDAMENTALS – COMPLETE LIBRARY*
- *ORACLE DATABASE 11G: ADMINISTRATION I*

Suggested Next Courses

Administrators may wish to proceed onto more focused and specialized courses with these modules:

- *ORACLE DATABASE 11G: ADMINISTRATION II*
- *ORACLE DATABASE 11G: PERFORMANCE TUNING*
- *ORACLE DATABASE 11G: SQL TUNING*
- *ORACLE DATABASE 11G: PARTITIONING & PARALLEL SQL*
- *ORACLE DATABASE 11G: DATA WAREHOUSING & ORACLE WAREHOUSE BUILDER*

Certification Examination

This course covers a portion of the requirements to complete the certification test *ORACLE DATABASE 11G: CERTIFIED MASTER EXAM (OCM)*.

ILT Course Schedule

When presented as a standalone instructor-led training (ILT) live or virtual presentation, this module is scheduled for two days. It is frequently combined with other modules from the Sideris Oracle curriculum for database administrators and system implementers.

Learning Resources

Online resources and e-learning modules for this training course are available from the Sideris portal at http://www.SiderisPress.com.

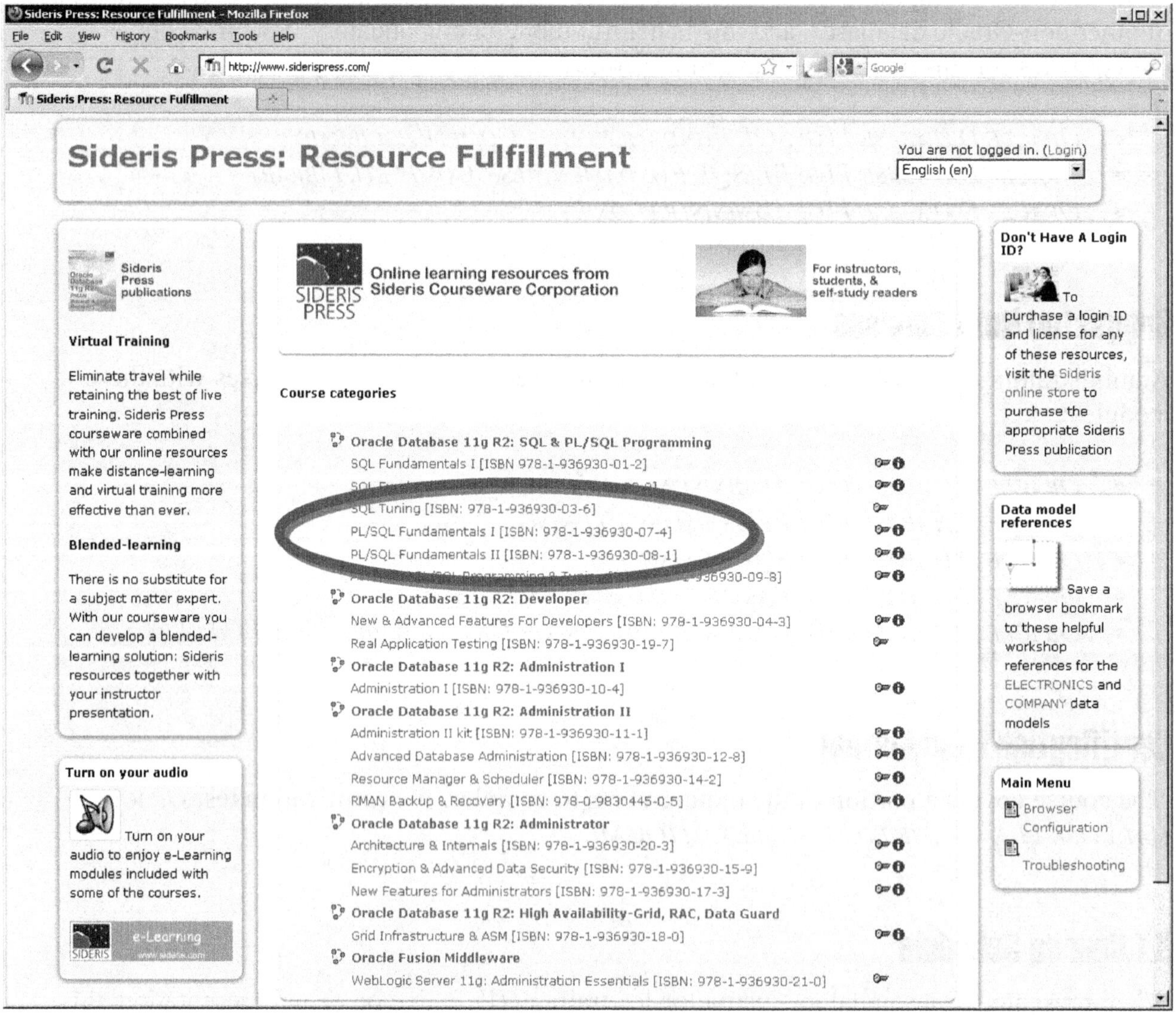

These resources from the Sideris portal may be used along with this textbook for any of the following training formats:

- Self-study – This textbook includes extensive examples and workshop solutions, allowing it to be used both on a self-study basis and as a long-term individual reference.
- Enhanced ILT – Integrate these online resources into the ILT presentations to improve the learning experience and extend beyond the traditional instructor-led training model.
- Distance-learning – Use low-cost web-based conference and training services to deliver live virtual training sessions.

Resource Files

Each course offers electronic resources useful for instructors and students. Included with these resources is a package which contains workshop files for exercises in this course. You can download these and other resources, from the appropriate course link within the Sideris portal.

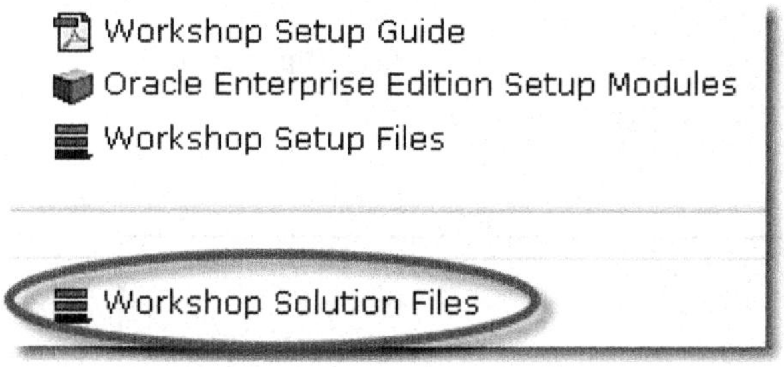

This is a summary of the resource files package available for this course module.

File	*Explanation*
CustomersAddDeleteLoop.sql	Workshop file for Section 6 – ASM Instance Administration

To access these files, visit the Sideris portal, click on the course link which corresponds to this course and login to the site.

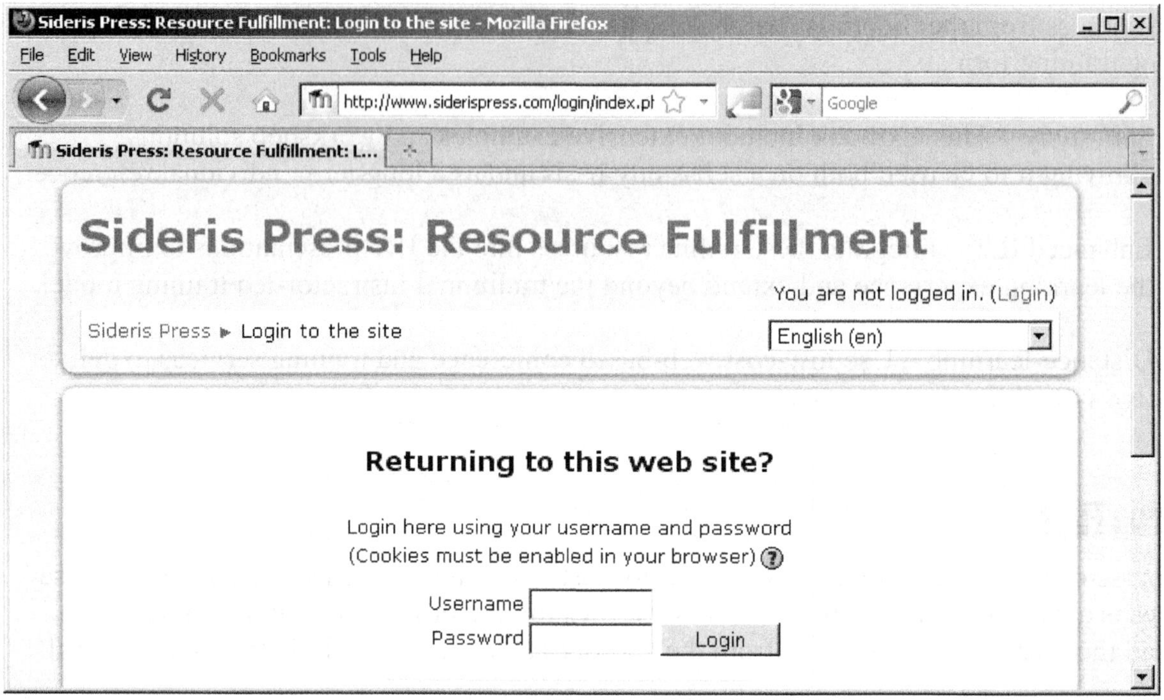

Your login credentials for this course are Username `978-1-936930-15-9` and Password `gridasm.sL312` and these should be entered when you are prompted for these.

> ***Note***
>
> Note that a variety of database instances and servers are used in the examples throughout this course. Thus, the instance names, server names, port numbers and so on, will vary. Obviously you will need to note the values for these items which are applicable to your local workshop database and consistently use these when performing the exercises yourself.

About The Sample Databases

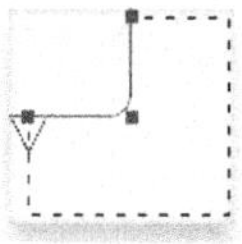

This course uses the sample data models known as the COMPANY and ELECTRONICS databases. These are highly simplified transactional data models which adequately support the objectives of the workshops without introducing unnecessary complexity. A useful description of these data models is available online from the Sideris portal.

Data model references

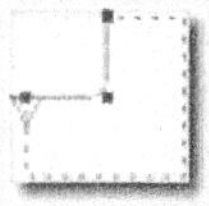

Save a browser bookmark to these helpful workshop references for the ELECTRONICS and COMPANY data models

It is usually good practice for one to reinitialize these sample databases at the start of each new workshop, unless specifically requested otherwise. The Workshop Setup Guide will provide instructions on initializing the sample databases.

Workshop Setup Guide

About The Workshop Setup

If you wish to download the Guide and complete the setup in advance of the start of the course, that may be useful. In this way you will confirm that you workshop environment is appropriate to support an Enterprise Edition installation of the Oracle database.

However, this is not necessary since a large part of this course is devoted to configuration and installation of both the Enterprise Edition of the Oracle database as well as installation of the Oracle Grid Infrastructure. Nevertheless, you should at the very least confirm that your workshop system meets the minimum requirements set forth in the Workshop Setup Guide.

Use these resources before the start of the course to configure the workshop environment

- Workshop Setup Guide
- Oracle Enterprise Edition Setup Modules
- Workshop Setup Files

Important System Requirements Note

In addition, note that for this course your host system must have a secondary disk device available for the exclusive use of the workshops. All data presently stored in that secondary device will be destroyed during the exercises of this course as the device is utilized for database storage.

Section 1
Configuring The Server For Grid Infrastructure Installation

Objectives

- ✓ What Is The Grid Infrastructure?
- ✓ Identify System Requirements
- ✓ Managing Linux Devices
- ✓ Managing MS Windows Devices
- ✓ Configure A Linux Installation

Section Overview

A fundamentally new configuration of the Oracle Installer exists when compared with older versions of the database. Part of this effort is the distinct separation of a database installation from a *grid infrastructure* installation. Within this section we will discuss these topics regarding how one prepares a host system for such an installation:

- Learn about the capabilities provided by a successful grid infrastructure installation
- Review the system requirements for such an installation
- Learn how to manage Linux devices and label these for ASM storage
- Learn how to manage MS Windows devices and stamp these for ASM storage
- Configure a Linux system for a grid infrastructure installation

Version Note

A Grid Infrastructure installation is available starting with Oracle 11g Release 2 (R2).

What Is The Grid Infrastructure?

In earlier releases of the database the Automatic Storage Management (ASM) volume manager was optionally installed as part of the database installation. This has now been separated into a separate grid infrastructure installation which includes these components:

- Automatic Storage Management – enhanced from earlier releases but otherwise similar to what has existed within the overall Oracle architecture.

- Listener – the Oracle database instance listener, initially provided for access to the ASM instance.

- Oracle Restart – a facility which provides for automatic restart of all Oracle software instances and related software components.

- Oracle Clusterware – system area network (SAN) cluster node communication and management software for an Oracle Real Application Cluster (RAC) configuration.

Note

It is recommended that the Grid Infrastructure Installation be performed before a database installation. While this is not mandatory, the setup is far more seamless and automatic when performed in this order. This section is based upon the recommended sequence of a Grid Infrastructure Installation followed by an Oracle database installation on a new, standalone server.

Identify System Requirements

The following system requirements exist as a practical minimum for installation of the grid infrastructure.

System Resource	*Recommended Requirements*
Physical memory	A minimum of 1 GB of RAM.
Virtual memory	The required swap space configuration required for the server will depend upon the amount of physical memory. These are the recommended guidelines: • Physical memory between 1 and 2 GB – swap space should be 1.5 times physical memory • Physical memory 2 8 GB – swap space should be equal to physical memory.
Disk space	Disk space requirements are as follows: • Temporary system disk space: 1 GB + • Grid infrastructure software disk space: 2.5 GB +
Processor speed	2 GHz or greater. In a large scale production environment, multiprocessing systems offer substantial performance benefits.
Processor architecture	On an MS Windows platform a grid infrastructure installation is only supported on a 64-bit processor running the 64-bit version of MS Windows. Either a 32-bit or 64-bit architecture is suitable on a Linux platform.

Note

These requirements apply solely to the grid infrastructure installation. They are in excess of what exists for a subsequent database installation that will be performed on the same system.

ASM Storage

There will be one or more disk devices available on any server which may be used for a variety of purposes. These might include serving as the boot device, providing swap space and temporary storage for the operating system, as well as running the operating system itself.

In addition one must have secondary storage space available from which ASM candidate disks and ASM storage may be configured. The following are common options from which such space may be obtained:

- The most sophisticated and costly option is the use of a storage subsystem. Oracle Corporation provides one such product in the form of the Oracle Exadata Storage Server. Other vendors such as EMC and IBM offer comparable products.

- At the other end of the spectrum, one could configure such space using something as simple as a USB-connected external disk. Such devices would also need to be compatible with the host operating system.

- While it is a potentially dangerous task, one could carefully configure ASM storage from un-partitioned space left over from the primary disk devices used for the operating system. This option is not generally recommended, although it is certainly possible.

ASM Candidate Disks

In order to successfully install ASM and the larger grid infrastructure, one must prepare available storage for use by ASM as part of the prerequisite system configuration.

During the installation one selects disks from a set of ASM *candidates* for inclusion into that storage framework. In order for a disk to be a candidate for ASM, it must undergo the following procedure:

1. There must be unformatted partitions available on the device
2. Once formatted, a partition must be *labeled* or *stamped* for ASM

We will demonstrate how this is done in advance of the actual installation.

Managing Linux Devices

A hard disk is a physical device used for storage. It may be segmented into logical devices known as *partitions*. When first configuring the Linux operating system, it is useful to leave some disk space or devices un-partitioned so that such logical devices may be created later as needed.

About Linux Devices

The following brief explanation about Linux disk devices is helpful to consider when contemplating the assignment of ASM storage:

- Small Computer System Interface (SCSI) devices appear as `/dev/sd*`
- Integrated Drive Electronics (IDE) devices appear as `/dev/hd*`
- A major identifier is used to refer to an entire disk, such as `/dev/sda`
- A minor identifier is used to refer to a partition on a disk, such as `/dev/sda1`, `/dev/sda2`

IDE Devices & Partitions

Notice in this example the IDE devices and partitions available on a particular system.

```
[administrator@siderislab2 ~]$ ls -l /dev/hda*
brw-r----- 1 root disk 3, 0 Apr 21 11:29 /dev/hda
brw-r----- 1 root disk 3, 1 Apr 21 11:30 /dev/hda1
brw-r----- 1 root disk 3, 2 Apr 21 12:55 /dev/hda2
brw-r----- 1 root disk 3, 3 Apr 21 11:29 /dev/hda3
```

We might be interested in the size of each device and partition.

```
[administrator@siderislab2 ~]$ cat /proc/partitions
major minor  #blocks  name

   3     0   78150744 hda
   3     1     104391 hda1
   3     2    1020127 hda2
   3     3   77023642 hda3
 253     0   74907648 dm-0
 253     1    2097152 dm-1
```

SCSI Devices & Partitions

Similar information is obtained for SCSI devices on another system.

```
[administrator@siderislab4 ~]$ ls -l /dev/sd*
brw-r----- 1 root disk 8,  0 Apr 23 11:32 /dev/sda
brw-r----- 1 root disk 8,  1 Apr 23 11:32 /dev/sda1
brw-r----- 1 root disk 8,  2 Apr 23 11:32 /dev/sda2
brw-r----- 1 root disk 8,  3 Apr 23 15:32 /dev/sda3
brw-r----- 1 root disk 8,  4 Apr 23 11:32 /dev/sda4
brw-r----- 1 root disk 8,  5 Apr 23 11:32 /dev/sda5
brw-r----- 1 root disk 8, 16 Apr 27 20:10 /dev/sdb
brw-r----- 1 root disk 8, 17 Apr 27 20:10 /dev/sdb1

[administrator@siderislab4 ~]$ cat /proc/partitions
major minor  #blocks  name

   8     0  244140625 sda
   8     1      56196 sda1
   8     2    2104515 sda2
   8     3     104422 sda3
   8     4          1 sda4
   8     5  241874608 sda5
 253     0  237731840 dm-0
 253     1    4128768 dm-1
   8    16    2000880 sdb
   8    17    1999749 sdb1
```

Note

One may also find Redundant Array of Independent Disks (RAID) configurations, which may also be used.

Partitioning A Device

Once one has identified an un-partitioned device which could be designated as an ASM candidate, then it must be partitioned.

Using fdisk

The `fdisk` command will allow one to partition available space on a disk device, in preparation for labeling that partition as an ASM candidate device.

```
[administrator@siderislab4 ~]$ su -
Password: ***********
[root@siderislab4 ~]# fdisk /dev/sda5
Device contains neither a valid DOS partition table, nor Sun, SGI or OSF
disklabel
Building a new DOS disklabel. Changes will remain in memory only,
until you decide to write them. After that, of course, the previous
content won't be recoverable.

The number of cylinders for this disk is set to 30111.
There is nothing wrong with that, but this is larger than 1024,
and could in certain setups cause problems with:
1) software that runs at boot time (e.g., old versions of LILO)
2) booting and partitioning software from other OSs
   (e.g., DOS FDISK, OS/2 FDISK)
Warning: invalid flag 0x0000 of partition table 4 will be corrected by w(rite)
```

A variety of commands are available for use of this utility. One could list these with the "menu" command:

```
Command (m for help): m
Command action
   a   toggle a bootable flag
   b   edit bsd disklabel
   c   toggle the dos compatibility flag
   d   delete a partition
   l   list known partition types
   m   print this menu
   n   add a new partition
   o   create a new empty DOS partition table
   p   print the partition table
   q   quit without saving changes
   s   create a new empty Sun disklabel
   t   change a partition's system id
   u   change display/entry units
   v   verify the partition table
   w   write table to disk and exit
   x   extra functionality (experts only)
```

One can verify available space using the "verify" command.

```
Command (m for help): v
483749216 unallocated sectors
```

Having confirmed that available space exists, the "new" command creates a partition on the disk. One can create up to 4 primary partitions, and additional unallocated space may be used by creating a sub-partition within one of the primary partitions, known as an *extended* partition. In terms of ASM-suitable partitions, one should create a primary partition comprising the entire device.

```
Command (m for help): n
Command action
   e   extended
   p   primary partition (1-4)
p
Partition number (1-4): 1
First cylinder (1-30111, default 1): 1
Last cylinder or +size or +sizeM or +sizeK (1-30111, default 30111): 30111

Command (m for help): w
The partition table has been altered!
Calling ioctl() to re-read partition table.
Syncing disks.

[root@siderislab4 ~]#
```

Note

ASM is not always stable when using partitions which consume a portion of a disk device. It is recommended that a single partition for the entire disk be used.

Oracle ASMLib

Oracle ASMLib is a support library required for the administration of ASM on a Linux platform. Its corresponding packages must be downloaded from Oracle Corporation and installed in order for one to have access to the `oracleasm` utility. The following packages are required:

- oracleasmlib – primary package for the library
- oracleasm-support – support package
- oracleasm-x.x.x – kernel driver package

As of this writing, the current version is ASMLib 2.0

Installing The Appropriate Packages

One must locate and download the appropriate packages which match the hardware processor architecture and kernel on which the host system is based. There are literally dozens of variations of the ASMLib packages to match the Linux distributions and hardware platforms.

One begins by determining the Linux kernel and the hardware processor by means of the `uname` command.

```
# uname -rm
2.6.18-128.el5 i686
```

Using this information, one must download the oracleasmlib and oracleasm-support packages appropriate for the hardware architecture, and the oracleasmlib and associated packages appropriate for the Linux kernel. Once these have been downloaded, then they are installed using the `rpm` utility.

```
# cd /home/grid/Desktop
# ls oracleasm*
oracleasm-2.6.18-128.el5-2.0.5-1.el5.i686.rpm
oracleasmlib-2.0.4-1.el5.i386.rpm
oracleasm-support-2.1.3-1.el5.i386.rpm

# rpm -Uvh oracleasmlib-2.0.4-1.el5.i386.rpm \
           oracleasm-support-2.1.3-1.el5.i386.rpm \
           oracleasm-2.6.18-128.el5-debuginfo-2.0.5-1.el5.i686.rpm \
           oracleasm-2.6.18-128.el5-2.0.5-1.el5.i686.rpm

warning: oracleasmlib-2.0.4-1.el5.i386.rpm: Header V3 DSA signature: NOKEY,
key ID 1e5e0159
Preparing...                ########################################### [100%]
   1:oracleasm-support      ########################################### [ 25%]
   2:oracleasm-2.6.18-128.el########################################### [ 50%]
   3:oracleasmlib           ########################################### [ 75%]
   4:oracleasm-2.6.18-128.el########################################### [100%]
```

Configure oracleasm

With the oracleasm utility installed, one can configure the library driver. Using the –i option, one specifies the user and group which owns the interface, and whether or not the utility should automatically be started after system reboot.

```
[root@siderislab4 Desktop]# oracleasm configure -i
Configuring the Oracle ASM library driver.

This will configure the on-boot properties of the Oracle ASM library
driver.  The following questions will determine whether the driver is
loaded on boot and what permissions it will have.  The current values
will be shown in brackets ('[]').  Hitting <ENTER> without typing an
answer will keep that current value.  Ctrl-C will abort.

Default user to own the driver interface []: grid
Default group to own the driver interface []: asmadmin
Start Oracle ASM library driver on boot (y/n) [n]: y
Scan for Oracle ASM disks on boot (y/n) [y]: y
Writing Oracle ASM library driver configuration: done
```

Next, one initializes the library. It now functions as a virtualized storage system.

```
[root@siderislab4 Desktop]# oracleasm init
Creating /dev/oracleasm mount point: /dev/oracleasm
Loading module "oracleasm": oracleasm
Mounting ASMlib driver filesystem: /dev/oracleasm
```

Label A Disk For ASM

Most importantly, one must place an ASM label on a properly partitioned and configured device. The device will now be an ASM candidate disk. Notice these elements of the `createdisk` command:

- Assign a label to the candidate disk, which is DATA1 in our example
- Specify the path of the device which has been partitioned for use by ASM

```
[root@siderislab4 Desktop]# oracleasm createdisk DATA1 /dev/sda5
Writing disk header: done
Instantiating disk: done
[root@siderislab4 Desktop]#
```

Additional Commands

A variety of other commands are available with facility. For instance, one could obtain a status of the storage system driver.

```
# oracleasm status
Checking if ASM is loaded: yes
Checking if /dev/oracleasm is mounted: yes
```

One could also obtain a list of all devices configured for ASM storage.

```
[root@siderislab4 ~]# oracleasm listdisks
DATA
DATA1
DATA2
```

Managing MS Windows Devices

One must likewise partition available devices for later designation as an ASM candidate device when using the MS Windows platform.

Disk Partition

Define a disk partition using the Microsoft-supplied tool DISKPART. Using an administrator account, one would first launch the utility.

```
C:\> DiskPart
Microsoft DiskPart version 5.1.3565
Copyright (C) 1999-2003 Microsoft Corporation.
On computer: SIDERISLAB9

DISKPART>
```

Caution!

This next step will destroy all existing data on the disk device specified, so one will need to make the appropriate adjustments before proceeding.

Partition The Disk

One must next select the disk to be prepared for ASM, destroy all existing data, and create the partition. This would be repeated for each disk to be used.

```
DISKPART> select disk 2
Disk 1 is now the selected disk.

DISKPART> clean
DiskPart succeeded in cleaning the disk.

DISKPART> create partition primary size=1700
DiskPart succeeded in creating the specified partition.

DISKPART> list disk

  Disk ###  Status      Size     Free     Dyn  Gpt
  --------  ----------  -------  -------  ---  ---
  Disk 1    Online        17 GB      0 B
  Disk 2    Online        80 GB      0 B
  Disk 3    Online        60 GB      0 B
```

Finally one must assign a device letter or mount point to the device.

```
DISKPART> list volume

Volume ###  Ltr  Label        Fs     Type        Size     Status     Info
----------  ---  -----------  -----  ----------  -------  ---------  --------
Volume 0     E                       CD-ROM          0 B
Volume 1     C   LabDisk2a    NTFS   Partition     17 GB  Healthy    System
Volume 2                             Partition   1004 MB  Healthy

DISKPART> select volume 2
Volume 2 is the selected volume.

DISKPART> assign
DiskPart successfully assigned the drive letter or mount point.

DISKPART> list volume

Volume ###  Ltr  Label        Fs     Type        Size     Status     Info
----------  ---  -----------  -----  ----------  -------  ---------  --------
Volume 0     E                       CD-ROM          0 B
Volume 1     C   LabDisk2a    NTFS   Partition     17 GB  Healthy    System
*Volume 2    D                       Partition   1004 MB  Healthy

DISKPART> exit
Leaving DiskPart...

C:\>
```

Stamp Disk With ASMTOOL

The Oracle-supplied `asmtool` may be launched from the Installer by clicking on the Stamp Disks... button. It will label a candidate disk for ASM.

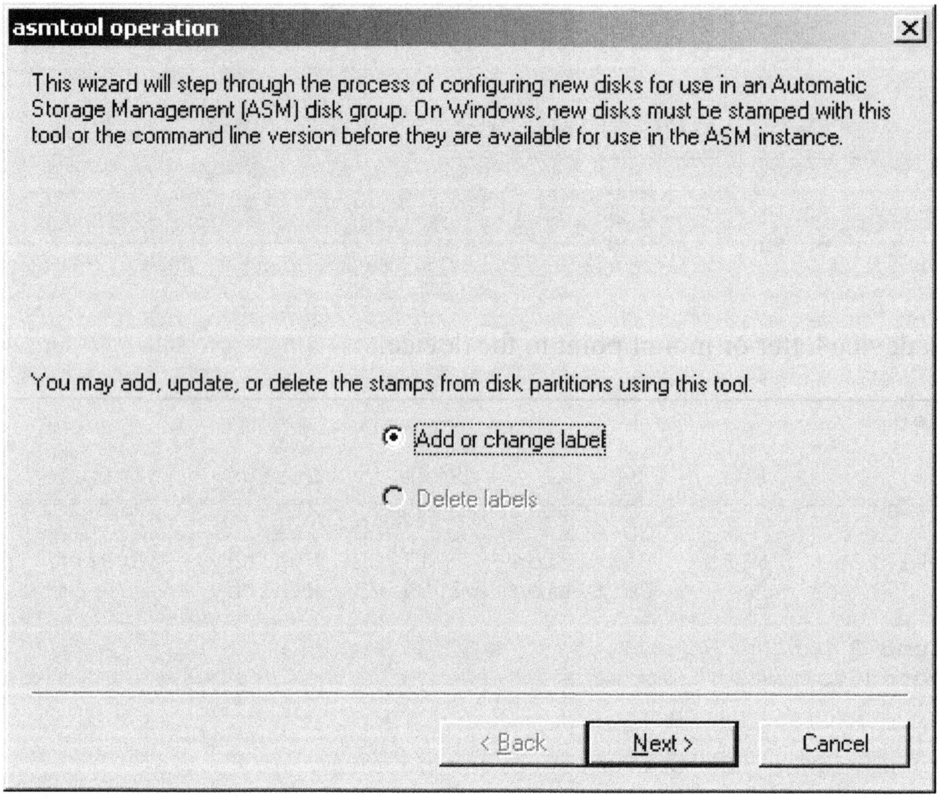

If a disk has not been stamped with an ASM-compliant header, select the Add Or Change Label option. If it has already been done and one wishes to change the label, then the Delete Labels option would first be selected.

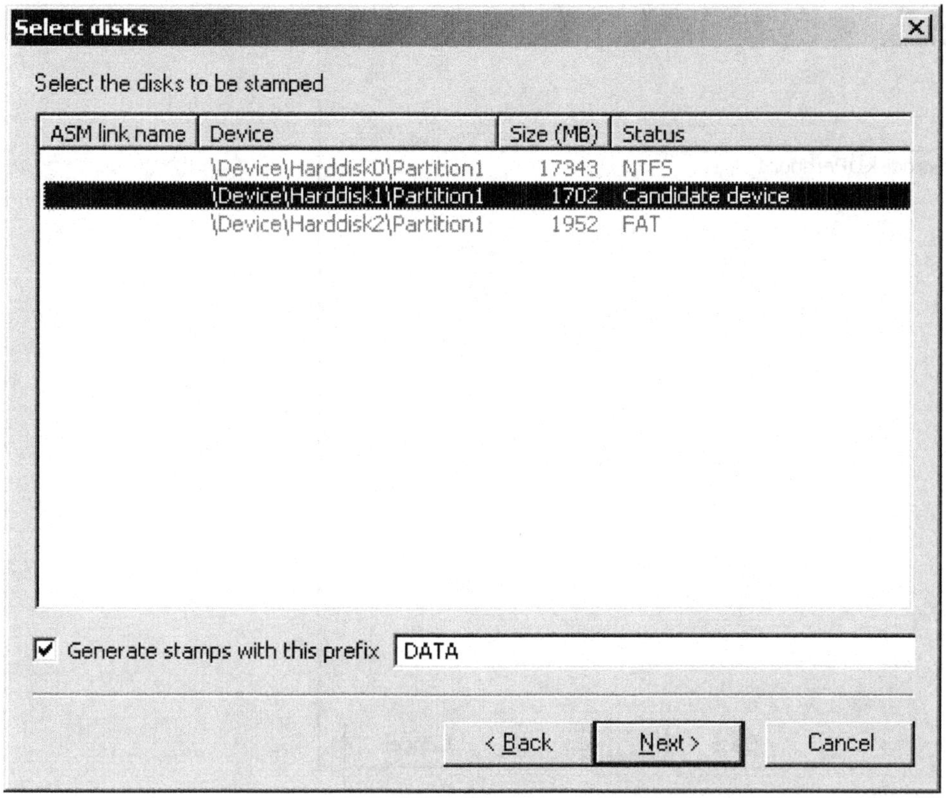

Of all available devices on the host system, one should select the devices to be stamped. The format of the label will be "ORCLDISK", followed by the prefix assigned on this screen, followed by a sequential number given to each device.

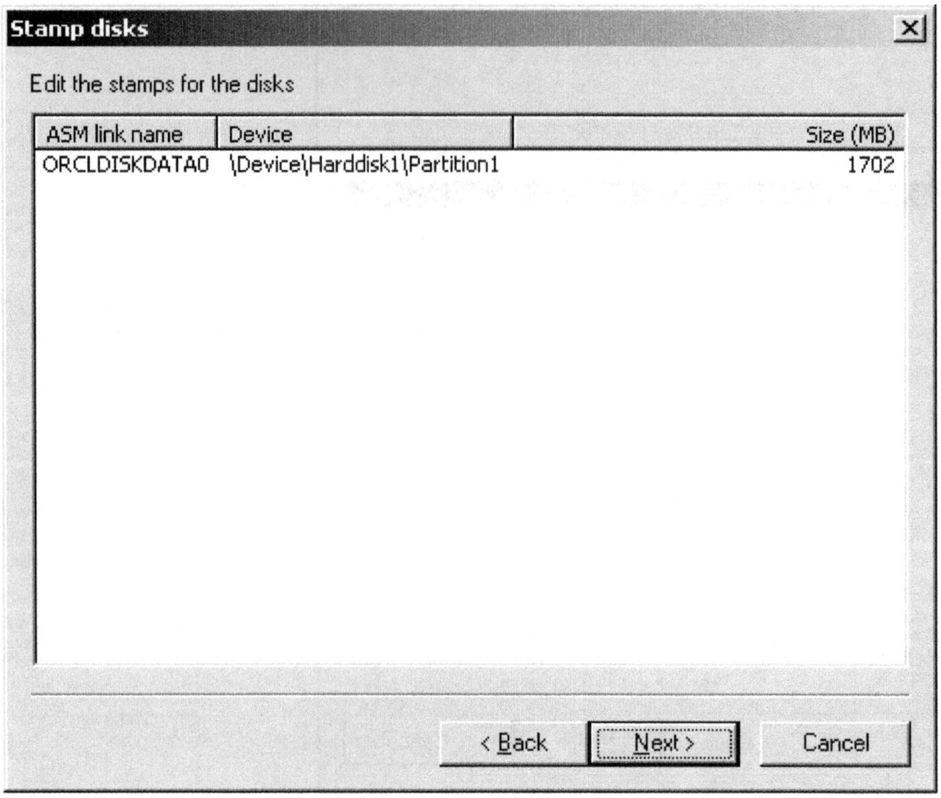

Using the label format described above, the actual label for each device is listed. One could customize a label for an individual disk by clicking in the ASM Link Name item. Otherwise, simply click the Next> button to complete the process.

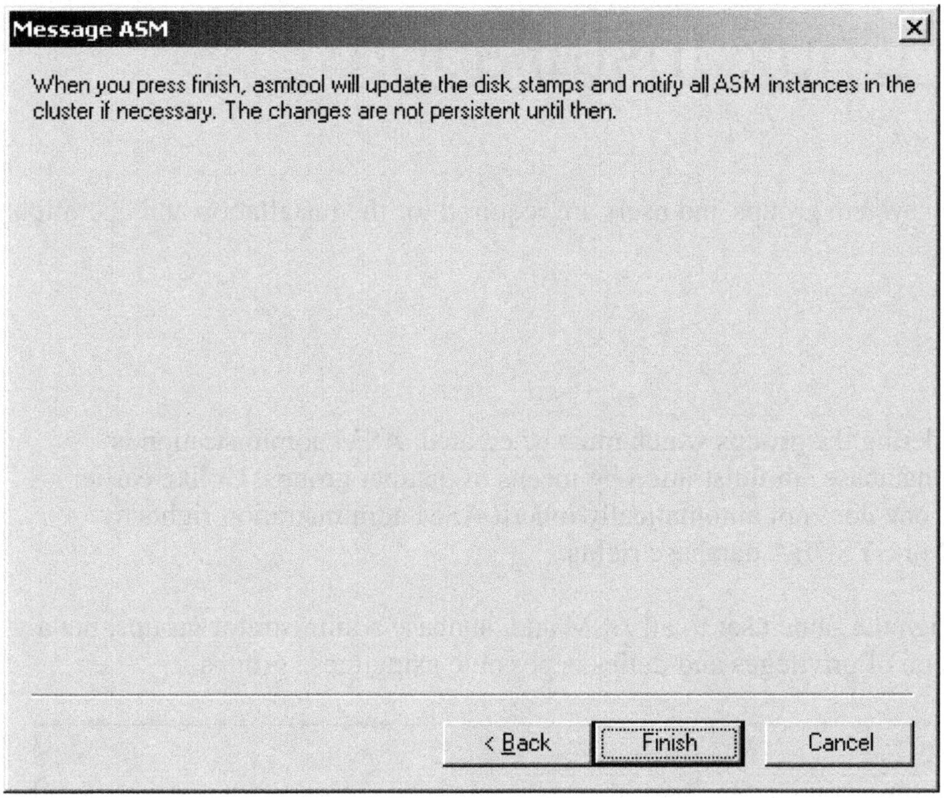

Click the Finish button and all selected devices will be stamped with the ASM label. These devices should now appear as candidate disks to the ASM installation.

Command-line asmtool

Alternately one could launch the "asmtool" utility directly from the command-line and assign the labels using the –add option. The set of available disk devices is visible using the –list option.

```
C:\> asmtool -add \device\Harddisk1\Partition1 ORCLDISKasm1
C:\> asmtool -add \device\Harddisk2\Partition1 ORCLDISKasm2
C:\> asmtool -add \device\Harddisk3\Partition1 ORCLDISKasm3
C:\> asmtool -list
        NTFS                \Device\Harddisk0\Partition1     17343M
        ORCLDISKasm1        \Device\Harddisk1\Partition1     1702M
        ORCLDISKasm2        \Device\Harddisk2\Partition1     17343M
        ORCLDISKasm3        \Device\Harddisk3\Partition1     17343M
C:\>
```

Configure Linux Installation

A set of operating system groups and users are required for the installation and operation of the grid infrastructure.

Begin by considering the groups which must be created. ASM administration is carefully separated from database administration by means of distinct groups. Unlike earlier versions of the database, one does not automatically inherit ASM administration rights by obtaining the SYSOPER or SYSDBA database rights.

Of course, one could assign the same user to all ASM and database administrator groups, but a more sophisticated division of privileges and duties is possible using these groups.

Group name	***Explanation***
asmadmin	Corresponds to the generic OSASM role – The purpose of this role is to distinguish ASM super administrator rights from SYSDBA database super administrator rights. Members of the OSASM role have full rights to ASM instances and to its storage administration. One can create and drop disk groups, manage individual devices within the groups, and so on. No rights are acquired to the database instance with this role.
asmdba	Corresponds to the generic OSDBA role – used by Oracle Restart for rights to start the database and ASM instances, among other components. It also provides access rights to the ASM files. This may be the same group as the OSDBA role for the database installation.
asmoper	Corresponds to the generic OSOPER role – This is an optional role not required for the installation but useful if one wishes to allow a subset of `asmdba` operations, similar to the manner in which SYSOPER provides a subset of SYSDBA rights for the database. Basically ASMOPER may start and stop an ASM instance, but otherwise is limited in what other administration tasks may be performed.

oinstall	Like a database installation, the grid infrastructure software components are recorded within the Oracle inventory for the server. This group must be defined if it does not already exist as a result of earlier Oracle software installations. Members of this group may install, deinstall and upgrade the binaries for an installation.

In addition, the following users are configured in advance of the installation.

User name	***Explanation***
grid	This user owns the Oracle Grid Infrastructure software installation. The primary group must be `oinstall` and it must secondarily be part of the `asmdba` and `asmadmin` groups.
oracle	This user owns the Oracle database installation. The primary group must be `oinstall` and it must secondarily be part of the `sysdba` and `sysoper` groups.

Note

It is not mandatory that the Grid Infrastructure and the Oracle database installations be owned by two different users, such as `grid` and `oracle` in our scenario above. One could have a single account own both installations if desired.

Defining The Groups & Users

One can list the groups and users which currently exist by means of the following commands respectively:

```
# cat /etc/group
...

# cat /etc/passwd
...
```

The following groups and users must next be created, if they do not already exist.

```
[administrator@siderislab4 ~]$ su -
Password: *******
# /usr/sbin/groupadd -g 520 oinstall
# /usr/sbin/groupadd -g 525 asmdba
# /usr/sbin/groupadd -g 530 asmoper
# /usr/sbin/groupadd -g 535 asmadmin
# /usr/sbin/useradd -u 1000 -g oinstall -G asmdba,asmadmin,asmoper grid
# passwd grid
Changing password for user grid.
New UNIX password:  ********
Retype new UNIX password: *******
passwd: all authentication tokens updated successfully.
#
```

Configure ORACLE_BASE Physical Directory

Define the ORACLE_BASE directory and assign appropriate ownership and permissions to the software owner account.

```
# mkdir -p  /u01/app/grid
# chown -R grid:oinstall /u01/app/grid
# chmod -R 775 /u01/app/grid
```

From this base directory the Installer will determine the ORACLE_HOME for the installation.

> *Note*
>
> Each software installation owner, such as `grid` and `oracle`, must have its own ORACLE_BASE directory.

Configure Oracle Inventory Physical Directory

Define the Oracle inventory directory and likewise assign appropriate ownership and permissions to the software owner account.

```
# mkdir -p  /u01/app/oraInventory
# chown -R grid:oinstall /u01/app/oraInventory
# chmod -R 775 /u01/app/oraInventory
```

Section Review

Remember These Points

- The Grid Infrastructure framework includes ASM, the listener, Oracle Restart and Oracle Clusterware.
- A Grid Infrastructure installation should generally precede a database installation.
- The Grid Infrastructure and the database installations may be owned by different system accounts or the same account.
- The ASMLib library includes the oracleasm utility which creates a storage virtualization layer on the host system.
- ASM candidate disks must be partitioned and labeled (stamped) to be recognized by ASM.
- ASM administration is segmented by the asmadmin, asmdba and asmoper roles.

Workshop Section
Configuring The Server For Grid Infrastructure Installation

Exercises

What You Will Do in This Workshop

In this workshop, you will:

- Confirm that your host system meets the basic system requirements for a Grid Infrastructure installation.
- Configure your host system to prepare for an installation of the Grid Infrastructure.
- Configure your storage devices for ASM usage.

> ***Note***
>
> This workshop assumes the Linux operating system is in use. You will need to make appropriate adjustments to complete this exercise on other platforms.

CONFIGURATION-1

❑ Confirm the following attributes for the host system on which you will perform the installation, and ensure that these meet the requirements.

- Operating system platform
- Processor speed
- Physical memory
- Virtual memory
- Available disk space

CONFIGURATION-2

❑ In this exercise you will examine the devices accessible to the server and partition one for use by ASM.

CONFIGURATION-3

❑ In this exercise you must locate the appropriate packages required for installation of the ASMLib library on your server. Thereafter, you will need to download these from the Oracle Corporation support web site and install these on your local system.

CONFIGURATION-4

❑ Our next step is to create the users, groups and directories which are necessary for a Grid Infrastructure installation and a subsequent database installation.

There are several different scenarios by which one could accomplish this task. In the lecture section we discussed having an account named grid own the Grid Infrastructure installation and another named oracle owning the database installation. While there are merits to such a configuration, within this workshop we will suggest that a single account named oracle own both installations.

Towards that end, create the account now and assign the oinstall group as the primary group for the account with the asmdba, asmadmin and asmoper groups as secondary.

CONFIGURATION-5

❑ Configure the ORACLE_BASE and Oracle Inventory physical directories, setting appropriate ownership and permissions for these locations.

CONFIGURATION-6

❑ With the ASMLib library installed on your system, launch the utility and configure the library driver. Thereafter, initialize the library and then use the library to label the designated device as an ASM candidate disk.

Solutions

CONFIGURATION-1

Begin this exercise by obtaining the Linux distribution and kernel providing the operating system for your server. This is not only necessary for this exercise but will be important information for completing a later exercise of this workshop.

```
[administrator@siderislab4 ~]$ cat /proc/version
Linux version 2.6.18-194.el5xen (mockbuild@ca-build10.us.oracle.com) (gcc
version 4.1.2 20080704 (Red Hat 4.1.2-48)) #1 SMP Mon Mar 29

[administrator@siderislab4 ~]$ uname -rm
2.6.18-194.el5xen i686
```

Proceed to check the memory, swap space and disk space available from this system.

```
[administrator@siderislab4 ~]$ grep MemTotal /proc/meminfo
MemTotal:       1810432 kB

[administrator@siderislab4 ~]$ grep SwapTotal /proc/meminfo
SwapTotal:      4128760 kB

[administrator@siderislab4 ~]$ free
             total       used       free     shared    buffers     cached
Mem:       1810432    1781268      29164          0     109508    1176364
-/+ buffers/cache:     495396    1315036
Swap:      4128760        244    4128516

[administrator@siderislab4 ~]$ df -k /dev/shm
Filesystem           1K-blocks      Used Available Use% Mounted on
tmpfs                   905304    282572    622732  32% /dev/shm

[administrator@siderislab4 ~]$ df -k
Filesystem           1K-blocks      Used Available Use% Mounted on
/dev/mapper/VolGroup00-LogVol00
                     230286224  36329644 182069988  17% /
/dev/sda3               101105     19288     76596  21% /boot
tmpfs                   905304    282572    622732  32% /dev/shm
none                    905216       104    905112   1% /var/lib/xenstored
```

CONFIGURATION-2

Look for IDE devices. In this case since there are none, we will try SCSI devices.

```
[administrator@siderislab4 ~]$ ls -l /dev/hda*
ls: /dev/hda*: No such file or directory
```

Examine SCSI devices. We find both a primary and a very small secondary disk. We will partition the secondary disk for use by ASM.

```
[administrator@siderislab4 ~]$ ls -l /dev/sd*

brw-r----- 1 root disk 8,  0 Jun 11 12:46 /dev/sda
brw-r----- 1 root disk 8,  1 Jun 11 12:46 /dev/sda1
brw-r----- 1 root disk 8,  2 Jun 11 12:46 /dev/sda2
brw-r----- 1 root disk 8,  3 Jun 11 16:46 /dev/sda3
brw-r----- 1 root disk 8,  4 Jun 11 12:46 /dev/sda4
brw-r----- 1 root disk 8,  5 Jun 11 12:46 /dev/sda5
brw-r----- 1 root disk 8, 16 Jun 11 16:49 /dev/sdb
brw-r----- 1 root disk 8, 17 Jun 11 16:49 /dev/sdb1

[administrator@siderislab4 ~]$ cat /proc/partitions
major minor  #blocks  name

   8     0  244140625 sda
   8     1      56196 sda1
   8     2    2104515 sda2
   8     3     104422 sda3
   8     4          1 sda4
   8     5  241874608 sda5
 253     0  153583616 dm-0
 253     1    4128768 dm-1
   8    16     244766 sdb
   8    17     244720 sdb1
```

From a root account, launch the `fdisk` utility on the appropriate device and verify that unallocated space is available for partitioning.

```
[administrator@siderislab4 ~]$ su -
Password: ***********
[root@siderislab4 ~]# fdisk /dev/sdb1
Device contains neither a valid DOS partition table, nor Sun, SGI or OSF
disklabel
Building a new DOS disklabel. Changes will remain in memory only,
until you decide to write them. After that, of course, the previous
content won't be recoverable.

The number of cylinders for this disk is set to 30111.
There is nothing wrong with that, but this is larger than 1024,
and could in certain setups cause problems with:
1) software that runs at boot time (e.g., old versions of LILO)
2) booting and partitioning software from other OSs
   (e.g., DOS FDISK, OS/2 FDISK)
Warning: invalid flag 0x0000 of partition table 4 will be corrected by w(rite)

Command (m for help): v
489439 unallocated sectors
```

While still running the `fdisk` program, create a new primary partition using all available storage and then exit the utility.

```
Command (m for help): n
Command action
   e   extended
   p   primary partition (1-4)
p
Partition number (1-4): 1
First cylinder (1-30111, default 1): 1
Last cylinder or +size or +sizeM or +sizeK (1-30111, default 30111): 30111

Command (m for help): w
The partition table has been altered!
Calling ioctl() to re-read partition table.
Syncing disks.

[root@siderislab4 ~]# exit
[administrator@siderislab4 ~]$
```

CONFIGURATION-3

The specific packages used in our solution may be different in your installation. Be sure to make whatever changes are appropriate based upon the results produced by your environment.

Navigate to the Oracle Corporation support site where the ASMLib downloads are located. In order to locate the appropriate packages, you will need the following information:

1. Your operating system distribution, e.g. Red Hat Enterprise Linux 4 or 5, SuSE Linux Enterprise Server 10 or 11, etc.
2. The hardware architecture upon which your host system is based. Examples are AMD64 / Intel em64T, Intel IA64, Intel IA32 (x86), and so on.
3. Your Linux kernel.

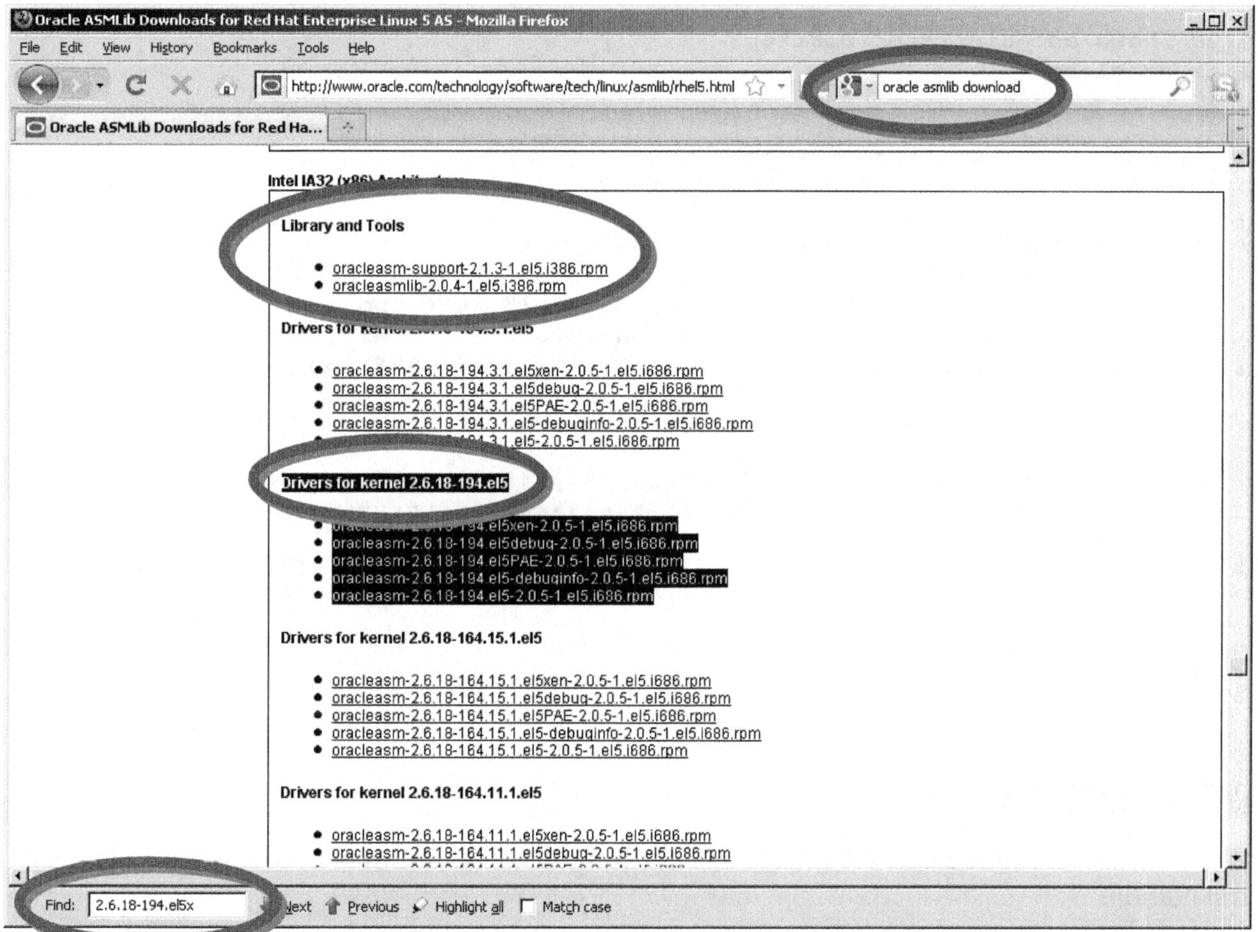

This browser screen sample demonstrates how one would navigate to the appropriate Oracle Corporation support download links for ASMLib. The particular links highlighted in this screen pertain to the Red Hat Linux 5 distribution, with a server using the Intel x86 processor architecture, and the Linux kernel 2.16.18-194.el5.

Based upon this research, download the following packages:

- `oracleasmlib` and `oracleasm-support` generic packages appropriate for your hardware architecture.

- `oracleasm` and `oracleasm-*-debuginfo` packages appropriate for your kernel.

Assuming that these were downloaded to the Desktop using an account named "administrator", launch a terminal session and login as the root user to install these packages.

```
[administrator@siderislab4 ~]$ su -
Password: ***********

# cd /home/administrator/Desktop
# ls oracleasm*
oracleasm-2.6.18-194.el5-2.0.5-1.el5.i686.rpm
oracleasm-2.6.18-194.el5-debuginfo-2.0.5-1.el5.i686.rpm
oracleasmlib-2.0.4-1.el5.i386.rpm
oracleasm-support-2.1.3-1.el5.i386.rpm

# rpm -Uvh oracleasmlib-2.0.4-1.el5.i386.rpm \
          oracleasm-support-2.1.3-1.el5.i386.rpm \
          oracleasm-2.6.18-194.el5-2.0.5-1.el5.i686.rpm \
          oracleasm-2.6.18-194.el5-debuginfo-2.0.5-1.el5.i686.rpm \
          oracleasm-2.6.18-194.el5PAE-2.0.5-1.el5.i686.rpm

warning: oracleasmlib-2.0.4-1.el5.i386.rpm: Header V3 DSA signature: NOKEY,
key ID 1e5e0159
Preparing...                ########################################### [100%]
   1:oracleasm-support      ########################################### [ 25%]
   2:oracleasm-2.6.18-194.el########################################### [ 50%]
   3:oracleasmlib           ########################################### [ 75%]
   4:oracleasm-2.6.18-194.el########################################### [100%]

[root@siderislab4 Desktop] #
```

CONFIGURATION-4

From the root account create the groups and software installation owner accounts needed for the installation.

```
[administrator@siderislab4 ~]$ su -
Password: *******
# /usr/sbin/groupadd -g 520 oinstall
# /usr/sbin/groupadd -g 525 asmdba
# /usr/sbin/groupadd -g 530 asmoper
# /usr/sbin/groupadd -g 535 asmadmin
# /usr/sbin/useradd -u 1000 -g oinstall -G asmdba,asmadmin,asmoper oracle
# passwd oracle
Changing password for user oracle.
New UNIX password:  ********
Retype new UNIX password: *******
passwd: all authentication tokens updated successfully.
#
```

CONFIGURATION-5

First configure the ORACLE_BASE directory.

```
# mkdir -p  /u01/app/oracle
# chown -R oracle:oinstall /u01/app/oracle
# chmod -R 775 /u01/app/oracle
```

Next configure Oracle Inventory directory in a similar manner.

```
# mkdir -p  /u01/app/oraInventory
# chown -R oracle:oinstall /u01/app/oraInventory
# chmod -R 775 /u01/app/oraInventory
```

CONFIGURATION-6

Having installed the library we should now be able to configure it for this system.

```
[root@siderislab4 Desktop]# oracleasm configure -i
Configuring the Oracle ASM library driver.

This will configure the on-boot properties of the Oracle ASM library
driver.  The following questions will determine whether the driver is
loaded on boot and what permissions it will have.  The current values
will be shown in brackets ('[]').  Hitting <ENTER> without typing an
answer will keep that current value.  Ctrl-C will abort.

Default user to own the driver interface []: oracle
Default group to own the driver interface []: asmadmin
Start Oracle ASM library driver on boot (y/n) [n]: y
Scan for Oracle ASM disks on boot (y/n) [y]: y
Writing Oracle ASM library driver configuration: done
```

With the configuration recorded, initialize the library.

```
[root@siderislab4 Desktop]# oracleasm init
Creating /dev/oracleasm mount point: /dev/oracleasm
Loading module "oracleasm": oracleasm
Mounting ASMlib driver filesystem: /dev/oracleasm
```

With the library initialized, label the designated disk as an ASM candidate disk. Thereafter, confirm that the disk is in fact accessible to the ASM storage system.

```
[root@siderislab4 Desktop]# oracleasm createdisk DATA1 /dev/sdb1
Writing disk header: done
Instantiating disk: done
[root@siderislab4 Desktop]#

[root@siderislab4 Desktop]# oracleasm listdisks
DATA1

[root@siderislab4 Desktop]#
```

Section 2
Grid Infrastructure Installation

Objectives

- ✓ Start The Installation
- ✓ Complete The Installation Dialog
- ✓ Verify The Installation
- ✓ Perform Subsequent Database Installation
- ✓ Post-Installation Configuration

Section Overview

Having sufficiently prepared your system for a Grid Infrastructure installation, this section will consider the following topics regarding the actual installation process:

- Perform a grid infrastructure installation and verify its success
- Perform a subsequent database installation with access to the grid infrastructure

Start The Installation

A distinct installation package exists for the grid infrastructure. It is not part of the database installation packages. One must download the package and uncompress the contents into an installation directory. The installation package is named similar to the following:

```
linux_11gR2_grid.zip
```

Thereafter, the Oracle Installer can be launched from an executable contained within the installation package.

Uncompress The Installation Package

Create an installation subdirectory which is owned by the user which will be the owner of the Grid Infrastructure installation. Into that subdirectory uncompress the installation package.

```
[administrator@siderislab4 ~]$ su grid
Password: *******
$ mkdir gridDirectory
$ unzip linux_11gR2_grid.zip -d gridDirectory
...
  inflating:
gridDirectory/grid/stage/properties/oracle.crs_Complete.properties
   creating: gridDirectory/grid/stage/sizes/
  inflating:
gridDirectory/grid/stage/sizes/oracle.crs11.2.0.1.0Complete.sizes.properties
  inflating: gridDirectory/grid/stage/OuiConfigVariables.xml
  inflating: gridDirectory/grid/stage/fastcopy.xml
...
```

Launch The Installation Session

Within the /grid subdirectory one will find the Oracle Universal Installer (OUI) executable. Launch the executable to start the installation session.

```
$ cd gridDirectory/grid
$ ./runInstaller
Starting Oracle Universal Installer...

Checking Temp space: must be greater than 80 MB.   Actual 52186 MB    Passed
Checking swap space: must be greater than 150 MB.   Actual 2047 MB    Passed
Checking monitor: must be configured to display at least 256 colors.    Actual
16777216    Passed
Preparing to launch Oracle Universal Installer from /tmp/OraInstall2010-04-
30_09-03-40AM. Please wait
...
```

You will find much of the installation dialog reminiscent of a database installation, with some notable differences.

The Installation Dialog

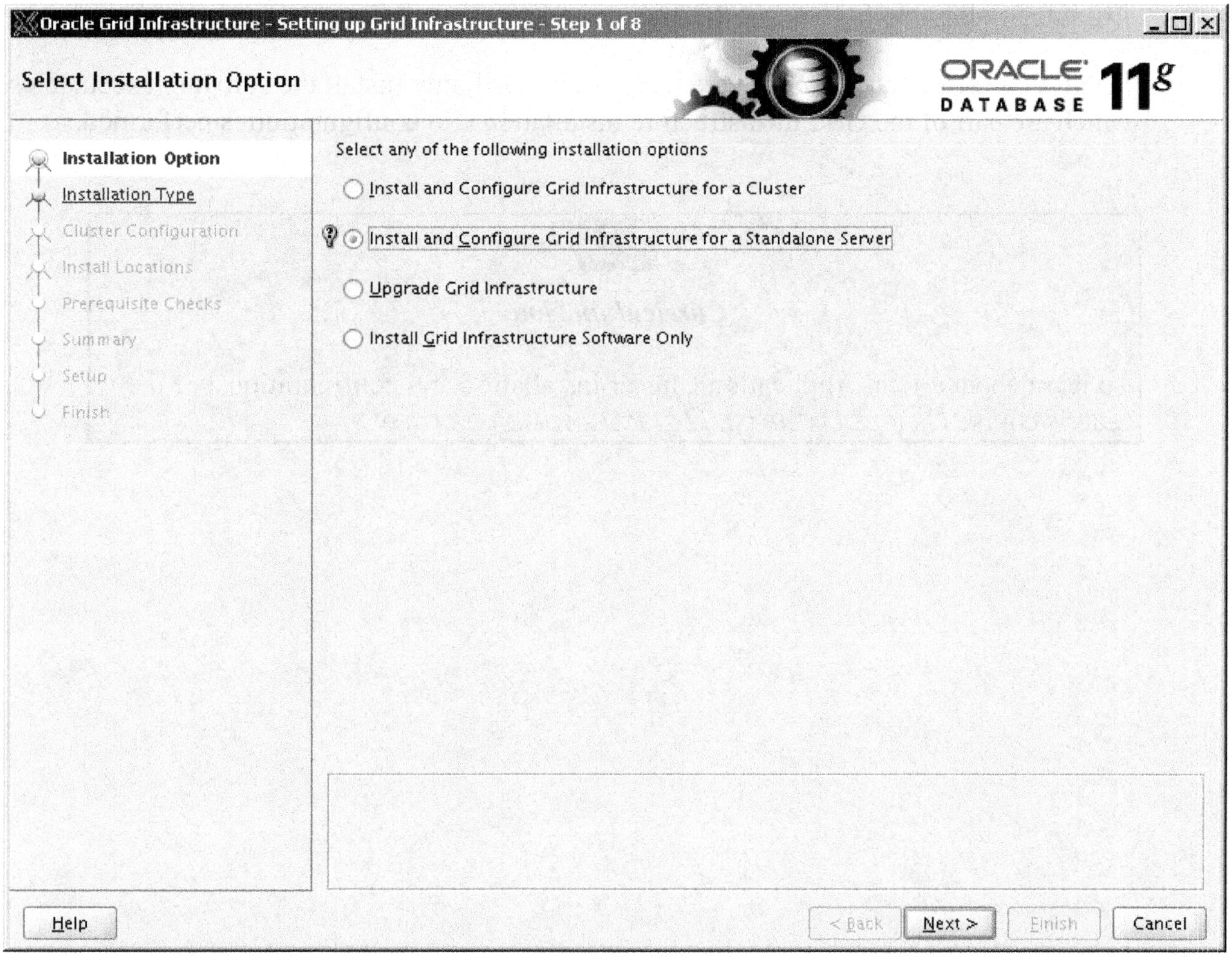

There are several different types of installations which may be performed, and the Select Installation Option will provide these choices:

- Install And Configure Grid Infrastructure For A Cluster – This performs Grid Infrastructure installation for a RAC configuration. It will include installation of Oracle Clusterware.

- Install And Configure Grid Infrastructure For A Standalone Server – A standalone installation will include both an ASM installation and an Oracle Restart installation and configuration.

- Upgrade Grid Infrastructure – While earlier releases of the database did not have a Grid Infrastructure installation per se, there did exist installations of Oracle Clusterware and ASM. This option will upgrade an existing Oracle 10g R1, Oracle 10g R2 or an Oracle 11g R1 installation of those products.

- Install Grid Infrastructure Software Only – This will only install the software executables which are part of the Grid Infrastructure installation. No configuration is performed.

> SIDERIS
> ***Curriculum Note***
>
> To learn about a Real Application Cluster installation and configuration, see the Sideris course *ORACLE DATABASE 11G: RAC ADMINISTRATION*.

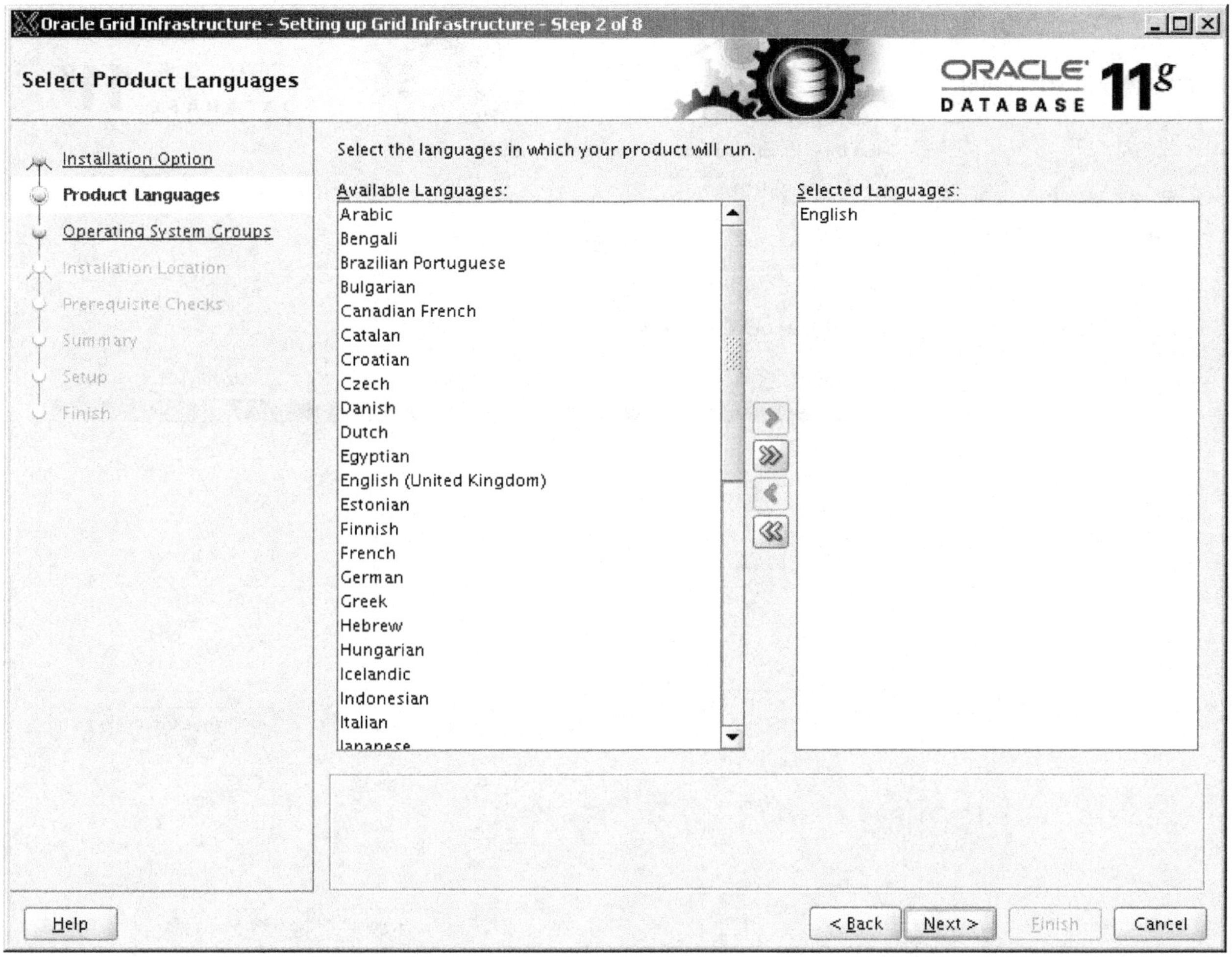

The Select Product Languages screen allows one to decide which language libraries to include in the installation, just as one would do for a database installation.

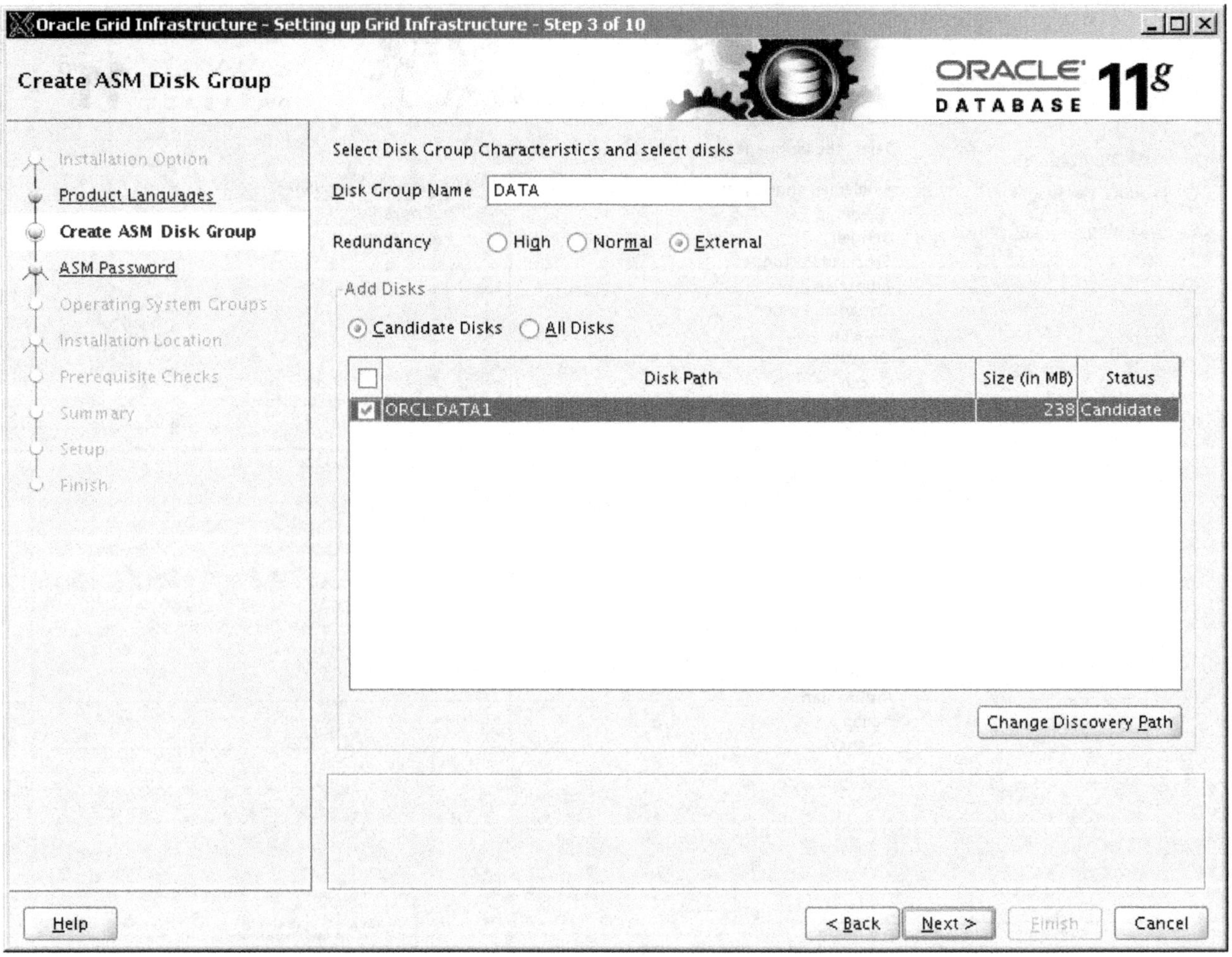

The Create ASM Disk Group screen allows one to define an initial disk group and the characteristics of that group. After the installation additional disk groups may be configured as desired.

ASM *candidate disks* are those which have been prepared for ASM as discussed earlier. Assuming that one or more candidate disks are visible, then one must select which ones should be included within the disk group. Depending upon the number of disks selected for the group, one may specify the Redundancy property as follows:

- Normal – this implements two-way mirroring and requires at least two candidate disks.
- High – this implements three-way mirroring and requires at least 3 candidate disks.

- External – this implements no mirroring within ASM and the assumption is that any needed mirroring is done by means of the storage system. A single disk could be included within the disk group. Or multiple disks specified for the disk group will combine their storage capacity to define the total capacity of the group.

One may click the All Disks option and choose raw devices for use in the ASM disk group. The Change Discovery Path allows one to modify the path through which disks are located. The default Disk Discovery Path specifies a regular expression which is used by the Installer to discover disks. One can include several different expressions by enclosing these in quotes and separating each path by commas.

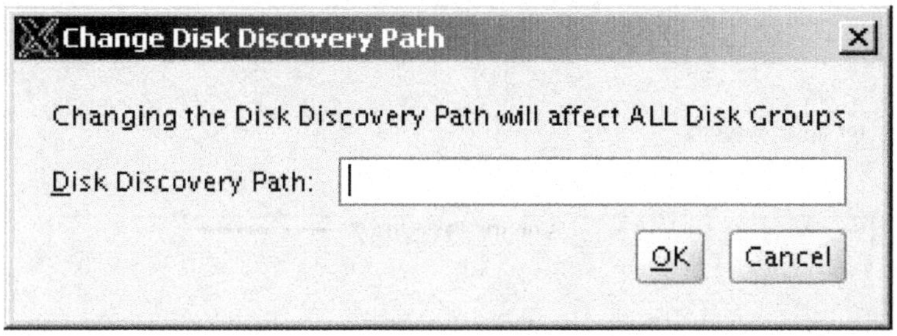

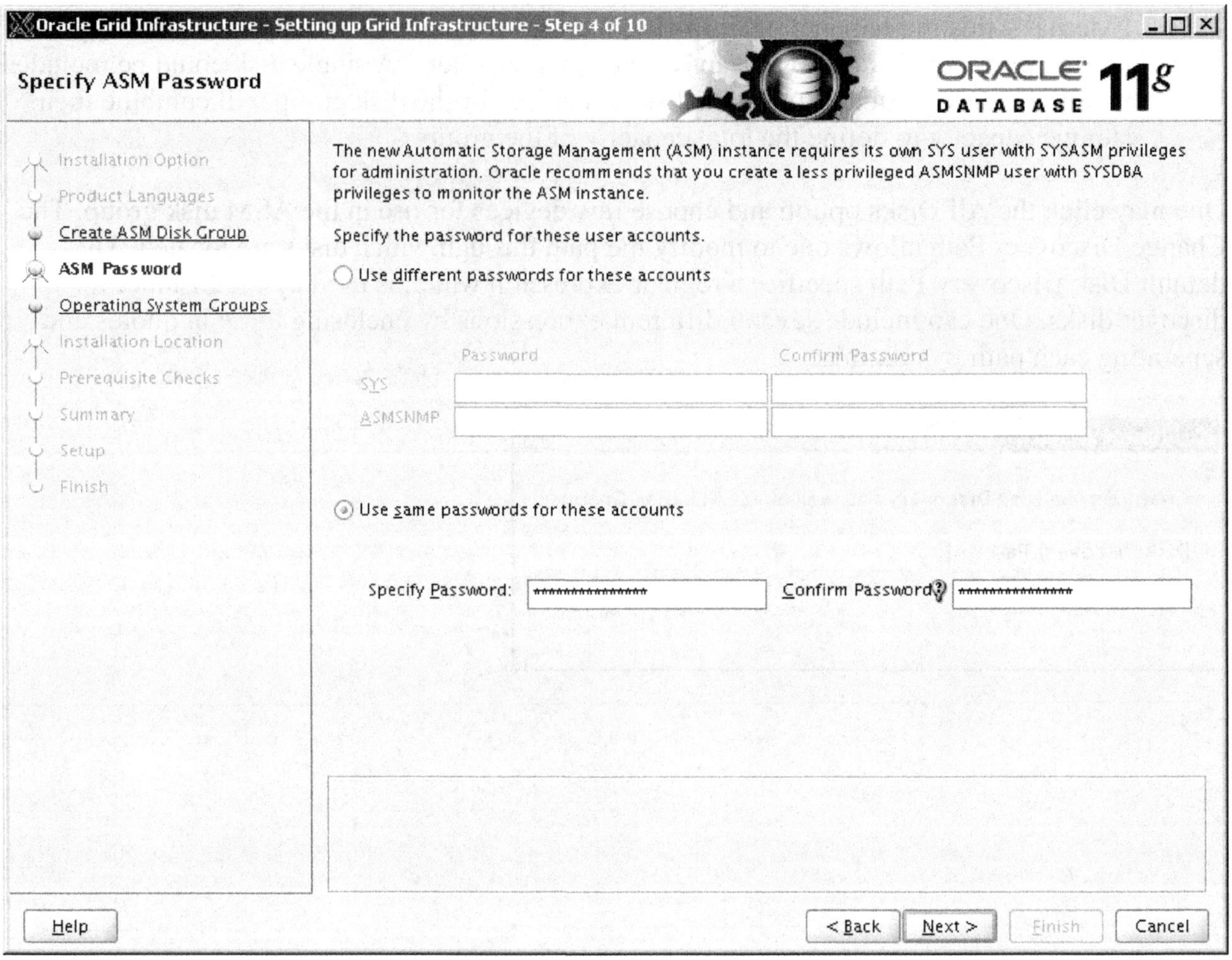

The ASM instance is governed by a super administrator account named SYS. It is also managed from the Enterprise Manager console and other system administration tools by means of metadata stored within the ASMSNMP account. One must assign passwords for these accounts which are created within the ASM instance as part of the installation.

Just like a database installation, one has the option to assign different passwords to each administrator account, or one can assign the same password to them all.

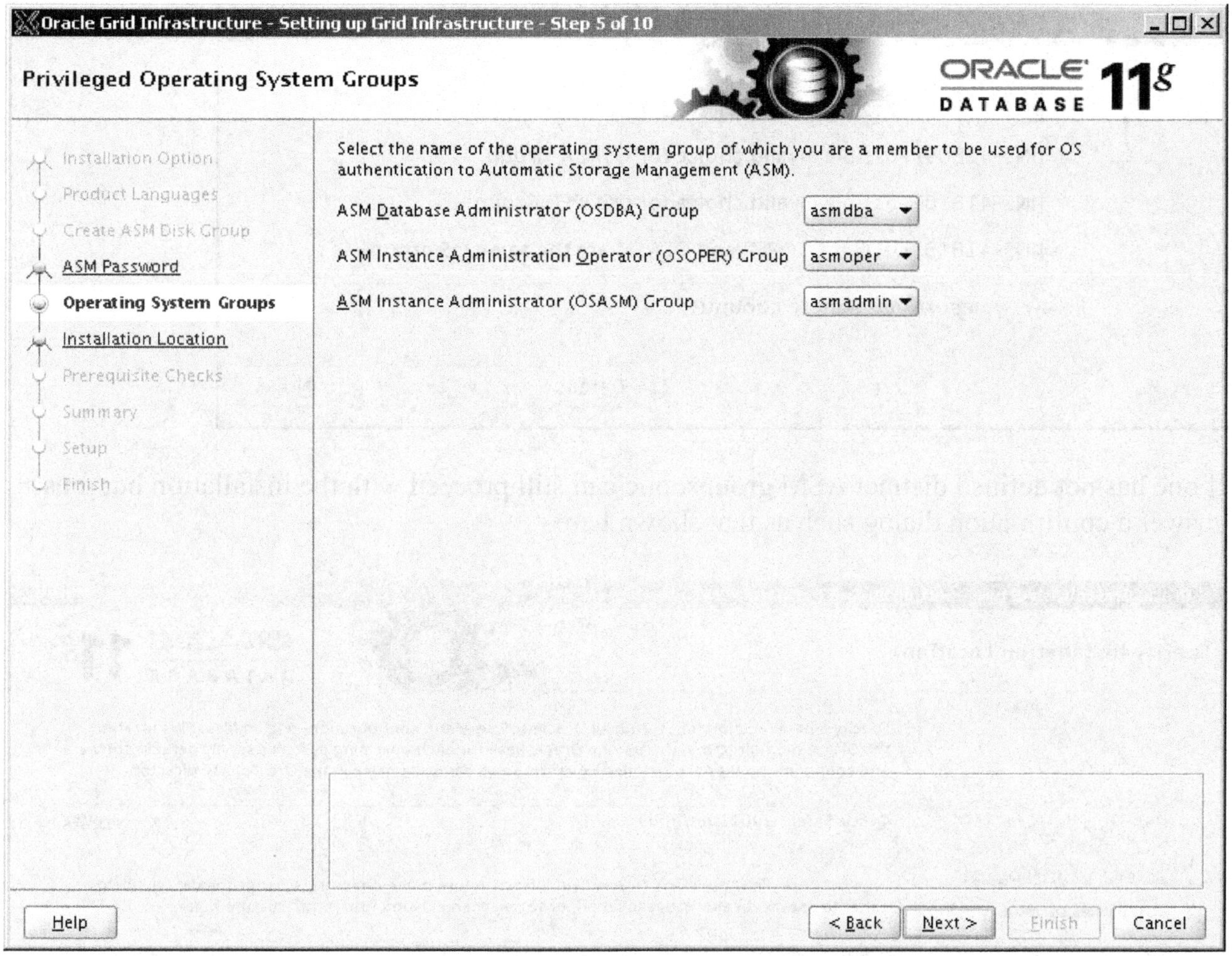

This screen allows one to specify which operating system groups will correspond to the generic roles defined for ASM administration. Ideally one has created a different group for each role. Following the well-establish security concept of the *principle of least privilege* (PoLP), one should define each role and then assign that role only to those users who need the corresponding rights. It is not desirable to create a single role and assign that to all administrators.

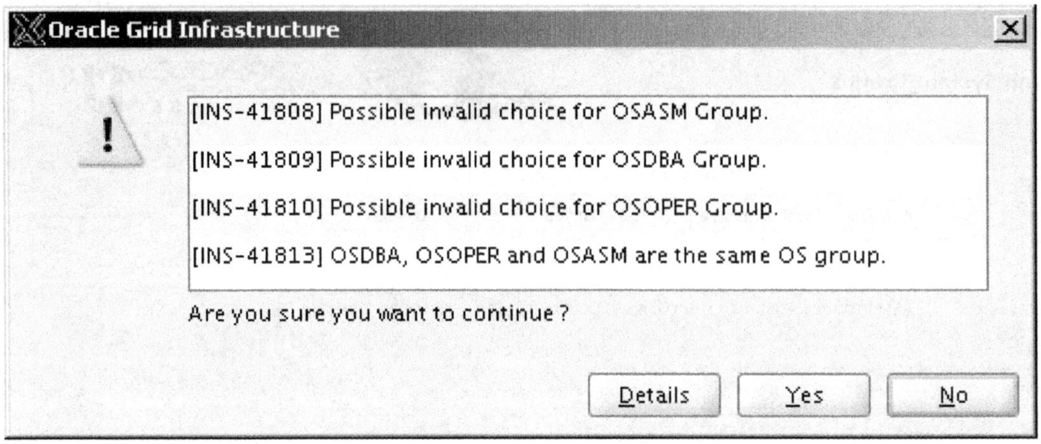

If one has not defined distinct ASM groups, one can still proceed with the installation but must answer a confirmation dialog such as that shown here.

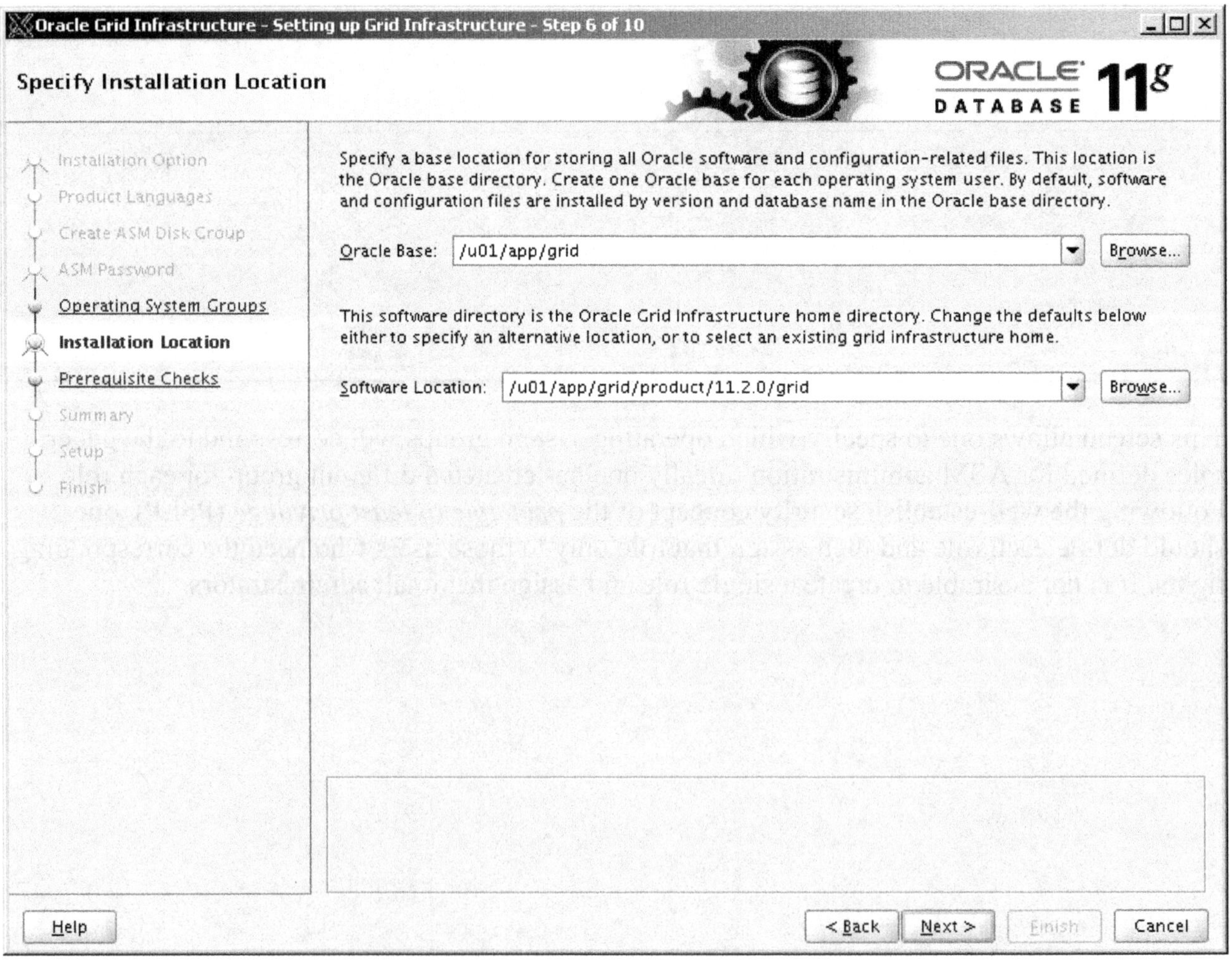

Next one must provide the paths for the Oracle Base and Oracle Home directories.

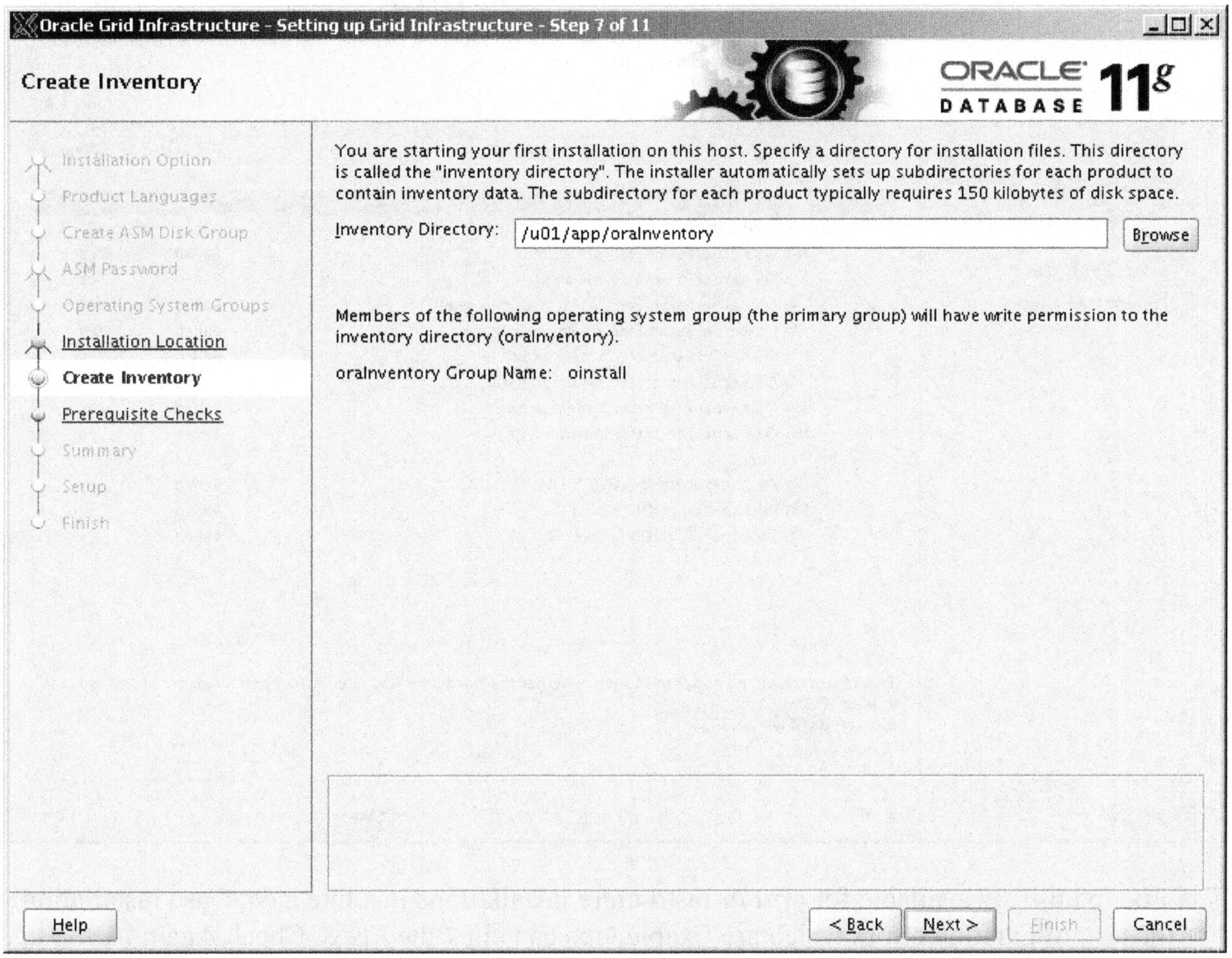

If this is the first Oracle installation on this host system, then one must specify the physical path of the Oracle Inventory directory.

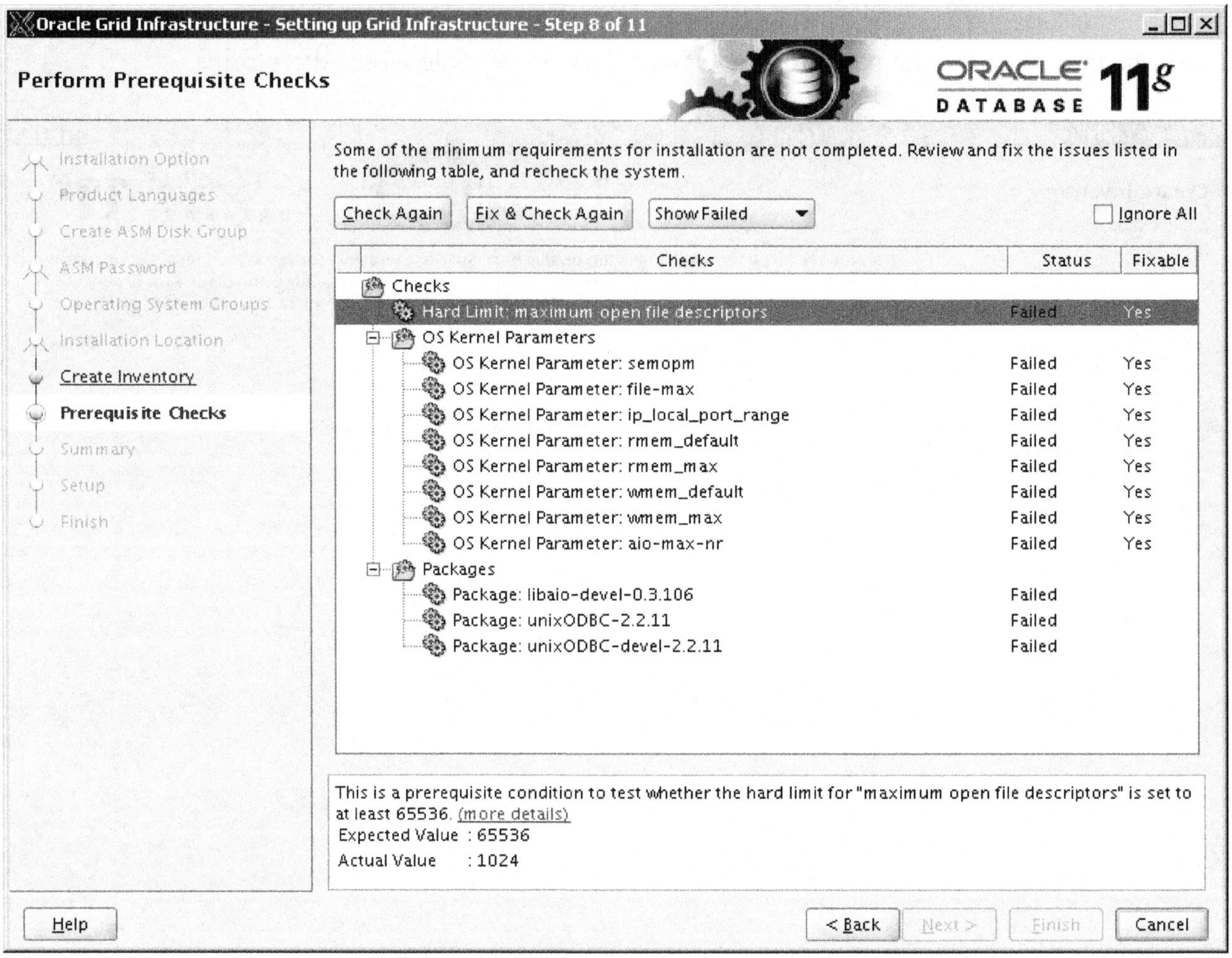

The FixUp utility is available for grid infrastructure installations just like a database installation. For those configuration errors which are fixable, one can click the Fix & Check Again button to generate a script which reconfigures the operating system to meet the installation prerequisites.

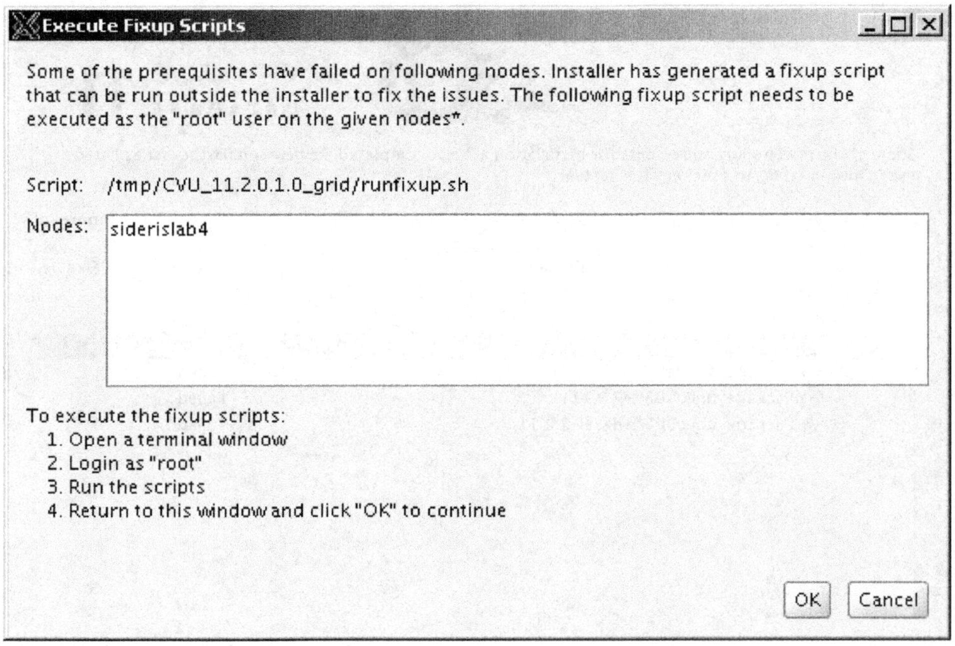

In this example a FixUp script is generated. One launches a separate terminal session to execute the script and can then proceed with the installation.

```
$ su -
Password: ******

# /tmp/CVU_11.2.0.1.0_grid/runfixup.sh
Response file being used is :/tmp/CVU_11.2.0.1.0_grid/fixup.response
Enable file being used is :/tmp/CVU_11.2.0.1.0_grid/fixup.enable
Log file location: /tmp/CVU_11.2.0.1.0_grid/orarun.log
Setting Kernel Parameters...
kernel.sem = 250 32000 100 128
fs.file-max = 6815744
net.ipv4.ip_local_port_range = 9000 65500
net.core.rmem_default = 262144
net.core.wmem_default = 262144
net.core.rmem_max = 4194304
net.core.wmem_max = 1048576
fs.aio-max-nr = 1048576
uid=1000(grid) gid=520(oinstall)
groups=520(oinstall),525(asmdba),535(asmadmin)
context=user_u:system_r:unconfined_t

#
```

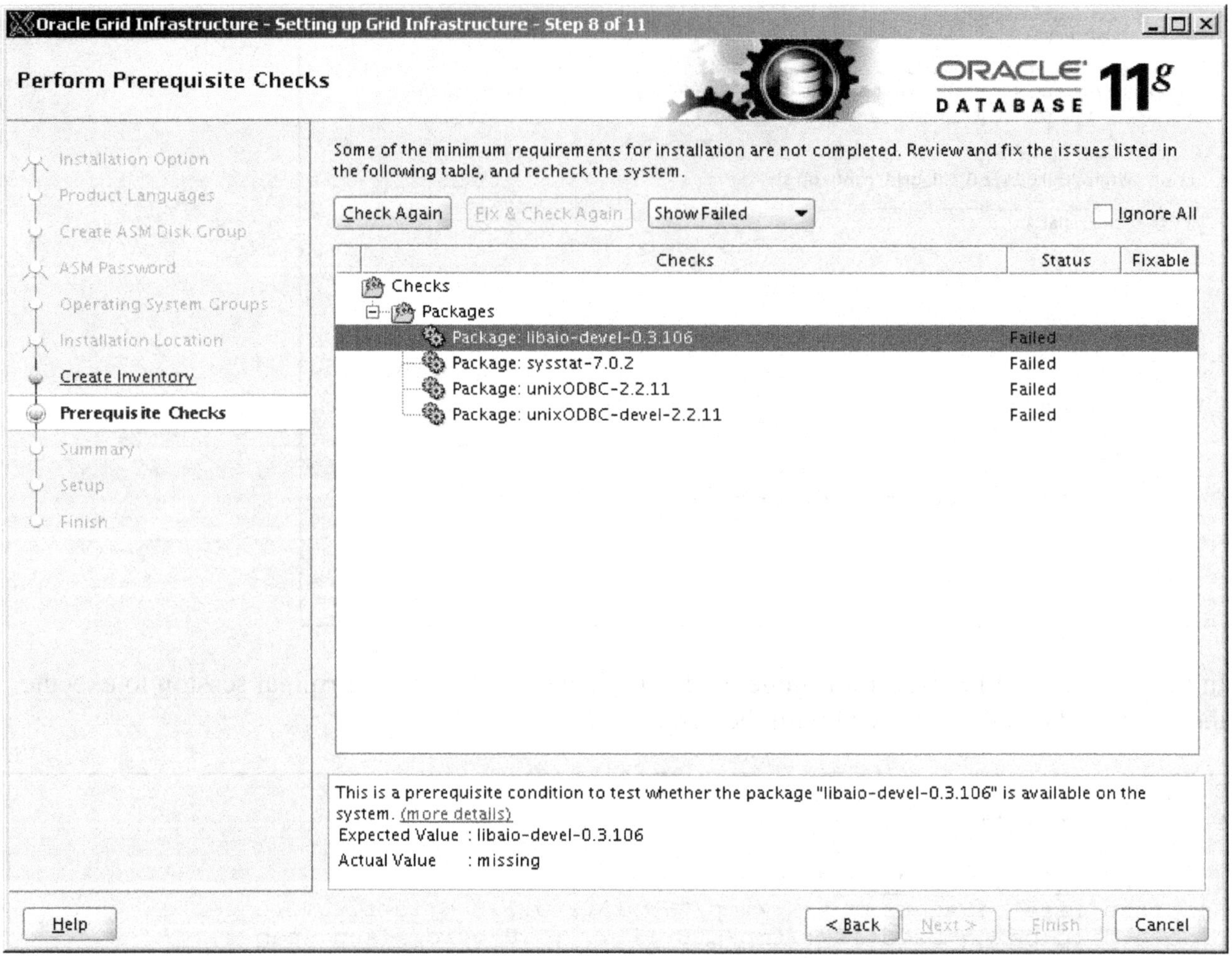

In our example, after executing this script we also need to install missing operating system packages.

> SIDERIS
>
> ***Curriculum Note***
>
> For a complete discussion of the use of the Installer, the FixUp utility, installation of missing packages and other standard Oracle software installation tasks, see the Sideris course *ORACLE DATABASE 11G: ADMINISTRATION I*.

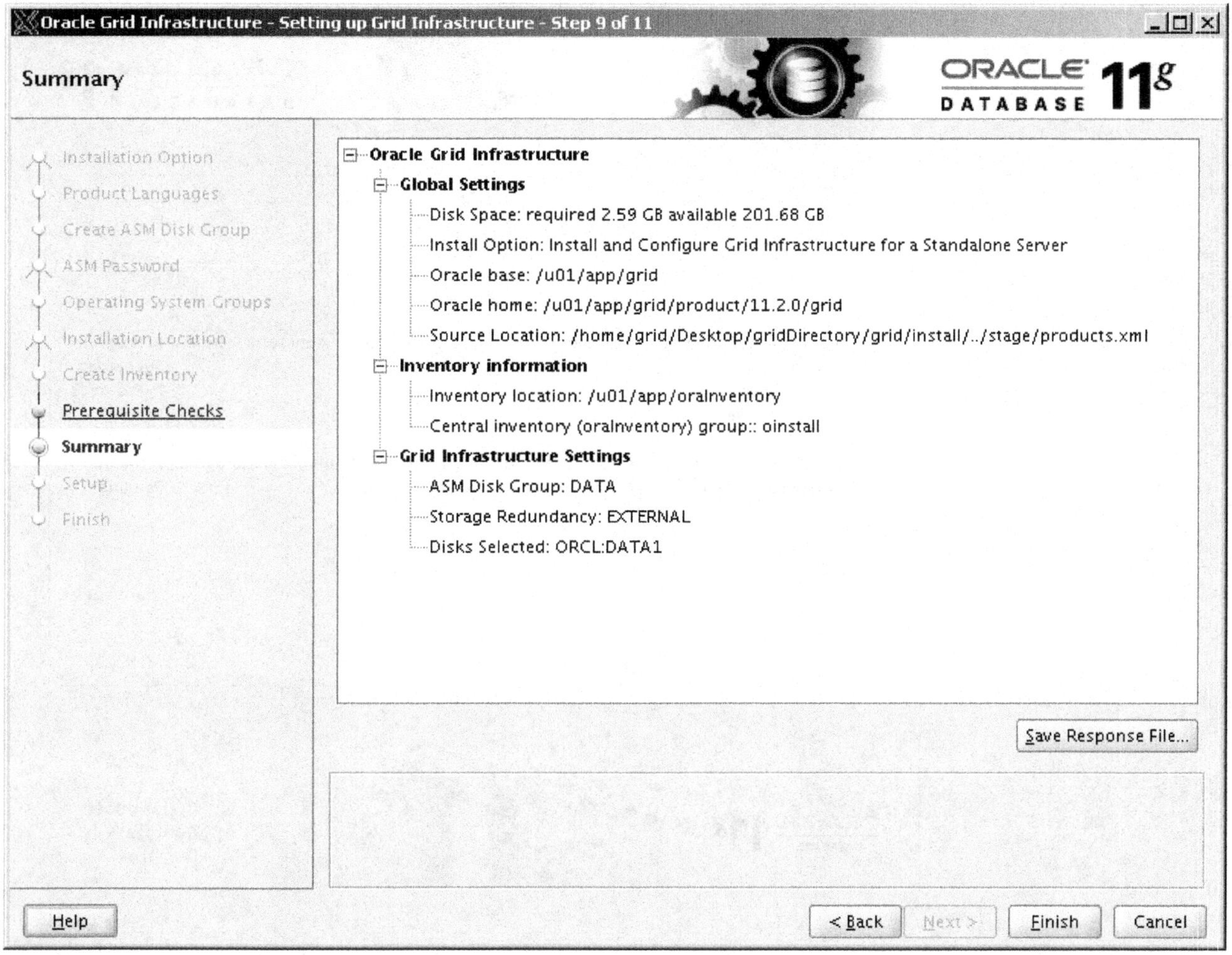

Finally the system configuration is confirmed to be valid and one can click the Finish button to complete the installation dialog and proceed with the actual installation.

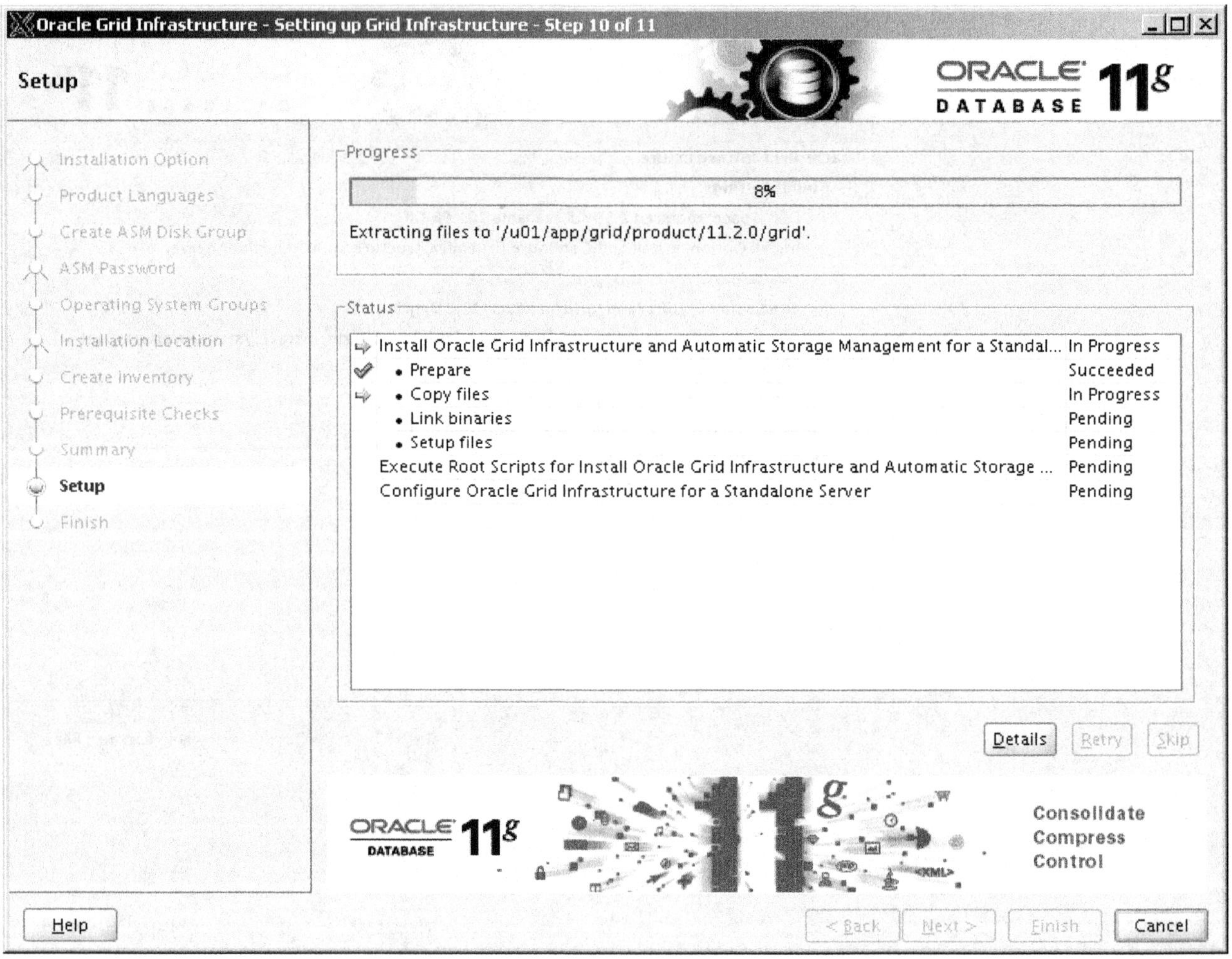
Oracle Grid Infrastructure - Setting up Grid Infrastructure - Step 10 of 11
Setup
ORACLE DATABASE 11g
Installation Option
Product Languages
Create ASM Disk Group
ASM Password
Operating System Groups
Installation Location
Create Inventory
Prerequisite Checks
Summary
Setup
Finish
Progress
8%
Extracting files to '/u01/app/grid/product/11.2.0/grid'.
Status
Install Oracle Grid Infrastructure and Automatic Storage Management for a Standal... In Progress
• Prepare Succeeded
• Copy files In Progress
• Link binaries Pending
• Setup files Pending
Execute Root Scripts for Install Oracle Grid Infrastructure and Automatic Storage ... Pending
Configure Oracle Grid Infrastructure for a Standalone Server Pending
Details
Retry
Skip
Consolidate
Compress
Control
Help
< Back
Next >
Finish
Cancel

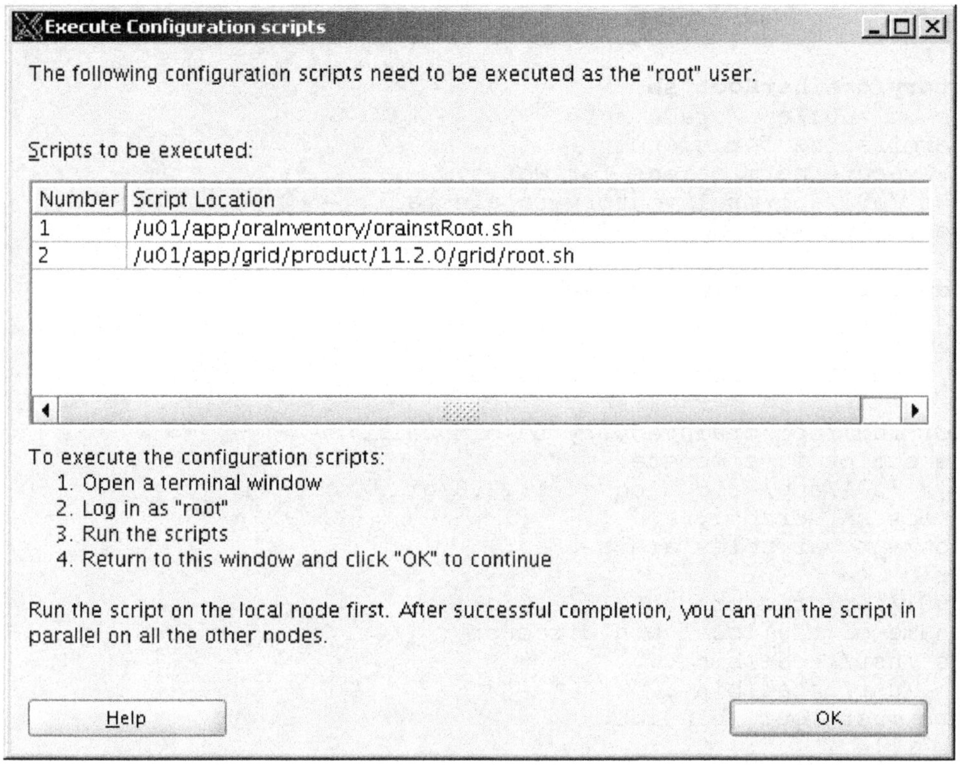

A post-installation set of scripts is generated to complete the installation. Launch a terminal session to execute the scripts and return to this screen and click the OK button.

An actual example of such a terminal session for a grid infrastructure installation is shown next.

```
$ su -
Password: ******
# /u01/app/oraInventory/orainstRoot.sh
Changing permissions of /u01/app/oraInventory.
Adding read,write permissions for group.
Removing read,write,execute permissions for world.
Changing groupname of /u01/app/oraInventory to oinstall.
The execution of the script is complete.

# /u01/app/grid/product/11.2.0/grid/root.sh
Changing permissions of /u01/app/oraInventory.
Adding read,write permissions for group.
Removing read,write,execute permissions for world.

Changing groupname of /u01/app/oraInventory to oinstall.
The execution of the script is complete.
[root@siderislab4 ~]# /u01/app/grid/product/11.2.0/grid/root.sh
Running Oracle 11g root.sh script...
The following environment variables are set as:
    ORACLE_OWNER= grid
    ORACLE_HOME=  /u01/app/grid/product/11.2.0/grid
Enter the full pathname of the local bin directory: [/usr/local/bin]:
   Copying dbhome to /usr/local/bin ...
   Copying oraenv to /usr/local/bin ...
   Copying coraenv to /usr/local/bin ...
Creating /etc/oratab file...
Entries will be added to the /etc/oratab file as needed by
Database Configuration Assistant when a database is created
Finished running generic part of root.sh script.
Now product-specific root actions will be performed.
2010-05-10 13:41:50: Checking for super user privileges
2010-05-10 13:41:50: User has super user privileges
2010-05-10 13:41:50: Parsing the host name
Using configuration parameter file:
/u01/app/grid/product/11.2.0/grid/crs/install/crsconfig_params
Creating trace directory
LOCAL ADD MODE
Creating OCR keys for user 'grid', privgrp 'oinstall'..
Operation successful.
CRS-4664: Node siderislab4 successfully pinned.
Adding daemon to inittab
CRS-4123: Oracle High Availability Services has been started.
ohasd is starting
siderislab4     2010/05/10 13:42:30
/u01/app/grid/product/11.2.0/grid/cdata/siderislab4/backup_20100510_134230.olr
Successfully configured Oracle Grid Infrastructure for a Standalone Server
Updating inventory properties for clusterware
Starting Oracle Universal Installer...
Checking swap space: must be greater than 500 MB.   Actual 4031 MB    Passed
The inventory pointer is located at /etc/oraInst.loc
The inventory is located at /u01/app/oraInventory
'UpdateNodeList' was successful.
```

Note

One should save a copy of the configuration scripts in the event that these need to be re-run at some future point. If a subsequent installation occurs within the same Oracle Home directory, the scripts may be overwritten.

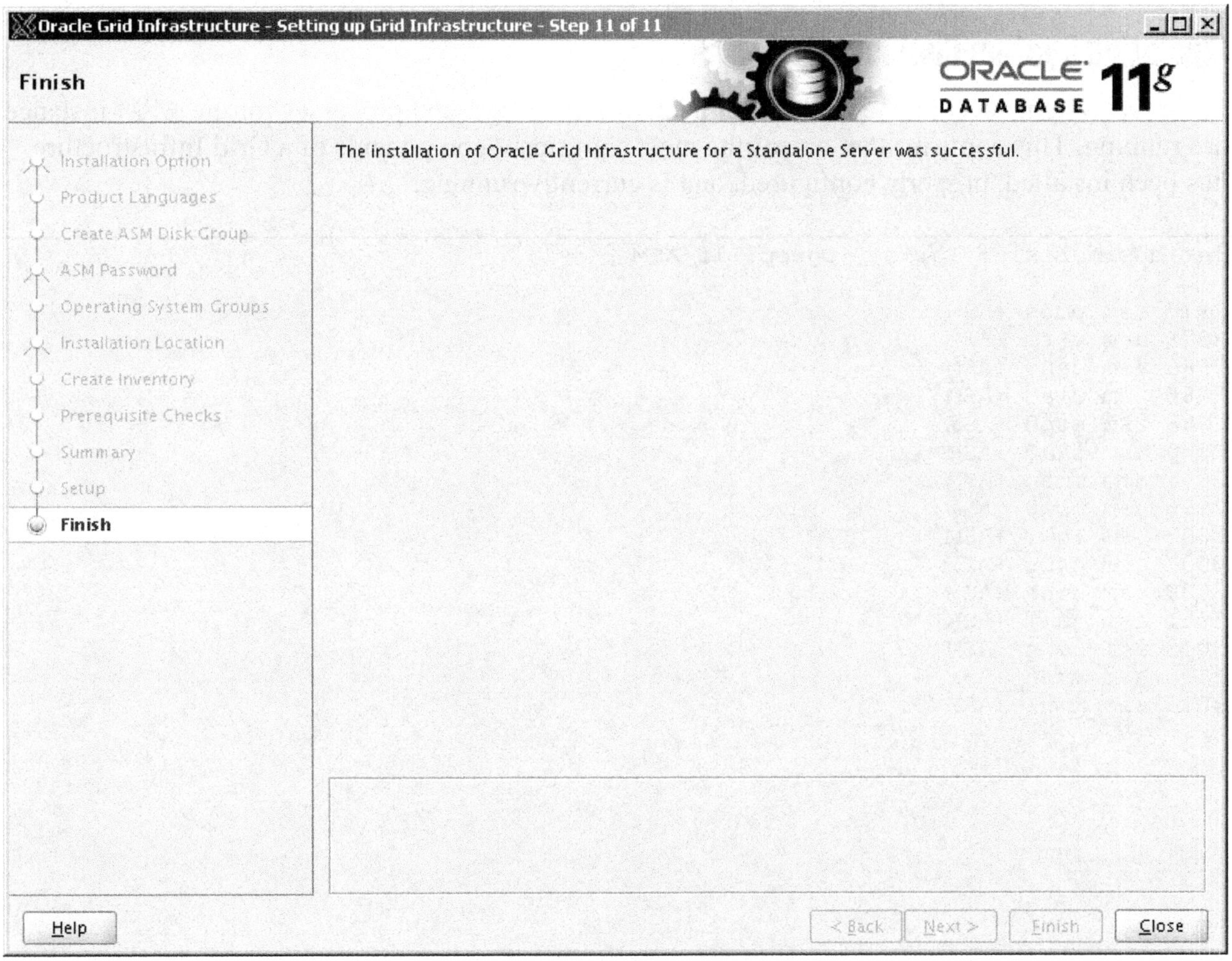

The Finish screen confirms that the installation was successful.

Verify The Installation

While the ultimate verification of the installation will be determined by a subsequent installation of the database and the use of ASM storage by the database, there are some preliminary steps which can be performed which provide initial confirmation that the installation and configuration of the Grid Infrastructure has likely succeeded.

Operating System Confirmation

From the system console one could examine that the background processes for the ASM instance are running. This confirms that one of the most significant components of a Grid Infrastructure has been installed, properly configured, and is currently running.

```
[grid@siderislab4 grid]$ pgrep -lf ASM

2977 asm_pmon_+ASM
2979 asm_vktm_+ASM
2983 asm_gen0_+ASM
2986 asm_diag_+ASM
2988 asm_psp0_+ASM
2990 asm_dia0_+ASM
2994 asm_mman_+ASM
2996 asm_dbw0_+ASM
3003 asm_lgwr_+ASM
3007 asm_ckpt_+ASM
3009 asm_smon_+ASM
3011 asm_rbal_+ASM
3013 asm_gmon_+ASM
3015 asm_mmon_+ASM
3017 asm_mmnl_+ASM
```

Note

While we will discuss the ASM instance in much greater detail later in this course, you can see that the name of the instance is +ASM, with the plus sign (+) serving as a special character which should distinguish the instance from user-assigned database instance names.

Another component of the installation is the system-wide listener. This command offers preliminary confirmation that the listener is configured and running.

```
[grid@siderislab4 bin]$ pgrep -lf tns

2568 /u01/app/grid/product/11.2.0/grid/bin/tnslsnr LISTENER -inherit
```

Oracle Utilities Confirmation

Similar to a database installation, there are environment variables which must be defined in order for the Oracle utilities to operate. These are examples of such definitions for the installation just performed.

```
export ORACLE_BASE=/u01/app/grid
export ORACLE_HOME=/u01/app/grid/product/11.2.0/grid
export ORACLE_SID=+ASM
export ORACLE_HOSTNAME=siderislab4.sideris
export ORACLE_PATH=/u01/app/grid/product/11.2.0/grid/bin:.
export PATH=$PATH:/u01/app/grid/product/11.2.0/grid/bin:.
export HOME=/u01/app/grid
```

Now, using the SQL*Plus utility and the SYSASM rights acquired during the system configuration and subsequent grid infrastructure installation, one could ensure that the ASM instance is accessible.

```
[grid@siderislab4 bin]$ sqlplus /nolog
SQL*Plus: Release 11.2.0.1.0 Production on Mon May 10 15:49:43 2010
Copyright (c) 1982, 2009, Oracle.  All rights reserved.

SQL> CONNECT sys/***** AS SYSASM;
Connected.

SQL> SELECT username, program
     FROM v$process;

USERNAME        PROGRAM
--------------- ------------------------------------------------
                PSEUDO
oracle          oracle@siderislab4.sideris (PMON)
oracle          oracle@siderislab4.sideris (VKTM)
oracle          oracle@siderislab4.sideris (GEN0)
oracle          oracle@siderislab4.sideris (DIAG)
oracle          oracle@siderislab4.sideris (PSP0)
oracle          oracle@siderislab4.sideris (DIA0)
oracle          oracle@siderislab4.sideris (MMAN)
oracle          oracle@siderislab4.sideris (DBW0)
oracle          oracle@siderislab4.sideris (LGWR)
oracle          oracle@siderislab4.sideris (CKPT)
oracle          oracle@siderislab4.sideris (SMON)
oracle          oracle@siderislab4.sideris (RBAL)
oracle          oracle@siderislab4.sideris (GMON)
oracle          oracle@siderislab4.sideris (MMON)
oracle          oracle@siderislab4.sideris (MMNL)
oracle          oracle@siderislab4.sideris (TNS V1-V3)

SQL> exit
[grid@siderislab4 bin]$
```

One could also confirm that the listener is running and that the ASM instance has successfully registered with the listener.

```
[grid@siderislab4 bin]$ lsnrctl status

LSNRCTL for Linux: Version 11.2.0.1.0 - Production on 10-MAY-2010 15:52:14
Copyright (c) 1991, 2009, Oracle.  All rights reserved.

Connecting to (DESCRIPTION=(ADDRESS=(PROTOCOL=IPC)(KEY=EXTPROC1521)))
STATUS of the LISTENER
------------------------
Alias                     LISTENER
Version                   TNSLSNR for Linux: Version 11.2.0.1.0 - Production
Start Date                10-MAY-2010 13:43:27
Uptime                    0 days 2 hr. 8 min. 46 sec
Trace Level               off
Security                  ON: Local OS Authentication
SNMP                      OFF
Listener Parameter File
/u01/app/grid/product/11.2.0/grid/network/admin/listener.ora
Listener Log File
/u01/app/grid/diag/tnslsnr/siderislab4/listener/alert/log.xml
Listening Endpoints Summary...
  (DESCRIPTION=(ADDRESS=(PROTOCOL=ipc)(KEY=EXTPROC1521)))
  (DESCRIPTION=(ADDRESS=(PROTOCOL=tcp)(HOST=siderislab4.sideris)(PORT=1521)))
Services Summary...
Service "+ASM" has 1 instance(s).
  Instance "+ASM", status READY, has 1 handler(s) for this service...
The command completed successfully
```

Subsequent Database Installation

One may next perform a standard database installation. For the most part the installation will be performed similar to a standalone database installation, with the following recommended differences:

- The database installation must be in a separate Oracle Home directory from the grid installation.

- A separate database software installation system user may be created to further distinguish the database installation from the grid installation software owner. These user accounts are `oracle` and `grid` respectively in our examples.

- The `oracle` account should be part of the ASMDBA group so that it may administer both the database and the ASM instances.

We will demonstrate a database installation on the same host system as the grid infrastructure installation next.

Create The Groups & Users

Since in our scenario the database installation will be owned by a separate user than the grid installation, we need to create the database groups and the software owner account in the normal manner.

```
[administrator@siderislab4 ~]$ su -
Password: ***********
# /usr/sbin/groupadd -g 510 dba
# /usr/sbin/groupadd -g 515 oper
# /usr/sbin/useradd -u 1200 -g oinstall -G dba,oper oracle

# passwd oracle
Changing password for user oracle.
New UNIX password:  ********
Retype new UNIX password: *******
passwd: all authentication tokens updated successfully.
```

Define ORACLE_BASE

Again, one would follow the pattern for any other database installation to create the ORACLE_BASE directory and assign appropriate ownership and permissions to that location.

```
# mkdir -p /u01/app/oracle
# chown -R oracle:oinstall /u01/app/oracle
# chmod -R 775 /u01/app/oracle
```

Unpack The Database Installation Files

One must download the installation packages for the database and unpack these into an installation directory.

```
$ su - oracle
Password: *******
$ mkdir installDirectory
$ unzip linux_11gR2_database_1of2.zip -d installDirectory
...
extracting:
11ginstall/database/stage/sizes/oracle.server11.2.0.1.0SE.sizes.properties
 extracting:
11ginstall/database/stage/sizes/oracle.server11.2.0.1.0Custom.sizes.properties
  inflating: 11ginstall/database/stage/OuiConfigVariables.xml
  inflating: 11ginstall/database/stage/oracle.server.11_2_0_1_0.xml
  inflating: 11ginstall/database/stage/fastcopy.xml
...

$ unzip linux_11gR2_database_2of2.zip -d installDirectory
  inflating:
11ginstall/database/stage/Components/oracle.ctx/11.2.0.1.0/1/DataFiles/filegro
up15.4.1.jar
  inflating:
11ginstall/database/stage/Components/oracle.ctx/11.2.0.1.0/1/DataFiles/filegro
up4.jar
  inflating:
11ginstall/database/stage/Components/oracle.ctx/11.2.0.1.0/1/DataFiles/filegro
up19.jar
  inflating:
11ginstall/database/stage/Components/oracle.ctx/11.2.0.1.0/1/DataFiles/filegro
up16.jar
...
$
```

Launch The Installation

It is recommended that the ORACLE_HOSTNAME environment variable be set in advance of launching the Installer. While many environments may not require this additional step, it will avoid installation problems in some environments and causes no problems in any case.

Thereafter, navigate to the Installer executable and launch the Installer process.

```
$ export ORACLE_HOSTNAME=siderislab4
$ cd installDirectory/database
$ ./runInstaller

Checking Temp space: must be greater than 80 MB.   Actual 203241 MB    Passed
Checking swap space: must be greater than 150 MB.   Actual 2490 MB    Passed
Checking monitor: must be configured to display at least 256 colors.    Actual
16777216    Passed
Preparing to launch Oracle Universal Installer from /tmp/OraInstall2009-09-
21_01-20-59PM. Please wait ...
```

Typical Install

We will not reproduce each step in the database installation as that should be familiar to you at this point in time. The following selections were made in the installation dialog demonstrated here:

1. Select Create And Configure A Database
2. Select a Server Class installation
3. Select a Single Instance Database Installation
4. Select a Typical Install

Typical Install Configuration

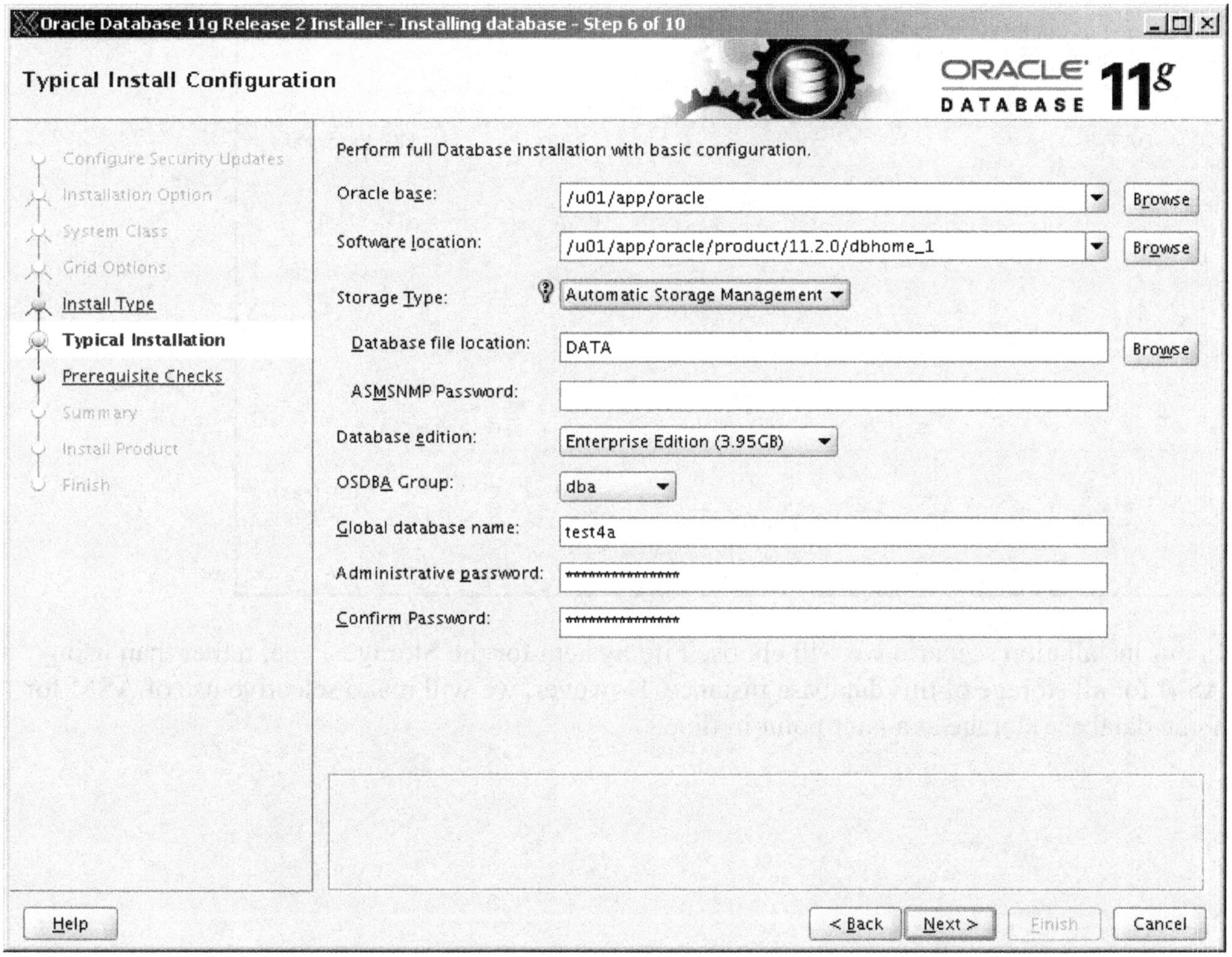

The Installer will detect the presence of an ASM instance and available ASM storage:

- It will therefore default to Automatic Storage Management for the Storage Type item
- It will default to the first ASM disk group located by the installer for the Database File Location item.
- One will also be required to enter the ASMSNMP password assigned when the ASM instance was created.

These default settings will use ASM for data files and database recovery files storage. If one wishes to use ASM storage but prefers a different disk group, one may click the Browse button to raise the ASM Group Selection screen and peruse the set of available disk groups and their basic attributes.

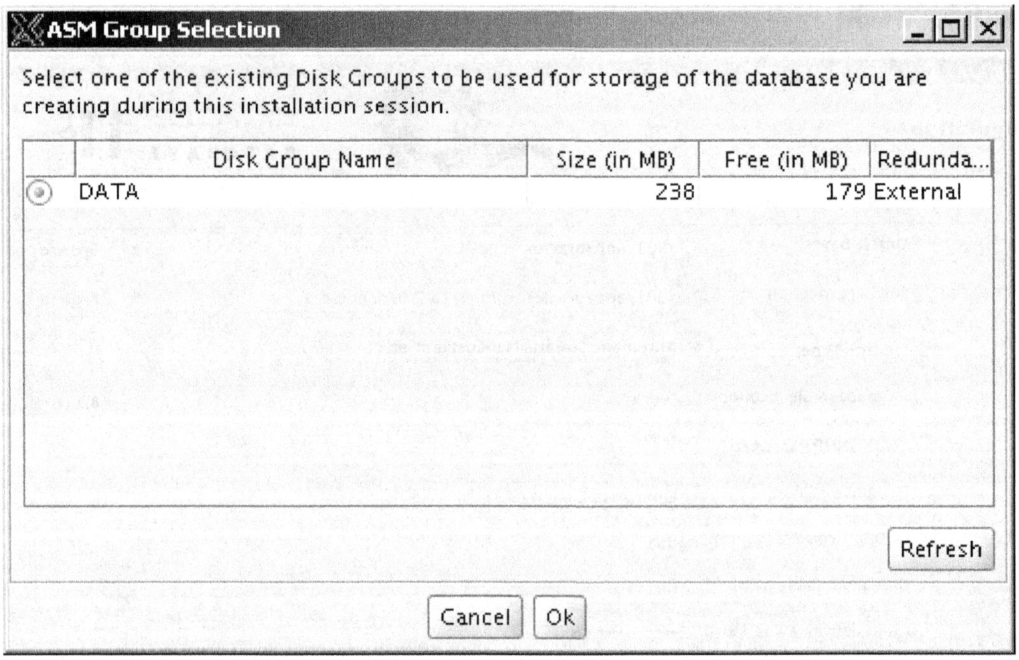

In our installation scenario we will choose File System for the Storage Type, rather than using ASM for all storage of this database instance. However, we will make selective use of ASM for some database storage at a later point in time.

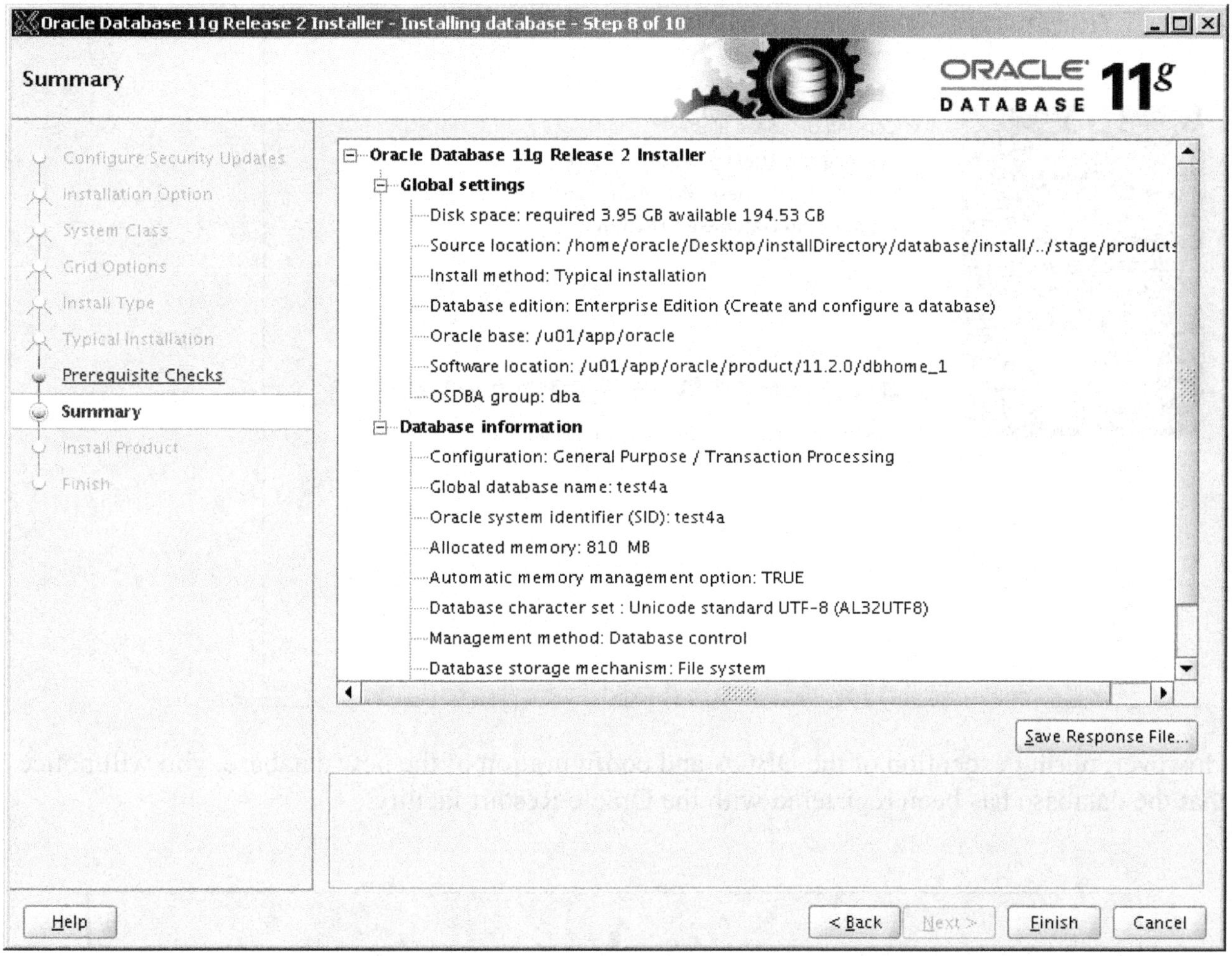

The installation will then generally proceed as you would expect for any other standalone database installation.

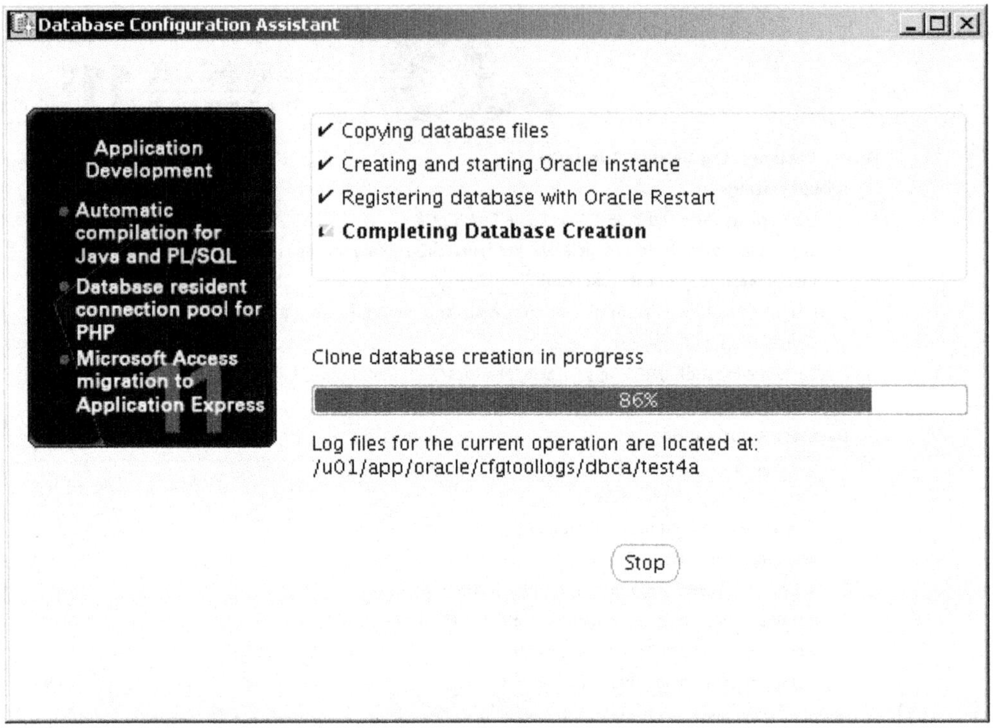

However, during execution of the DBCA and configuration of the new database, you will notice that the database has been registered with the Oracle Restart facility.

> ***Note***
>
> In the event that you create multiple database installations on this same server, you should ensure that each one is owned by a separate system account, for example `oracle`, `oracle1`, `oracle2` and so on. Only in this way will advanced security controls discussed within this course be possible.

Advanced Install

An advanced database installation will likewise proceed largely as it would in a standalone database environment. The following screens isolate those installation steps which are affected by the Grid Infrastructure installation.

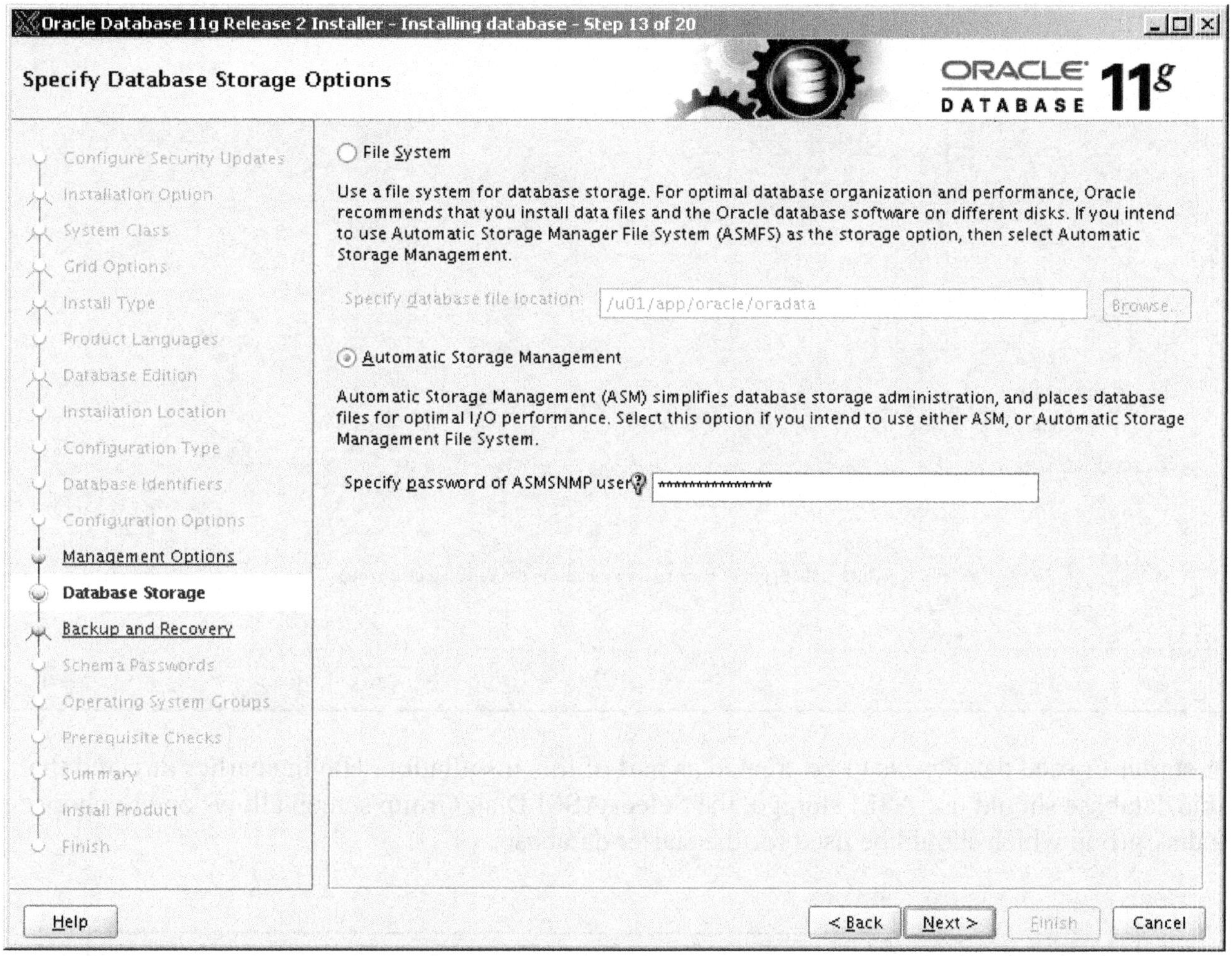

From the Specify Database Storage Options screen one has the option to choose Automatic Storage Management rather than File System storage since the Grid Infrastructure exists on this host system. If one chooses Automatic Storage Management then one must provide the password for the ASMSNMP account created during the Grid Infrastructure installation so that the ASM devices may be accessed later within this database installation.

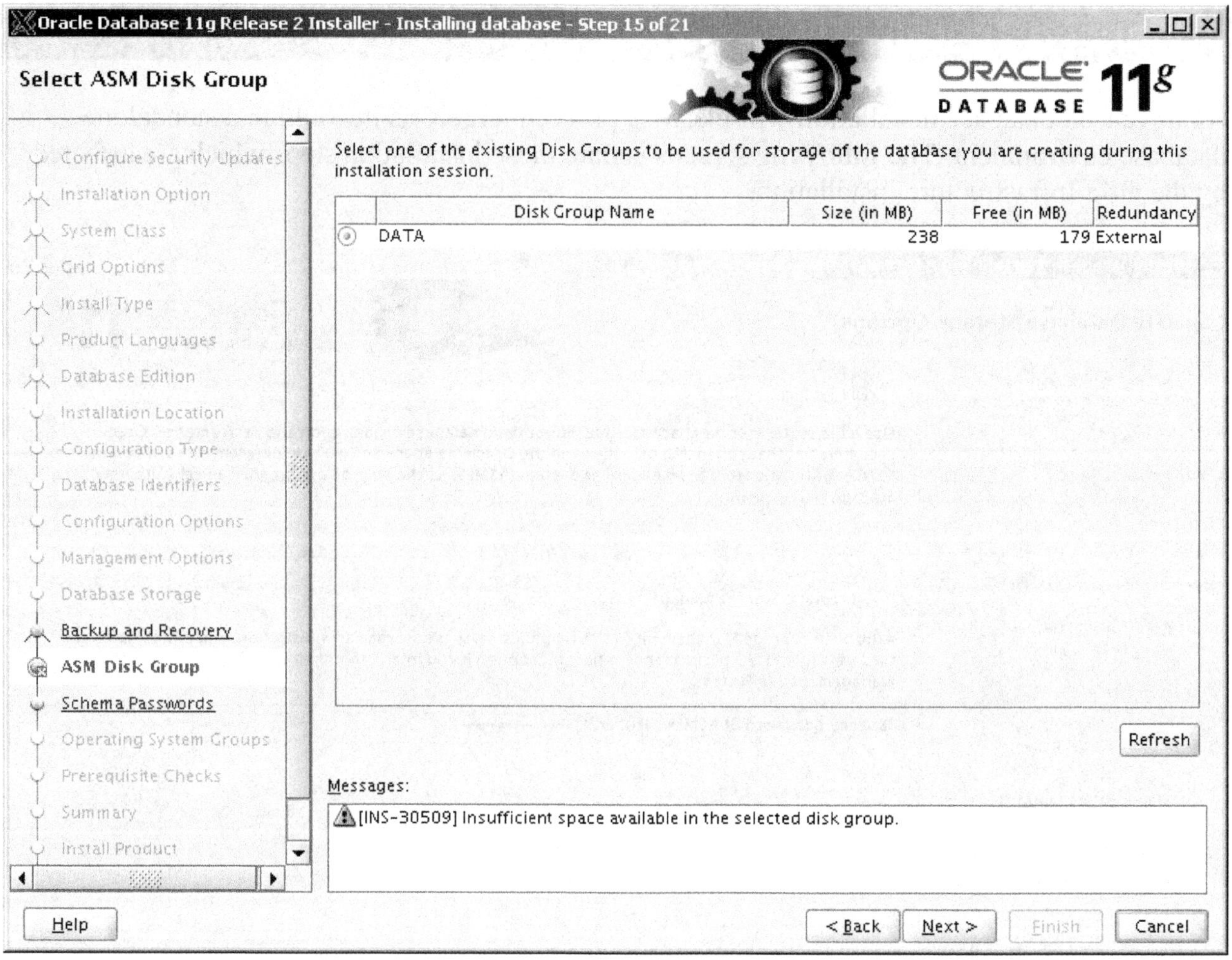

A starter or seed database is to be created as part of this installation. Having earlier directed that this database should use ASM storage, the Select ASM Disk Group screen allows one to choose a disk group which should be used for the starter database.

> ***Note***
>
> The starter database will typically require about 2 GB of storage.

Post-Installation Configuration

There are no special post-installation configuration steps required for a database installation within a Grid Infrastructure environment which are different from what would normally be required. For your reference we will briefly list such items next.

Firewall Configuration

Depending upon the firewall configuration of your database server system, along with other local circumstances, it may be necessary for you to open up pathways to specific ports within your firewall configuration. If this is necessary, keep in mind the following TCP ports which may require such a configuration within your firewall setup:

- Database listener port – often 1521, 1522, etc.
- Enterprise Manager HTTP listener port – often 5500, 5501, 1158 and so on

Required Environment Variables

In order to operate the database administration utilities, each terminal session is required to have environment variables set.

Variable	*Explanation*
ORACLE_BASE	This is the OFA variable which defines the Oracle software base directory.
ORACLE_HOME	This is the OFA variable which defines the home directory of the specific database instance to be used. If one is switching between several instances running on a single server, then this value must be changed each time.
ORACLE_SID	This is the name of the database SID to be operated.
ORACLE_PATH	This is the name of the binary directory within ORACLE_HOME where executables will be located.
PATH	This is an operating system environment variable which defines the path where all executables are to be found. One must include the ORACLE_PATH directory within this value.

HOME	This is an operating system environment variable which is the home directory for the user. For the `oracle` owner of the database instance, it should match ORACLE_BASE. If one is accessing system utilities from a different account than `oracle`, then this variable setting should remain unchanged.
JAVA_HOME	This is the path where Java executables are found. It must include the directory $ORACLE_HOME/jdk.

Optional Environment Variables

Variable	*Explanation*
ORACLE_HOSTNAME	This is used during installation and configuration of the administrator graphical interface Enterprise Manager. It should be set to the host name and domain name of the server system.
ORACLE_UNQNAME	This is used during startup of Enterprise Manager. It should be set to the same value as ORACLE_SID.

Defining The Environment Variables

The following is an example of a portion of a shell script which would make settings for these variables.

```
export ORACLE_BASE=/u01/app/oracle
export ORACLE_HOME=/u01/app/oracle/product/11.2.0/dbhome_1
export ORACLE_SID=test4g
export ORACLE_UNQNAME=test4g
export ORACLE_HOSTNAME=siderislab4.sideris
export ORACLE_PATH=/u01/app/oracle/product/11.2.0/dbhome_1/bin:.
export PATH=$PATH:/u01/app/oracle/product/11.2.0/dbhome_1/bin:.
export HOME=/u01/app/oracle
export JAVA_HOME=$ORACLE_HOME/jdk
```

Note

Remember that if you are using an Oracle utility such as SQL*Plus to administer the ASM instance, these environment variables settings will be different than when you are using that utility to administer the database instance. Some obvious differences will be ORACLE_SID and ORACLE_HOME.

Section Review

Remember These Points

- The installation package for the Grid Infrastructure must be unpacked and a Grid Infrastructure installation performed.
- During the Grid Infrastructure installation one may create an initial ASM Disk Group based upon available candidate disks.
- The asmdba, asmoper and asmadmin groups are typically used for the OSDBA, OSOPER and OSASM administration roles.
- When the Grid Infrastructure installation is complete one should find the +ASM instance configured and running on the system. It should also have been registered with Oracle Restart.
- The listener is also configured, running and registered with Oracle Restart as a result of the installation.
- One follows a Grid Infrastructure installation with a database installation on the same host system. The database is able to use the ASM disk groups for its storage.
- Such a database installation is very similar to any other database install. However, the ORACLE_HOME location of the Grid Infrastructure installation must be different than the database installation.

Workshop Section
Grid Infrastructure Installation

Exercises

What You Will Do in This Workshop

In this workshop, you will:

- Perform a Grid Infrastructure installation and verify the success of that installation.
- Perform a database installation and verify the success of that installation.

To begin this workshop, be sure that you have downloaded both the Grid Infrastructure installation and the database installation packages.

> *Note*
>
> As is usually the case for our workshop solutions, the solutions we provide are based upon the configuration of the Sideris data center. You will need to make appropriate changes to your solution to reflect local circumstances, such as host names, directory paths and so on.

INSTALLATION-1

❑ In an earlier workshop you configured the `oracle` system account to function as the owner of the Grid Infrastructure. This is a simpler scenario than the distinct `grid` and `oracle` installation ownership arrangement described in the lecture section, but it will serve us well in the workshop.

In this exercise, ensure that the Grid Infrastructure installation package is accessible to the `oracle` account. Create an installation directory and unpack the installation package into that directory.

Once this has completed, launch the Installer to begin the installation session.

INSTALLATION-2

❑ Complete the installation dialog using these selections:

1. Choose the option Install And Configure Grid Infrastructure For A Standalone Server.
2. Select the candidate disk(s) you prepared in the earlier workshop to comprise the starting disk group for ASM.
3. Take note of the passwords which you assign to the SYS and ASMSNMP accounts.
4. Ensure that you specify the asmdba, asmoper and asmadmin groups for the OSDBA, OSPOPER and OSASM roles respectively.

Otherwise, you should be able to complete the installation dialog using the default values provided by the Installer.

INSTALLATION-3

❑ Before proceeding with the database installation it would be good to verify the success of the Grid Infrastructure installation. Perform these steps:

- Using the operating system utilities confirm that ASM and the host listener are running.
- Create a shell script or otherwise configure a terminal session so that it can access the Oracle Grid Infrastructure utilities.
- Use SQL*Plus and the Listener Control to confirm that ASM and the host listener are running.

INSTALLATION-4

❑ You are now ready to perform a database installation. Before actually launching the database installation session, perform these preparatory steps:

- Create a system group named dba which will serve as the OSDBA role for the database installation.

- Modify the oracle account so that this group is added to the secondary groups for that user.

- Create an ORACLE_HOME subdirectory which conforms to the OFA standard for database installations and which is different from the ORACLE_HOME used by the Grid Infrastructure.

- Unpack the database installation package into an installation subdirectory which you create for this purpose.

INSTALLATION-5

❑ Define the ORACLE_HOSTNAME environment variable and launch the database installer. Make these selections when prompted to do so by the Installer. As you can see, we will initially use File System storage for the database but in a later workshop you will selectively utilize ASM for database storage.

1. Select Create And Configure A Database
2. Select a Server Class installation
3. Select a Single Instance Database Installation
4. Select a Typical Install
5. Choose the ORACLE_HOME directory path created earlier in this workshop for the Software Location
6. Choose File System storage

INSTALLATION-6

❑ Using the environment variable settings established earlier for the ASM instance, you could confirm the configuration of the database instance using the Listener Control utility. Obtain a status and see if the database instance has been registered with the listener alongside the ASM instance.

INSTALLATION-7

❑ This is an optional exercise but one which will be helpful to complete now for the benefit of later workshops. Define a terminal session which provides access to the database instance and connect to the database using the SYSTEM administrator account. Execute the script SiderisClassIDs.sql referenced in the Workshop Setup Guide to create one or two sample student IDs.

You will be able to use these student IDs to perform simulated database application activity later in this course.

Solutions

INSTALLATION-1

```
[administrator@siderislab4 ~]$ su oracle
Password: *******
$ mkdir gridDirectory
$ unzip linux_11gR2_grid.zip -d gridDirectory
...
  inflating:
gridDirectory/grid/stage/properties/oracle.crs_Complete.properties
   creating: gridDirectory/grid/stage/sizes/
  inflating:
gridDirectory/grid/stage/sizes/oracle.crs11.2.0.1.0Complete.sizes.properties
  inflating: gridDirectory/grid/stage/OuiConfigVariables.xml
  inflating: gridDirectory/grid/stage/fastcopy.xml
...
```

```
$ cd gridDirectory/grid
$ ./runInstaller
Starting Oracle Universal Installer...

Checking Temp space: must be greater than 80 MB.   Actual 52186 MB    Passed
Checking swap space: must be greater than 150 MB.   Actual 2047 MB    Passed
Checking monitor: must be configured to display at least 256 colors.    Actual
16777216    Passed
Preparing to launch Oracle Universal Installer from /tmp/OraInstall2010-04-
30_09-03-40AM. Please wait
...
```

INSTALLATION-2

We will not reproduce the screens for each step in the installation dialog, but you will want to take particular note of those screens which are noted next.

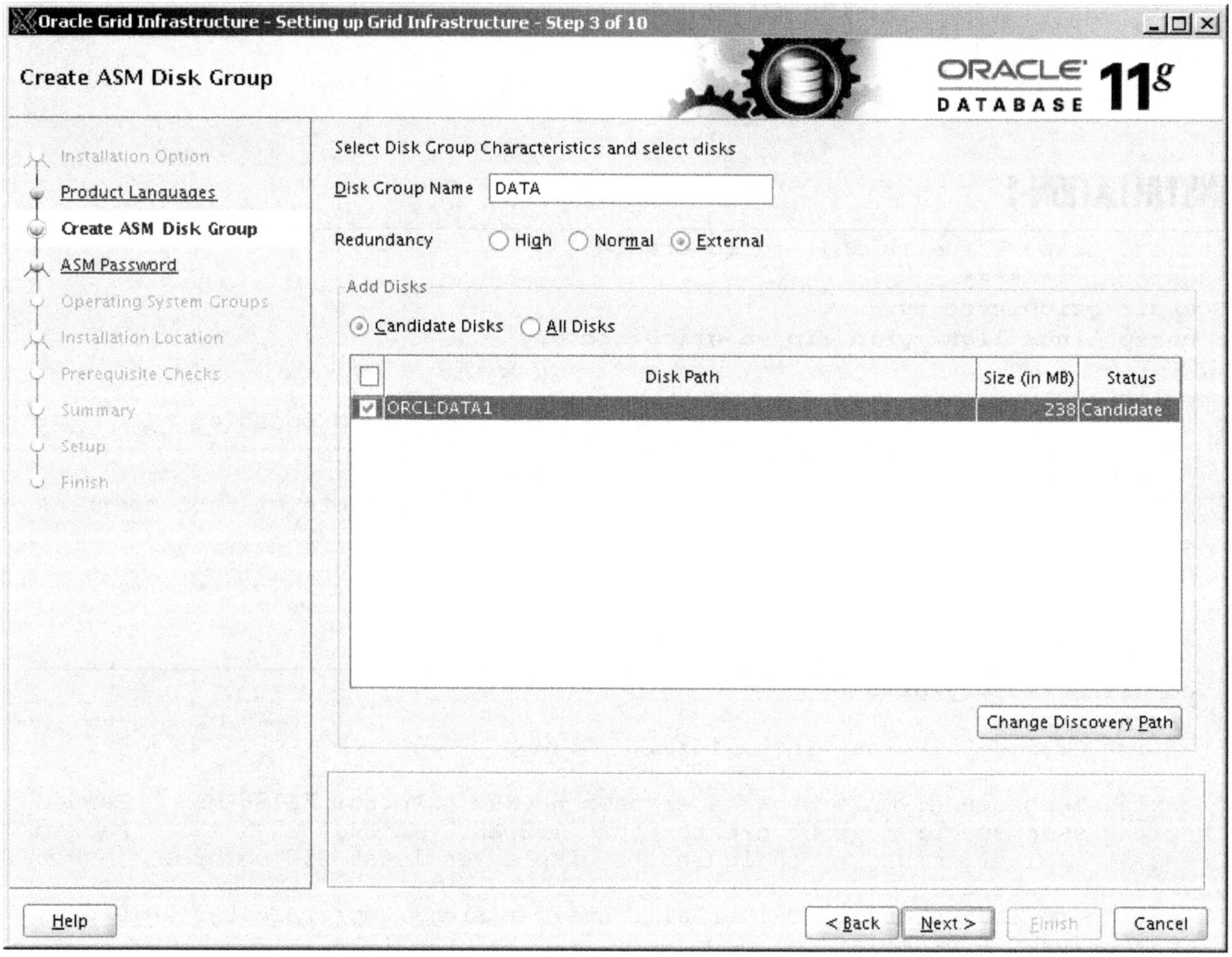

Hopefully the Installer will discover the candidate disk(s) which you prepared during the previous workshop. If so, be sure to select all such disks from the Create ASM Disk Group screen.

Unless you have multiple candidate disks available, ensure that you choose the Redundancy option External.

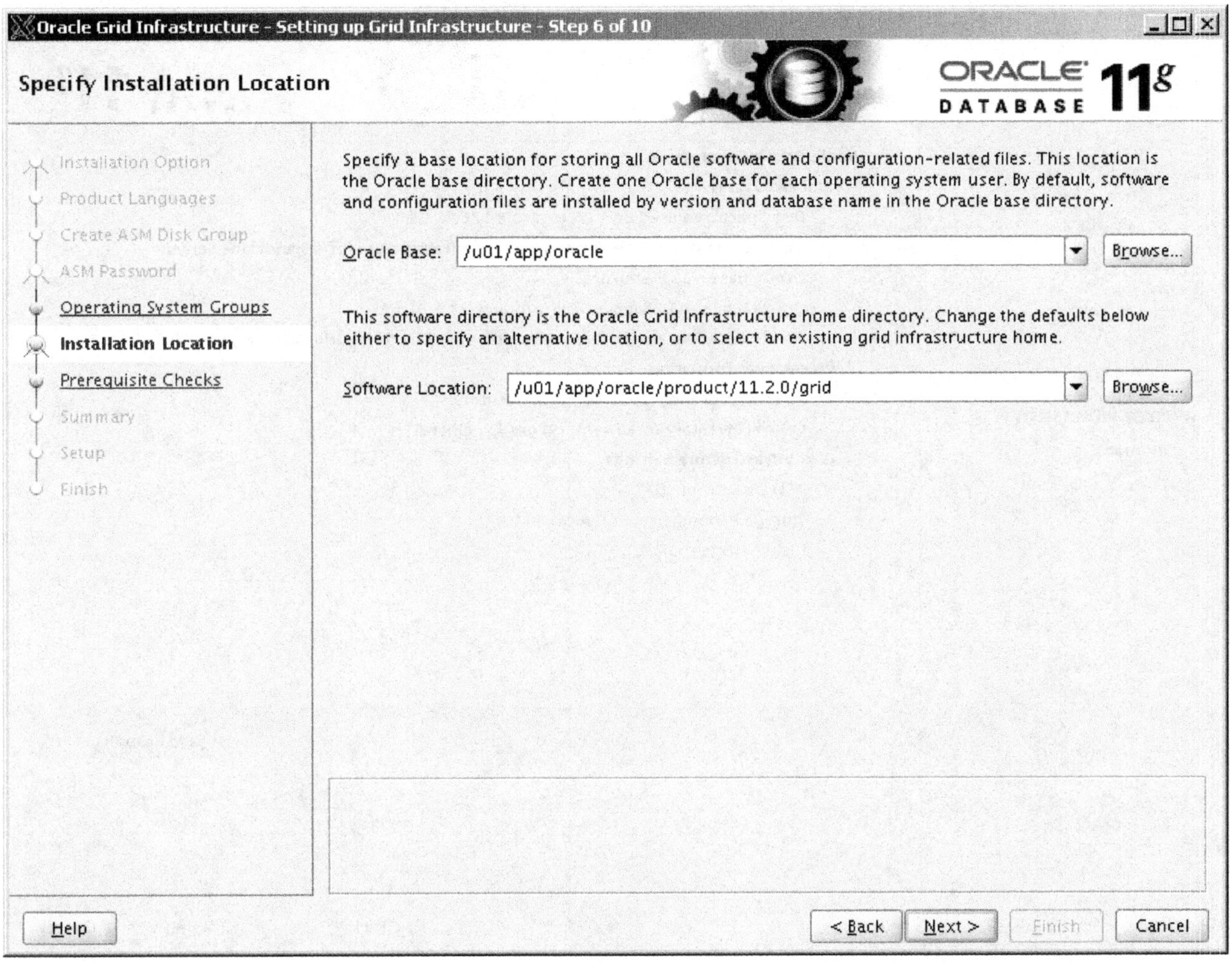

The default ORACLE_BASE and ORACLE_HOME locations should be adequate for the installation. Take particular note of the ORACLE_HOME location as the subsequent database installation must use a different ORACLE_HOME than whatever is provided from the Specify Installation Location screen of the Grid Infrastructure installation.

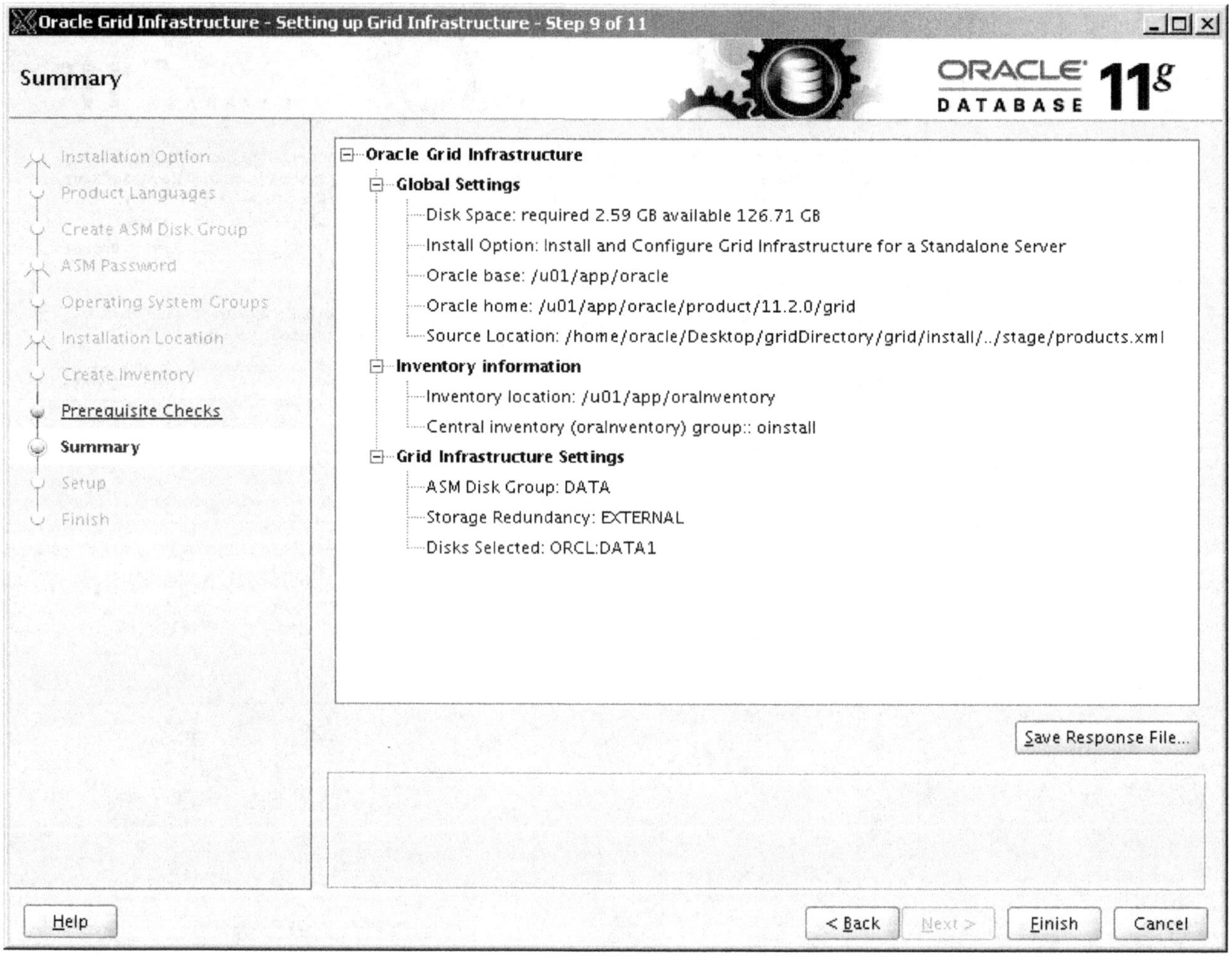

The Summary screen should appear similar to what is depicted here. Click the Finish button to proceed with the installation.

You may be asked to perform other tasks by the FixUp utility and for post-installation configuration. Complete these tasks in exactly the same manner that you would for a database installation.

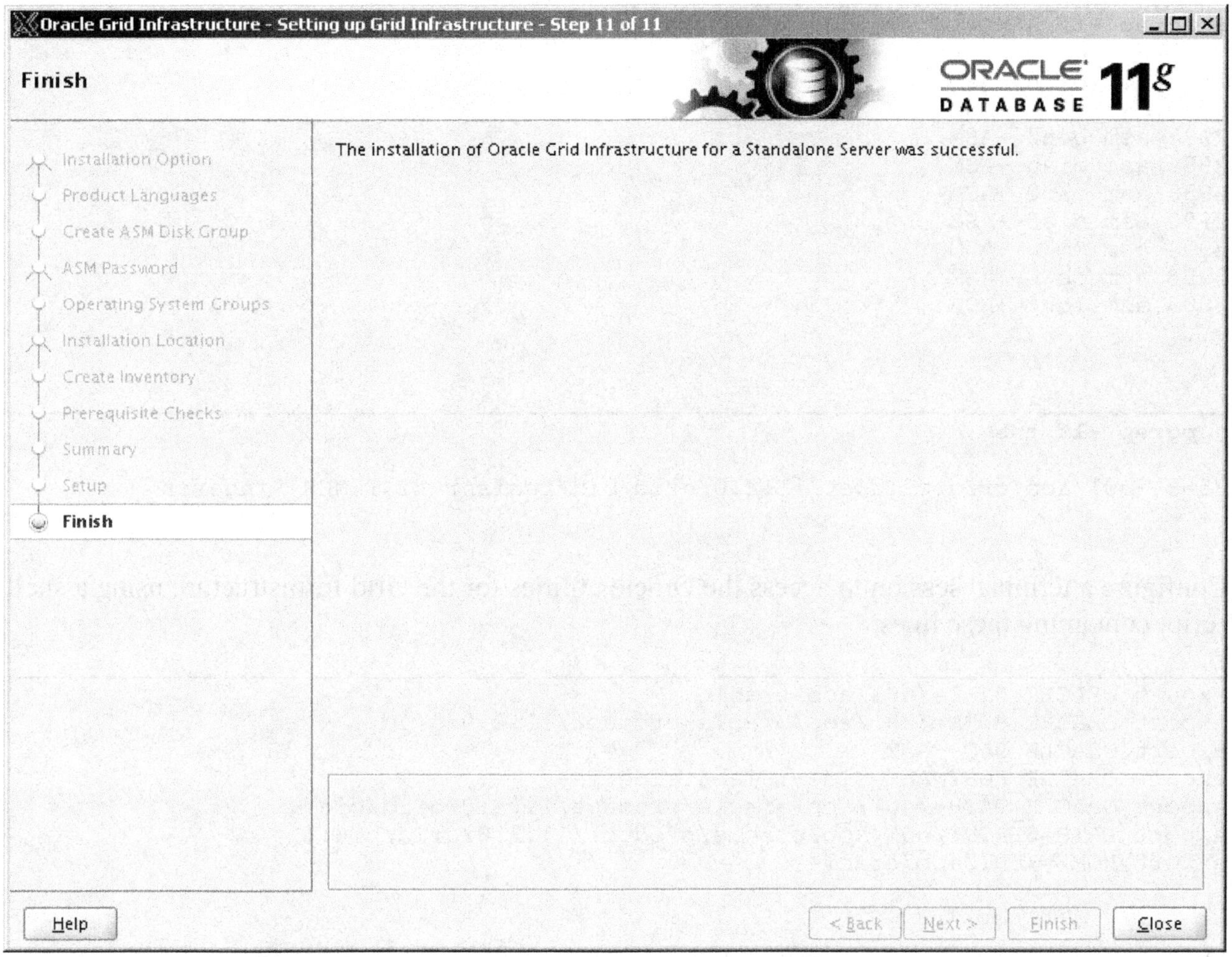

Ideally at the end of the installation process you will encounter the Finish screen. Click to Close button to complete the Grid Infrastructure installation.

INSTALLATION-3

Use the operating system utilities to confirm that ASM and the host listener are running.

```
$ pgrep -lf ASM

2977 asm_pmon_+ASM
2979 asm_vktm_+ASM
2983 asm_gen0_+ASM
2986 asm_diag_+ASM
2988 asm_psp0_+ASM
2990 asm_dia0_+ASM
2994 asm_mman_+ASM
2996 asm_dbw0_+ASM
3003 asm_lgwr_+ASM
...
```

```
$ pgrep -lf tns

2568 /u01/app/grid/product/11.2.0/grid/bin/tnslsnr LISTENER -inherit
```

Configure a terminal session to access the Oracle utilities for the Grid Infrastructure using a shell script containing these lines:

```
export ORACLE_BASE=/u01/app/oracle
export ORACLE_HOME=/u01/app/oracle/product/11.2.0/grid
export ORACLE_SID=+ASM
export ORACLE_HOSTNAME=siderislab4.sideris
export ORACLE_PATH=/u01/app/oracle/product/11.2.0/grid/bin:.
export PATH=$PATH:/u01/app/oracle/product/11.2.0/grid/bin:.
export HOME=/u01/app/oracle
```

Use the Oracle utilities to confirm that ASM and the host listener are running.

```
$ sqlplus /nolog
SQL*Plus: Release 11.2.0.1.0 Production on Mon May 10 15:49:43 2010
Copyright (c) 1982, 2009, Oracle.  All rights reserved.

SQL> CONNECT sys/***** AS SYSASM;
Connected.

SQL> SELECT username, program
     FROM v$process;

USERNAME        PROGRAM
--------------- ------------------------------------------------
                PSEUDO
oracle          oracle@siderislab4.sideris (PMON)
oracle          oracle@siderislab4.sideris (VKTM)
oracle          oracle@siderislab4.sideris (GEN0)
...
```

```
$ lsnrctl status

LSNRCTL for Linux: Version 11.2.0.1.0 - Production on 10-MAY-2010 15:52:14
Copyright (c) 1991, 2009, Oracle.  All rights reserved.

Connecting to (DESCRIPTION=(ADDRESS=(PROTOCOL=IPC)(KEY=EXTPROC1521)))
STATUS of the LISTENER
------------------------
Alias                     LISTENER
Version                   TNSLSNR for Linux: Version 11.2.0.1.0 - Production
Start Date                10-MAY-2010 13:43:27
Uptime                    0 days 2 hr. 8 min. 46 sec
Trace Level               off
Security                  ON: Local OS Authentication
SNMP                      OFF
Listener Parameter File
/u01/app/oracle/product/11.2.0/grid/network/admin/listener.ora
Listener Log File
/u01/app/oracle/diag/tnslsnr/siderislab4/listener/alert/log.xml
Listening Endpoints Summary...
  (DESCRIPTION=(ADDRESS=(PROTOCOL=ipc)(KEY=EXTPROC1521)))
  (DESCRIPTION=(ADDRESS=(PROTOCOL=tcp)(HOST=siderislab4.sideris)(PORT=1521)))
Services Summary...
Service "+ASM" has 1 instance(s).
  Instance "+ASM", status READY, has 1 handler(s) for this service...
The command completed successfully
```

INSTALLATION-4

From the root account create the dba group and add it to the oracle account.

```
[oracle@siderislab4 ~]$ su -
Password: ***********
# /usr/sbin/groupadd -g 510 dba
# /usr/sbin/usermod -G dba oracle
# exit
[oracle@siderislab4]$
```

You could confirm the group membership of the account thereafter if you wish.

```
[oracle@siderislab4]$ id oracle
uid=1000(oracle) gid=520(oinstall)
groups=520(oinstall),525(asmdba),535(asmadmin),510(dba)
```

Create a subdirectory within the existing ORACLE_BASE which will serve as an ORACLE_HOME directory distinct from the home directory of the grid installation.

```
[oracle@siderislab4 ~]$ mkdir -p /u01/app/oracle/product/11.2.0/dbhome_1
[oracle@siderislab4 ~]$
```

Create an installation subdirectory for the database installation and unpack the database installation packages into that location.

```
[oracle@siderislab4 ~]$ mkdir installDirectory
[oracle@siderislab4 ~]$ unzip linux_11gR2_database_1of2.zip -d
installDirectory
...
extracting:
11ginstall/database/stage/sizes/oracle.server11.2.0.1.0SE.sizes.properties
 extracting:
11ginstall/database/stage/sizes/oracle.server11.2.0.1.0Custom.sizes.properties
  inflating: 11ginstall/database/stage/OuiConfigVariables.xml
  inflating: 11ginstall/database/stage/oracle.server.11_2_0_1_0.xml
  inflating: 11ginstall/database/stage/fastcopy.xml
...

[oracle@siderislab4 ~]$ unzip linux_11gR2_database_2of2.zip -d
installDirectory
  inflating:
11ginstall/database/stage/Components/oracle.ctx/11.2.0.1.0/1/DataFiles/filegro
up15.4.1.jar
  inflating:
11ginstall/database/stage/Components/oracle.ctx/11.2.0.1.0/1/DataFiles/filegro
up4.jar
  inflating:
11ginstall/database/stage/Components/oracle.ctx/11.2.0.1.0/1/DataFiles/filegro
up19.jar
  inflating:
11ginstall/database/stage/Components/oracle.ctx/11.2.0.1.0/1/DataFiles/filegro
up16.jar
...
$
```

INSTALLATION-5

Define the environment variable ORACLE_HOSTNAME and launch the database installer.

```
$ export ORACLE_HOSTNAME=siderislab4.sideris
$ cd installDirectory/database
$ ./runInstaller
```

Proceed through the installation dialog, making the selections indicated in the exercise instructions, until you encounter the Typical Install Configuration screen.

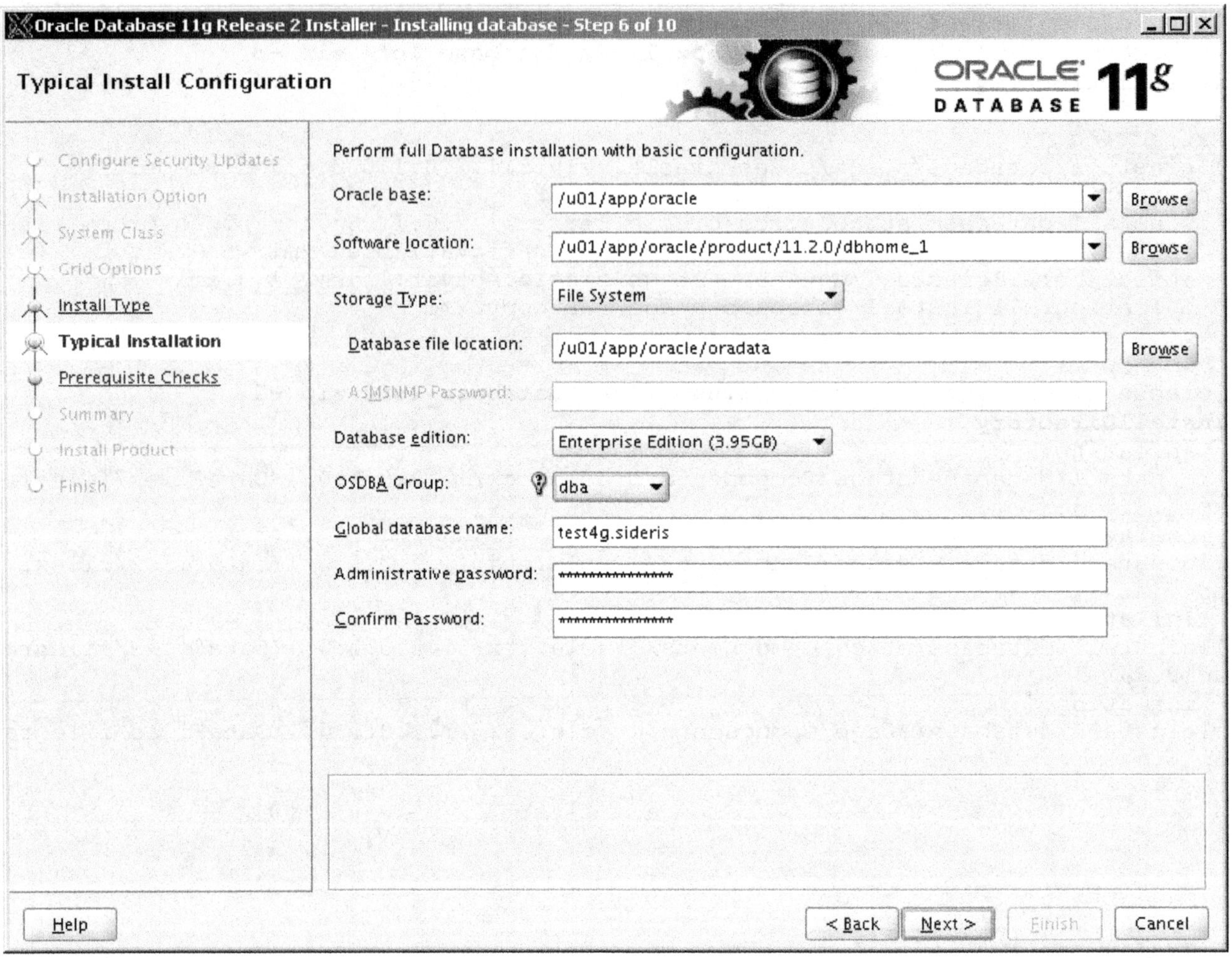

Note these important items as shown on the Typical Install Configuration page:

- Ensure that the Software Location matches the ORACLE_HOME directory you just created for the database installation.

- Although you should ultimately select File System for the Storage Type, try to temporarily select Automatic Storage Management. If that is possible, it will indicate that the database installation is detecting the ASM instance and the ASM disk groups. But as mentioned, for now select the traditional File System storage.

- You may specify any Global Database Name you wish, but we have used test4g in our example.

- Ensure that the OSDBA Group is set to dba.

Click the Next button and continue through the installation dialog.

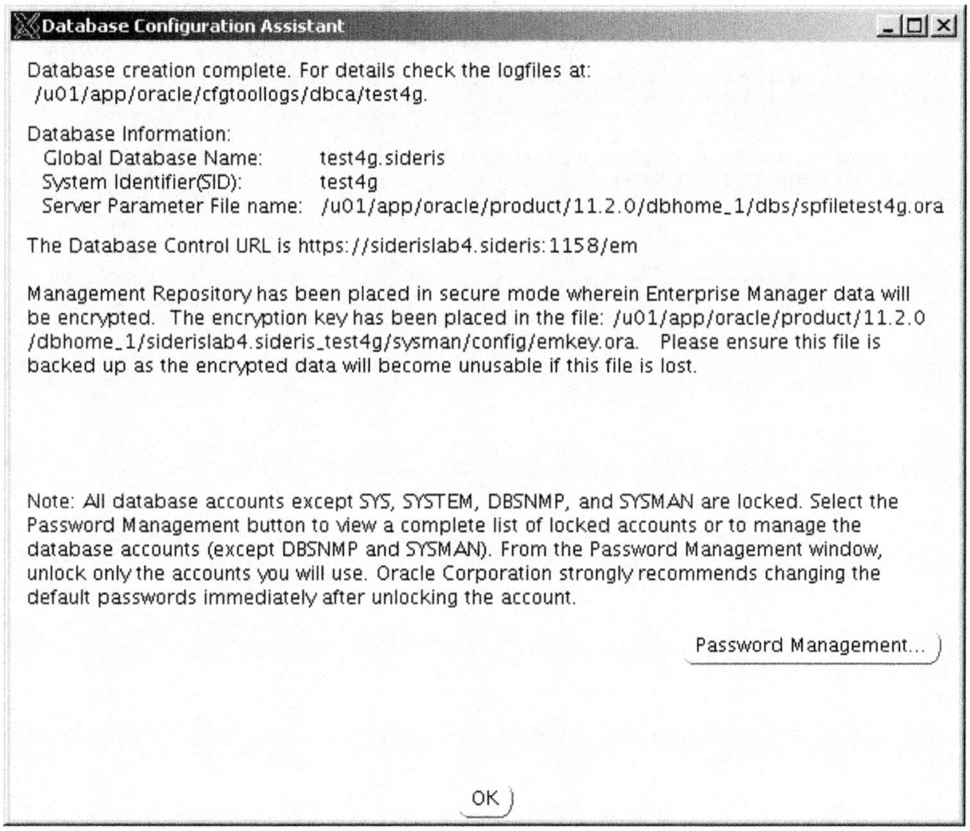

You should eventually see the DBCA launch and create the starter database. Click the OK button to acknowledge successful installation, creation and configuration of the database.

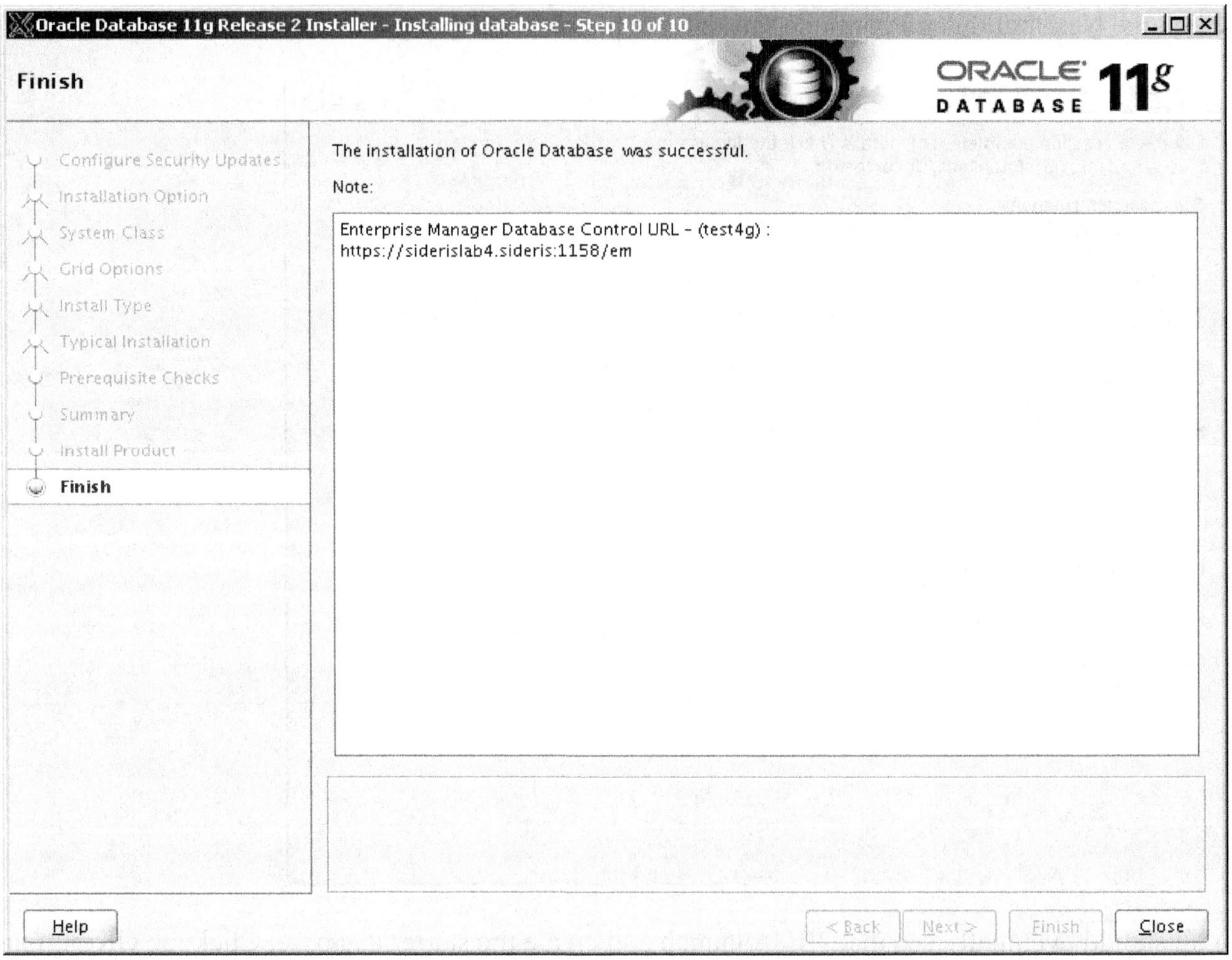

After performing required post-installation tasks the database installation dialog should complete with a successful indication from the Finish screen.

Note that if you wish to use the Oracle utilities to manage the database instance that you will need to invoke a shell script which has these environment variable settings.

```
export ORACLE_BASE=/u01/app/oracle
export ORACLE_HOME=/u01/app/oracle/product/11.2.0/dbhome_1
export ORACLE_SID=test4g
export ORACLE_UNQNAME=test4g
export ORACLE_HOSTNAME=siderislab4.sideris
export ORACLE_PATH=/u01/app/oracle/product/11.2.0/dbhome_1/bin:.
export PATH=$PATH:/u01/app/oracle/product/11.2.0/dbhome_1/bin:.
export HOME=/u01/app/oracle
export JAVA_HOME=$ORACLE_HOME/jdk
```

INSTALLATION-6

```
$ lsnrctl status

LSNRCTL for Linux: Version 11.2.0.1.0 - Production on 25-JUN-2010 16:09:09
Copyright (c) 1991, 2009, Oracle.  All rights reserved.

Connecting to (DESCRIPTION=(ADDRESS=(PROTOCOL=IPC)(KEY=EXTPROC1521)))
STATUS of the LISTENER
------------------------
Alias                     LISTENER
Version                   TNSLSNR for Linux: Version 11.2.0.1.0 - Production
Start Date                24-JUN-2010 08:53:14
Uptime                    1 days 7 hr. 15 min. 55 sec
Trace Level               off
Security                  ON: Local OS Authentication
SNMP                      OFF
Listener Parameter File
/u01/app/oracle/product/11.2.0/grid/network/admin/listener.ora
Listener Log File
/u01/app/oracle/diag/tnslsnr/siderislab4/listener/alert/log.xml
Listening Endpoints Summary...
  (DESCRIPTION=(ADDRESS=(PROTOCOL=ipc)(KEY=EXTPROC1521)))
  (DESCRIPTION=(ADDRESS=(PROTOCOL=tcp)(HOST=siderislab4.sideris)(PORT=1521)))
Services Summary...
Service "+ASM" has 1 instance(s).
  Instance "+ASM", status READY, has 1 handler(s) for this service...
Service "test4g.sideris" has 1 instance(s).
  Instance "test4g", status READY, has 1 handler(s) for this service...
Service "test4gXDB.sideris" has 1 instance(s).
  Instance "test4g", status READY, has 1 handler(s) for this service...
The command completed successfully
```

Section 3
Oracle Restart

Objectives

- ✓ What Is Oracle Restart?
- ✓ Component Status Using srvctl
- ✓ Configuration Using srvctl
- ✓ Startup / Shutdown Using srvctl
- ✓ Using crsctl

Section Overview

The Oracle Restart facility is part of the High Availability features of the database. Its intent is to ensure that the database and related facilities operate on a non-stop basis, or at least recover as quickly as possible when a failure does occur. Within this section we will explore these subjects:

- Learn about the intent and purpose of Oracle Restart
- Registration of software components with Oracle Restart
- Managing the configuration using `srvctl`
- Manual startup and shutdown using `srvctl`
- Accessing `srvctl` via the Enterprise Manager interface
- Managing Oracle Restart with `crsctl`

> ***Note***
>
> Oracle Restart is available starting with the Oracle 11g R2 version of the database and related database services.

What Is Oracle Restart?

Traditionally the database instance and related services needed to be restarted manually in the event that a failure occurred or a system reboot was performed. This became an increasingly difficult task as more and more services related to the database were created, with each one having its own startup procedure. Furthermore, the order in which these various services needed to be started and shutdown was sometimes critical.

A legacy solution was to create system scripts which executed upon system startup or which could be called upon in the event of a failure. However, such scripts were platform-specific and version-dependent.

About Oracle Restart

Oracle Restart is a facility included within the Grid Infrastructure installation for standalone database installations. It will automatically restart all database instances and services which have been registered with the facility when the system is started.

If a system is shutdown, Oracle Restart activates and shuts down all database services in an orderly manner and in the proper sequence.

Additionally, when the system is running Oracle Restart will issue periodic check to ensure that the registered facilities are running. If the check fails, the service is shutdown and restarted. As of this writing these are the services which may be managed by Oracle Restart:

- Database instance(s)
- Oracle Net listener
- ASM instance
- ASM disk groups
- Oracle Notification Services (ONS) within a Data Guard environment

Note

As of this writing the Database Control or Grid Control services which activate the Enterprise Manager interface are not included within the Oracle Restart framework. Thus one must still manually use the `emctl` utility to manually manage these services.

Registering With Oracle Restart

Most Oracle utilities which create database instances or database related services will register the newly created component with Oracle Restart. Thereafter, these services will automatically be included in the restart framework. Consider examples of facilities which will integrate their respective components with Oracle Restart:

- DBCA – database instances
- ASMCA – ASM disk groups
- NETCA – Oracle Net listeners
- EM – Oracle Enterprise Manager
- Oracle Universal Installer – database and ASM instances and Oracle Net listeners

Of course, these same utilities will also remove the component from the Oracle Restart configuration if they remove or deinstall a particular service or component.

In the event that a component is not registered with Oracle Restart, the registration may be manually managed using the Server Control `srvctl` utility. However, by installing the Grid Infrastructure first on a server, all subsequent installations will automatically perform appropriate Oracle Restart registrations.

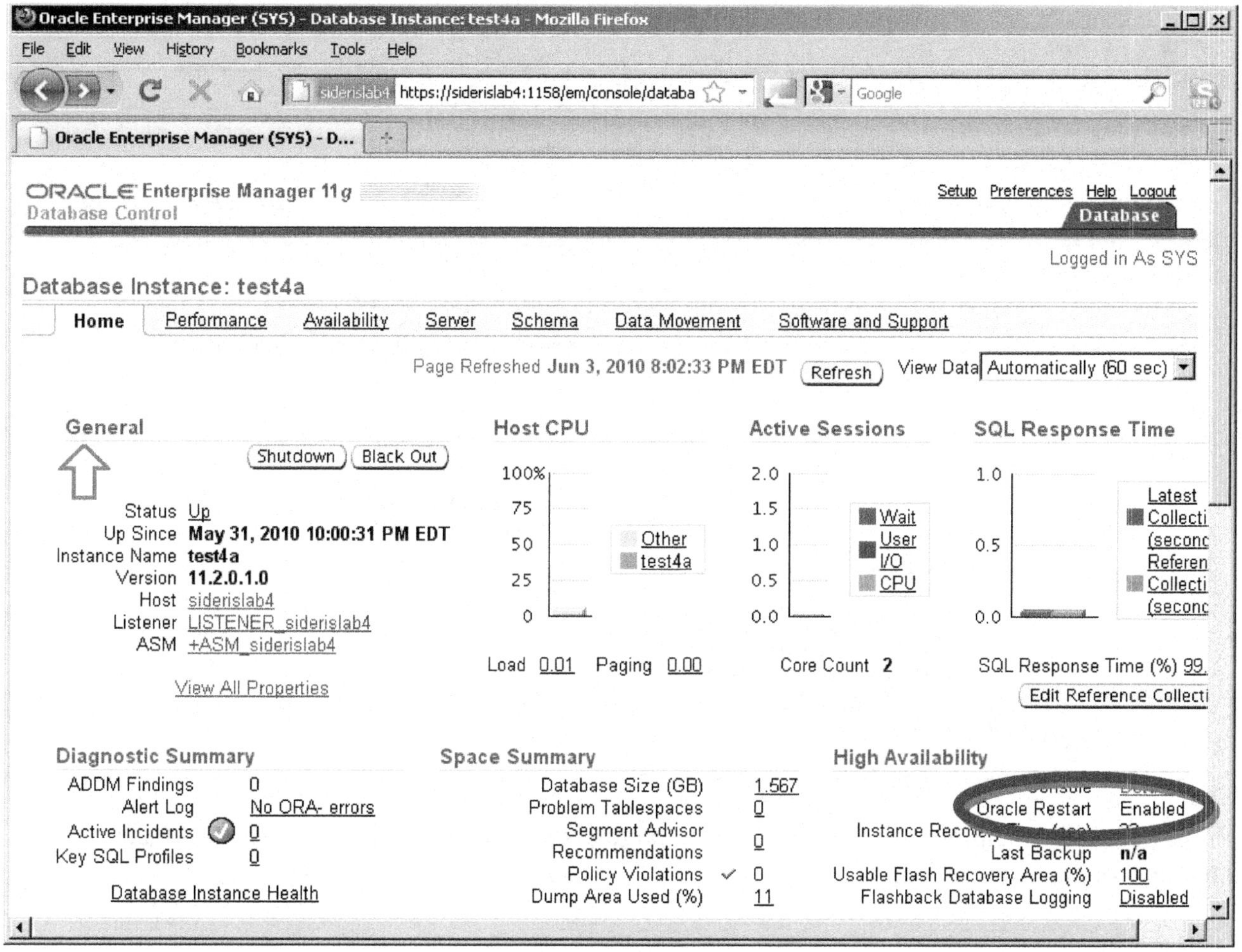

Notice in this example of the EM home page for a database instance how the instance has been registered with Oracle Restart.

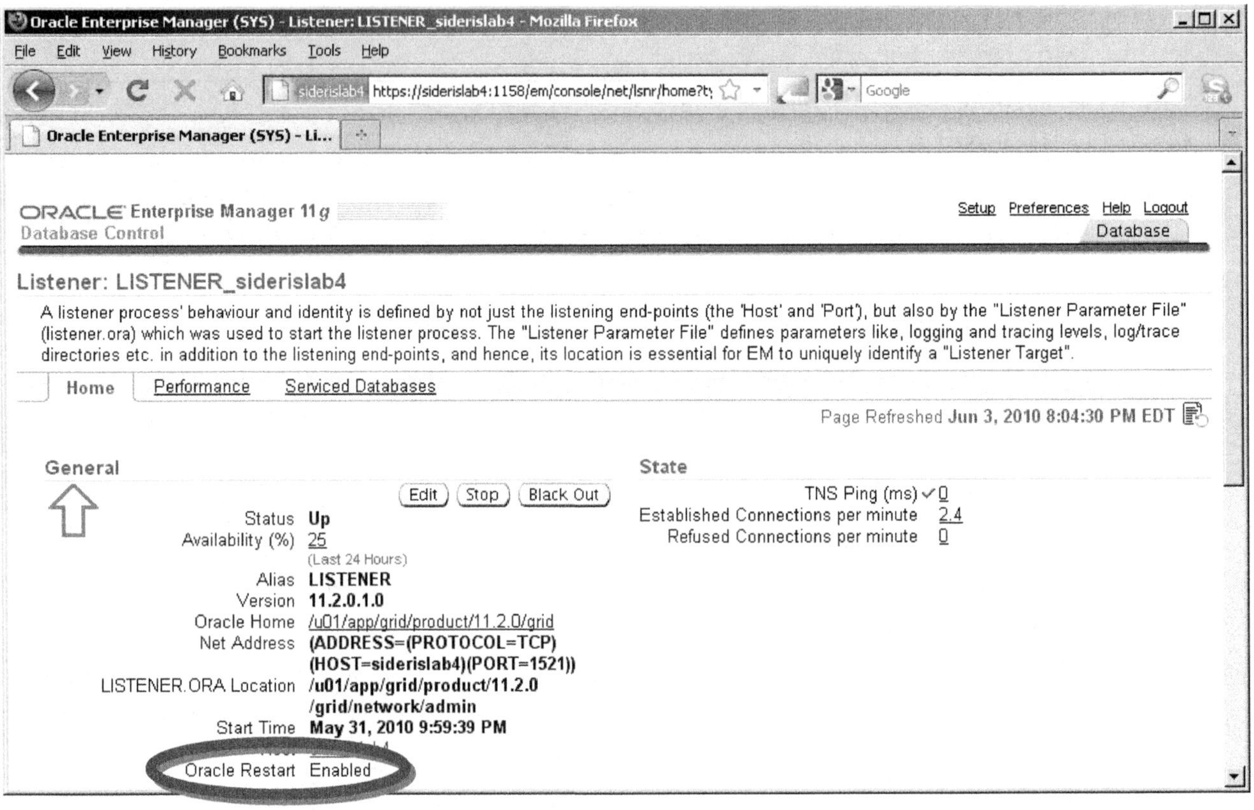

Similarly, the Oracle Net Listener EM home page also indicates that Oracle Restart has been enabled for this component.

> *Note*
>
> While Oracle Restart only exists within a standalone database environment, its functionality does exist within a RAC environment as part of Oracle Clusterware.

About srvctl

Traditionally the database instance and related services had control utilities by which one could obtain status information, perform startup and shutdown operations, and so on. For example, the Enterprise Manager Control (`emctl`) utility managed the database administrator interface to the database, the Listener Control (`lsnrctl`) utility performed similar functions for the listener, and so on.

The Server Control (`srvctl`) is a single utility which allows the administrator to manually manage all database related services. This facility is also used by the Oracle Restart component to perform its automatic restart operations as well.

Our discussion will next consider how the administrator may use this utility directly. While there are many detailed options available with `srvctl`, those which we have selected to demonstrate are representative of what you are most likely to need in a production environment.

Component Status Using srvctl

The `srvctl` utility allows one to manage the Oracle Restart configuration. One might begin by learning to use the utility to obtain basic status information.

Obtaining A Component Status

When using `srvctl` the command elements often conform to the following form:

```
$ srvctl command component -option componentIdentifier
```

For example, suppose one wanted to obtain the status of a database instance. The STATUS command might be used along with the component keyword and an identifier as to which database instance is being queried:

```
[oracle@siderislab4 ~]$ srvctl status database -d test4g
Database is running.
```

Similarly, if one wished to obtain the status of the Oracle Net listener, with a name of listener1, then the following command would be used:

```
[oracle@siderislab4 ~]$ srvctl status listener -l listener1
Listener LISTENER1 is enabled
Listener LISTENER1 is running on node(s): siderislab4
```

Referencing The Oracle Home Directory

Another way to obtain identify a component is to specify its Oracle Home directory. All components installed within that Oracle Home are addressed. Thus, in this case where one issues the STATUS command, the status of all components in that Oracle Home directory are listed. When using the HOME keyword one must also specify a state file by means of the –s option. The state file is used to record the results of the command.

```
[oracle@siderislab4 ~]$ srvctl status home -o
/u01/app/oracle/product/11.2.0/dbhome_1 -s test4gState.txt

Database test4g is running on node siderislab4
```

Notice in this example how several components which exist with the Grid Infrastructure home directory are examined by use of the HOME keyword.

```
[oracle@siderislab4 ~]$ srvctl status home -o
/u01/app/oracle/product/11.2.0/grid -s gridState.txt

Disk Group ora.DATA.dg is running on siderislab4
ASM is running on siderislab4
Listener LISTENER is running on node siderislab4
ONS daemon is running on node: siderislab4
eONS daemon is running on node: siderislab4
```

ASM Components Status

This command obtains the status of the ASM instance. In this case no component identifier is required since only one ASM instance may be running on a given host system.

```
[oracle@siderislab4 ~]$ srvctl status asm -a
ASM is running on siderislab4
ASM is enabled.
```

ASM disk groups must be mounted in order to be accessible. In the context of Oracle Restart, a mounted disk group is considered to be running. This command obtains the status of disk group DATA.

```
[oracle@siderislab4 ~]$ srvctl status diskgroup -g data -a
Disk Group data is running on siderislab4
Disk Group data is enabled
```

Configuration Using srvctl

In order for Oracle Restart to manage a service it must be configured or registered. Normally, this is automatically done if the Grid Infrastructure has been installed first on a host system. In such a circumstance, when the Installer creates a new database instance it will register and configure the instance with Oracle Restart. Or, when the DBCA drops a database, it is de-registered with Oracle Restart.

However, there may be circumstances where one needs to manually modify the configuration. This is especially the case if existing software installations exist before the Grid Infrastructure is installed. There are many other circumstances in the practical use of the database environment in which manual configuration may be required.

Specifically we will consider these configuration options:

- Examining existing configurations or registrations
- Manually registering a component
- Modifying a registered component configuration

Examining Registrations

Examining A Database Configuration

One can examine the current registration with Oracle Restart, including its attributes. In this example, notice that the database configuration which is queried. When the START option is specified by `srvctl` it will bring the database to an open state. Or, when the STOP option is specified it will perform an IMMEDIATE shutdown.

```
[oracle@siderislab4 oracle]$ srvctl config database -d test4g

Database unique name: test4g
Database name: test4g
Oracle home: /u01/app/oracle/product/11.2.0/dbhome_1
Oracle user: oracle
Spfile:
Domain: sideris
Start options: open
Stop options: immediate
Database role: PRIMARY
Management policy: AUTOMATIC
Disk Groups:
Services:
```

The management policy indicates how Oracle Restart should respond to a failure. The policy of AUTOMATIC will include the instance in the restart sequence. A policy of MANUAL will not perform an automatic restart, but the Oracle Restart facility will still monitor and report changes to the status of the database component.

Note

One could omit the –d specifier and obtain a brief list of all databases registered with ASM. One could thereafter use the database name to obtain a detailed configuration output such as is shown above.

Examining The Listener Configuration

The listener configuration is also available.

```
[oracle@siderislab4 ~]$ srvctl config listener
Name: LISTENER
Home: /u01/app/oracle/product/11.2.0/grid
End points: TCP:1521
```

Examining The ASM Configuration

The ASM configuration is produced by this command.

```
[oracle@siderislab4 ~]$ srvctl config asm
ASM home: /u01/app/oracle/product/11.2.0/grid
ASM listener: LISTENER
Spfile: +DATA/asm/asmparameterfile/registry.253.722508959
ASM diskgroup discovery string:
```

Manual Registration

Suppose that in advance of the Grid Infrastructure installation one had already created a database instance named TEST4A. Now, with the Grid Infrastructure in place, one wishes to register that database manually with Oracle Restart. This could be done as follows, including the –o option which specifies the Oracle Home path.

```
[oracle@siderislab4 ~]$ srvctl add database -d test4a -o
/u01/app/oracle/product/11.2.0/dbhome_2
```

Similarly one could manually remove or de-register a component from the Oracle Restart framework.

```
[oracle@siderislab4 ~]$ srvctl remove database -d test4a
Remove the database test4a? (y/[n]) y

[oracle@siderislab4 ~]$
```

Modifying Configurations

There may be circumstances in which one wishes to modify the configuration of a component.

Listener Modification

For example, suppose that one were going to shutdown the listener in order to perform troubleshooting and reconfiguration of Oracle Net Services. In such a case one may want to disable automatic restart, while otherwise preserving the configuration of the listener within Oracle Restart. The following command would accomplish this objective:

```
[oracle@siderislab4 ~]$ srvctl disable listener
[oracle@siderislab4 ~]$ srvctl status listener
Listener LISTENER is disabled
Listener LISTENER is running on node(s): siderislab4
```

The component is no longer managed by Oracle Restart or by `srvctl`. It must now be managed using lsnrctl, unless it is enabled once again:

```
[oracle@siderislab4 ~]$ srvctl enable listener
[oracle@siderislab4 ~]$ srvctl status listener
Listener LISTENER is enabled
Listener LISTENER is not running
```

Database Modification

Suppose one wanted to modify the configuration for a database instance. One might expect extensive database recovery operations to be performed after any failure. Therefore, one might set the management policy to MANUAL. Additionally, when one does manually start the database, one might wish to bring the database only to a mounted, but not opened state. This would be accomplished using the –y and –s options respectively.

```
[oracle@siderislab4 ~]$ srvctl modify database -d test4g -y MANUAL -s MOUNT
[oracle@siderislab4 ~]$ srvctl config database -d test4g
Database unique name: test4g
Database name: test4g
Oracle home: /u01/app/oracle/product/11.2.0/dbhome_1
Oracle user: oracle
Spfile:
Domain: sideris
Start options: MOUNT
Stop options: immediate
Database role: PRIMARY
Management policy: MANUAL
Disk Groups:
Services:
```

Startup/Shutdown Using srvctl

Any component may be manually started or shutdown using the universal control utility `srvctl`. Notice how this is done for the listener component.

```
[oracle@siderislab4 ~]$ srvctl stop listener
[oracle@siderislab4 ~]$ srvctl status listener
Listener LISTENER is enabled
Listener LISTENER is not running
```

```
[oracle@siderislab4 ~]$ srvctl start listener
[oracle@siderislab4 ~]$ srvctl status listener
Listener LISTENER is enabled
Listener LISTENER is running on node(s): siderislab4
```

Similar operations are possible for any other component, such as the database or ASM instances.

Why Use srvctl?

In addition to simple convenience, components should be started and shutdown using `srvctl` rather than the legacy control utilities for the following important reasons:

- The *component dependency* is only maintained by `srvctl`. For example, if one performs a SHUTDOWN ABORT operation on an ASM instance before performing a shutdown of database instances using ASM disk groups, one could corrupt the ASM configuration. On the other hand, `srvctl` will ensure that the shutdown sequence among any dependent components is properly implemented.

- Oracle Restart configuration options are only accessed by `srvctl`. For example, if a database instance was configured for startup only to the mounted state, as demonstrated earlier, this is only implemented by `srvctl`. Manual restart procedures using SQL*Plus would not access the latest Oracle Restart configuration settings.

Using srvctl Via EM

The Enterprise Manager (EM) interface allows one to startup and shutdown the database instance from that vantage point. If the instance is registered with Oracle Restart, one will also have the option to invoke `srvctl` from the EM interface similar to the way in which this could be manually invoked from the SQL command line.

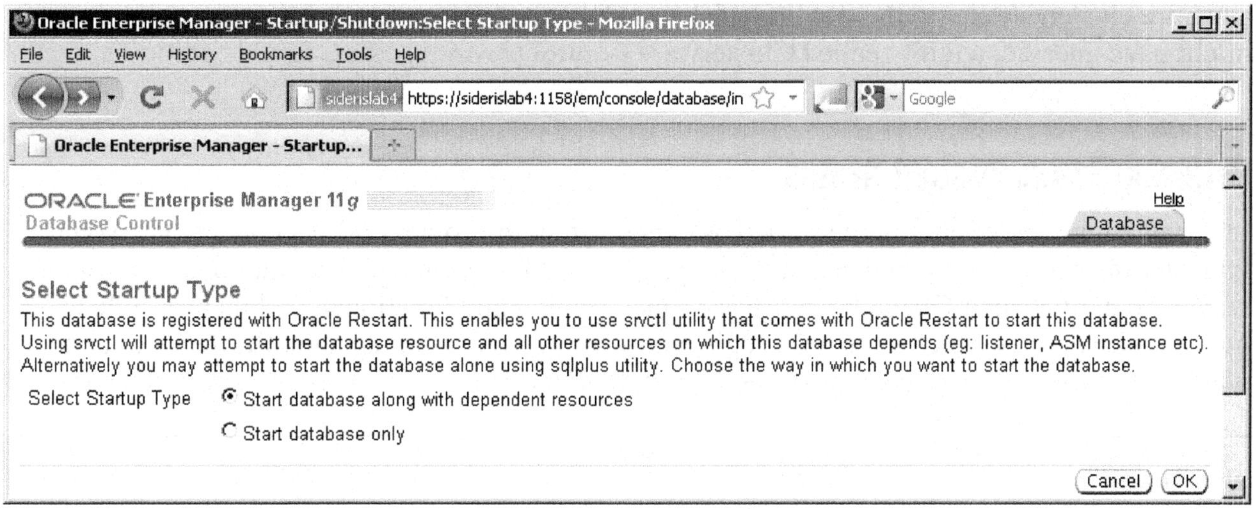

This is an example of a startup dialog within EM when the database has been registered with Oracle Restart. The option Start Database Along With... invokes the `srvctl` utility. This screen does not appear when starting an unregistered database.

Managing The Oracle Restart Facility

While outside the scope of this course, Oracle Clusterware includes restart facilities for an entire cluster, similar to the way in which Oracle Restart does for a standalone server. As you might have guessed, a utility called Clusterware Control (`crsctl`) exists for this purpose.

Obtaining Oracle Restart Status

In a standalone server environment such as exists within the context of this course, one would typically only use `crsctl` to manage the Oracle Restart facility itself. For example, suppose one wanted to confirm that Oracle Restart was in fact running and functional, and thereby able to oversee the services which have been registered with it. One could use the following command, with the keyword HAS referring to Oracle *high-availability services*, such as Oracle Restart.

```
[oracle@siderislab4 ~]$ crsctl check has
CRS-4638: Oracle High Availability Services is online
```

Start/Stop & Enable/Disable Oracle Restart

On occasion one may need to patch the Grid Infrastructure software installation. In such a circumstance, one would proceed with the following basic outline:

1. Stop all component services managed by Oracle Restart.
2. Use `crsctl` to disable Oracle Restart automatically restarting itself in the event of a system reboot.
3. Use `crsctl` to stop the current Oracle Restart operation.

Consider an example of how using `crsctl` in this manner would appear on our demonstration server:

```
[oracle@siderislab4 ~]$ crsctl disable has
CRS-4621: Oracle High Availability Services autostart is disabled.

[oracle@siderislab4 ~]$ crsctl stop has
CRS-2791: Starting shutdown of Oracle High Availability Services-managed
resources on 'siderislab4'
CRS-2673: Attempting to stop 'ora.cssd' on 'siderislab4'
CRS-2677: Stop of 'ora.cssd' on 'siderislab4' succeeded
CRS-2673: Attempting to stop 'ora.diskmon' on 'siderislab4'
CRS-2677: Stop of 'ora.diskmon' on 'siderislab4' succeeded
CRS-2793: Shutdown of Oracle High Availability Services-managed resources on
'siderislab4' has completed
CRS-4133: Oracle High Availability Services has been stopped.
```

> ***Note***
>
> The first step noted above which manually stops all registered services is not necessary but done using an abundance of caution. The `crsctl stop has` command will first shutdown all registered services before Oracle Restart is shutdown.

After the software update was completed, one would essentially reverse the process:

1. Use `crsctl` to enable Oracle Restart in the event that the host system must be restarted.
2. Use `crsctl` to start the current Oracle Restart operations.
3. Start all component services managed by Oracle Restart, or perhaps just reboot the server if you prefer.

```
[oracle@siderislab4 ~]$ crsctl enable has
CRS-4622: Oracle High Availability Services autostart is enabled.
[oracle@siderislab4 ~]$ crsctl start has
CRS-4123: Oracle High Availability Services has been started.
```

Section Review

Remember These Points

- Oracle Restart is part of the High Availability Services (HAS) features for standalone servers, similar to the way in which Oracle Clusterware provides such features for clustered servers.
- Components may be registered with Oracle Restart to ensure that startup and shutdown operations are performed in sequence, considering appropriate component dependencies.
- Oracle HAS will detect when a registered service has failed, and will invoke Oracle Restart to restart all appropriate services automatically.
- One manages the Oracle Restart configuration using the Clusterware Control (crsctl) utility.
- One manages the components using the Server Control (srvctl) utility.

Workshop Section
Oracle Restart

Exercises

What You Will Do in This Workshop

In this workshop, you will:

- Use the Clusterware Control utility to examine the status of High Availability Services
- Use the Server Control utility to examine the status of grid infrastructure and database components
- Examine the Oracle Restart configurations of all software components
- Simulate a crash of an Oracle Restart registered component and watch the automatic restart occur.

RESTART-1

❑ Launch a terminal session to the host system, either directly or using an SSH connection. After doing so, define the environment variables necessary to access Grid Infrastructure utilities.

RESTART-2

❑ Use the Clusterware Control utility to ensure that Oracle Restart and the Oracle High Availability services are running on the server at present.

RESTART-3

❑ Use the Server Control utility to examine the status of all components within the Grid Infrastructure and database installations.

RESTART-4

❑ Examine the Oracle Restart configuration of one or two components.

RESTART-5

❑ Using the unified Server Control utility, demonstrate the alternative to the component-specific Listener Control by manually starting and stopping the listener. You could still use the Listener Control to examine the status of the component.

RESTART-6

❑ In this exercise we will demonstrate the automatic restart capabilities of Oracle High Availability services. Perform these steps:

1. Locate the TNS listener process using the Process Status command in Linux.
2. Kill the process.
3. Quickly examine the status of the listener to confirm that it is in fact down.
4. After a few moments, query the status of the listener once again to confirm that it has automatically restarted.

It is important that you are fluent in the use of Linux process commands to ensure that you can correctly identify the appropriate process.

Solutions

RESTART-1

These are typical settings for environment variables required to function within the Grid Infrastructure installation. Of course you will need to make appropriate adjustments for your local installation.

```
export ORACLE_BASE=/u01/app/oracle
export ORACLE_HOME=/u01/app/oracle/product/11.2.0/grid
export ORACLE_SID=+ASM
export ORACLE_HOSTNAME=siderislab4.sideris
export ORACLE_PATH=/u01/app/oracle/product/11.2.0/grid/bin:.
export PATH=$PATH:/u01/app/oracle/product/11.2.0/grid/bin:.
```

RESTART-2

```
[oracle@siderislab4 ~]$ crsctl check has
CRS-4638: Oracle High Availability Services is online
```

RESTART-3

You might begin by examining the status of the Grid Infrastructure components.

```
[oracle@siderislab4 ~]$ srvctl status listener -l listener
Listener LISTENER is enabled
Listener LISTENER is running on node(s): siderislab4
```

```
[oracle@siderislab4 ~]$ srvctl status asm -a
ASM is running on siderislab4
ASM is enabled.
```

```
[oracle@siderislab4 ~]$ srvctl status diskgroup -g data -a
Disk Group data is running on siderislab4
Disk Group data is enabled
```

Next one could examine the status of the database installation.

```
[oracle@siderislab4 ~]$ srvctl status database -d test4g
Database is running.
```

It is possible to obtain this information more readily by referencing the Oracle Home directories of the installations. In this example we do so using the Grid Infrastructure home.

```
[oracle@siderislab4 ~]$ srvctl status home -o
/u01/app/oracle/product/11.2.0/grid -s gridState.txt

Disk Group ora.DATA.dg is running on siderislab4
ASM is running on siderislab4
Listener LISTENER is running on node siderislab4
```

And in this case we reference the database installation home.

```
[oracle@siderislab4 ~]$ srvctl status home -o
/u01/app/oracle/product/11.2.0/dbhome_1 -s test4gState.txt

Database test4g is running on node siderislab4
```

RESTART-4

This command queries the Oracle Restart configuration for the ASM instance.

```
[oracle@siderislab4 ~]$ srvctl config asm
ASM home: /u01/app/oracle/product/11.2.0/grid
ASM listener: LISTENER
Spfile: +DATA/asm/asmparameterfile/registry.253.722508959
ASM diskgroup discovery string:
```

This command examines the configuration for the database instance.

```
[oracle@siderislab4 oracle]$ srvctl config database -d test4g

Database unique name: test4g
Database name: test4g
Oracle home: /u01/app/oracle/product/11.2.0/dbhome_1
Oracle user: oracle
Spfile:
Domain: sideris
Start options: open
Stop options: immediate
Database role: PRIMARY
Management policy: AUTOMATIC
Disk Groups:
Services:
```

RESTART-5

Using the legacy Listener Control utility we confirm what the Server Control reported earlier, namely that the listener is up and running and has recognized all instances created on this server.

```
[oracle@siderislab4 ~]$ lsnrctl status

LSNRCTL for Linux: Version 11.2.0.1.0 - Production on 02-JUL-2010 14:14:03

Copyright (c) 1991, 2009, Oracle.  All rights reserved.

Connecting to (DESCRIPTION=(ADDRESS=(PROTOCOL=IPC)(KEY=EXTPROC1521)))
STATUS of the LISTENER
------------------------
Alias                     LISTENER
Version                   TNSLSNR for Linux: Version 11.2.0.1.0 - Production
Start Date                02-JUL-2010 13:46:32
Uptime                    0 days 0 hr. 27 min. 31 sec
Trace Level               off
Security                  ON: Local OS Authentication
SNMP                      OFF
Listener Parameter File
/u01/app/oracle/product/11.2.0/grid/network/admin/listener.ora
Listener Log File
/u01/app/oracle/diag/tnslsnr/siderislab4/listener/alert/log.xml
Listening Endpoints Summary...
  (DESCRIPTION=(ADDRESS=(PROTOCOL=ipc)(KEY=EXTPROC1521)))
  (DESCRIPTION=(ADDRESS=(PROTOCOL=tcp)(HOST=siderislab4.sideris)(PORT=1521)))
Services Summary...
Service "+ASM" has 1 instance(s).
  Instance "+ASM", status READY, has 1 handler(s) for this service...
Service "test4g.sideris" has 1 instance(s).
  Instance "test4g", status READY, has 1 handler(s) for this service...
Service "test4gXDB.sideris" has 1 instance(s).
  Instance "test4g", status READY, has 1 handler(s) for this service...
The command completed successfully
```

Next we use the Server Control to stop the listener, and the Listener Control to obtain an updated status.

```
[oracle@siderislab4 ~]$ srvctl stop listener
[oracle@siderislab4 ~]$ lsnrctl status

LSNRCTL for Linux: Version 11.2.0.1.0 - Production on 02-JUL-2010 14:15:20

Copyright (c) 1991, 2009, Oracle.  All rights reserved.

Connecting to (DESCRIPTION=(ADDRESS=(PROTOCOL=IPC)(KEY=EXTPROC1521)))
TNS-12541: TNS:no listener
 TNS-12560: TNS:protocol adapter error
  TNS-00511: No listener
   Linux Error: 2: No such file or directory
Connecting to
(DESCRIPTION=(ADDRESS=(PROTOCOL=TCP)(HOST=siderislab4.sideris)(PORT=1521)))
TNS-12541: TNS:no listener
 TNS-12560: TNS:protocol adapter error
  TNS-00511: No listener
   Linux Error: 111: Connection refused
```

The Server Control reports the same status for the listener. But it does confirm that the component remains within the Oracle Restart framework in the event that unplanned stoppage occurs.

```
[oracle@siderislab4 ~]$ srvctl status listener
Listener LISTENER is enabled
Listener LISTENER is not running
```

Manually restart the listener and confirm its operation.

```
[oracle@siderislab4 ~]$ srvctl start listener
[oracle@siderislab4 ~]$ lsnrctl status

LSNRCTL for Linux: Version 11.2.0.1.0 - Production on 02-JUL-2010 14:18:49

Copyright (c) 1991, 2009, Oracle.  All rights reserved.

Connecting to (DESCRIPTION=(ADDRESS=(PROTOCOL=IPC)(KEY=EXTPROC1521)))
STATUS of the LISTENER
------------------------
Alias                     LISTENER
Version                   TNSLSNR for Linux: Version 11.2.0.1.0 - Production
Start Date                02-JUL-2010 14:17:18
Uptime                    0 days 0 hr. 1 min. 31 sec
Trace Level               off
Security                  ON: Local OS Authentication
SNMP                      OFF
Listener Parameter File
/u01/app/oracle/product/11.2.0/grid/network/admin/listener.ora
Listener Log File
/u01/app/oracle/diag/tnslsnr/siderislab4/listener/alert/log.xml
Listening Endpoints Summary...
  (DESCRIPTION=(ADDRESS=(PROTOCOL=ipc)(KEY=EXTPROC1521)))
  (DESCRIPTION=(ADDRESS=(PROTOCOL=tcp)(HOST=siderislab4.sideris)(PORT=1521)))
Services Summary...
Service "+ASM" has 1 instance(s).
  Instance "+ASM", status READY, has 1 handler(s) for this service...
Service "test4g.sideris" has 1 instance(s).
  Instance "test4g", status READY, has 1 handler(s) for this service...
Service "test4gXDB.sideris" has 1 instance(s).
  Instance "test4g", status READY, has 1 handler(s) for this service...
The command completed successfully
```

RESTART-6

Using the Process Status command search for all processes with a command line which includes the string "tns". Carefully note the process for the listener component.

```
[oracle@siderislab4 ~]$ ps -ef | grep tns

oracle    5274     1  0 Jul01 ?        00:00:03
/u01/app/oracle/product/11.2.0/grid/bin/tnslsnr LISTENER -inherit
oracle   12156  1951  0 14:30 pts/1    00:00:00 grep tns
```

Use the `kill` command to abort the listener process. The Listener Control utility confirms that the listener has crashed.

```
[oracle@siderislab4 ~]$ kill 5274
[oracle@siderislab4 ~]$ lsnrctl status

LSNRCTL for Linux: Version 11.2.0.1.0 - Production on 02-JUL-2010 14:31:36

Copyright (c) 1991, 2009, Oracle.  All rights reserved.

Connecting to (DESCRIPTION=(ADDRESS=(PROTOCOL=IPC)(KEY=EXTPROC1521)))
TNS-12541: TNS:no listener
 TNS-12560: TNS:protocol adapter error
  TNS-00511: No listener
   Linux Error: 111: Connection refused
Connecting to
(DESCRIPTION=(ADDRESS=(PROTOCOL=TCP)(HOST=siderislab4.sideris)(PORT=1521)))
TNS-12541: TNS:no listener
 TNS-12560: TNS:protocol adapter error
  TNS-00511: No listener
   Linux Error: 111: Connection refused
```

After a few seconds the Oracle HAS will detect the listener crash and activate Oracle Restart to startup the listener. This can be confirmed by means of the Listener Control and the Process Status.

```
[oracle@siderislab4 ~]$ lsnrctl status

LSNRCTL for Linux: Version 11.2.0.1.0 - Production on 02-JUL-2010 14:32:47

Copyright (c) 1991, 2009, Oracle.  All rights reserved.

Connecting to (DESCRIPTION=(ADDRESS=(PROTOCOL=IPC)(KEY=EXTPROC1521)))
STATUS of the LISTENER
------------------------
Alias                     LISTENER
Version                   TNSLSNR for Linux: Version 11.2.0.1.0 - Production
Start Date                02-JUL-2010 14:32:22
Uptime                    0 days 0 hr. 0 min. 25 sec
Trace Level               off
Security                  ON: Local OS Authentication
SNMP                      OFF
Listener Parameter File
/u01/app/oracle/product/11.2.0/grid/network/admin/listener.ora
Listener Log File
/u01/app/oracle/diag/tnslsnr/siderislab4/listener/alert/log.xml
Listening Endpoints Summary...
  (DESCRIPTION=(ADDRESS=(PROTOCOL=ipc)(KEY=EXTPROC1521)))
  (DESCRIPTION=(ADDRESS=(PROTOCOL=tcp)(HOST=siderislab4.sideris)(PORT=1521)))
Services Summary...
Service "+ASM" has 1 instance(s).
  Instance "+ASM", status READY, has 1 handler(s) for this service...
Service "test4g.sideris" has 1 instance(s).
  Instance "test4g", status READY, has 1 handler(s) for this service...
Service "test4gXDB.sideris" has 1 instance(s).
  Instance "test4g", status READY, has 1 handler(s) for this service...
The command completed successfully
```

```
[oracle@siderislab4 ~]$ ps -ef | grep tns

oracle   12226     1  0 14:32 ?        00:00:00
/u01/app/oracle/product/11.2.0/grid/bin/tnslsnr LISTENER -inherit
oracle   12677  1951  0 14:37 pts/1    00:00:00 grep tns
```

Section 4
ASM Concepts & Architecture

Objectives

✓ ASM & The Database Architecture

Section Overview

The option to employ Automatic Storage Management (ASM) for the database represents one of the most powerful options available for both maximizing database performance while simplifying its administration. Within this section we will explore these subjects:

- The architecture of ASM and an ASM software instance
- Virtualization concepts, the Oracle stack and ASM
- ASM storage capabilities

ASM & The Database Architecture

Like so many technologies within the Oracle architecture, Automatic Storage Management (ASM) is best understood as one of several components which are intended to work together. The synergistic effect of all of these technologies allows one to realize the benefits that were envisioned for the overall Oracle architecture. Therefore, consider first a brief explanation of ASM in the context of these other technologies:

- Oracle Restart or Oracle Clusterware facilitates the integration of ASM into the broader database framework.

- Oracle-managed files (OMF) seek to hide the physical file names from the administrator. By simply identifying the disk device and path, the peculiarities of the actual files names are managed by the database.

- ASM seeks to hide the physical devices and paths from the administrator. One simply allocates a mass amount of storage from several devices to a *disk group*. When creating a logical database object such as a tablespace, one needs only to identify the disk group. ASM will determine how best to allocate all the data files and other database files among the total space available within the disk group.

- The flash recovery area seeks to automatically manage all of the backup files created in the event recovery of some sort is needed. By defining the flash recovery area as an ASM disk group, a higher level of abstraction is realized as well.

- The RMAN tool allows administrators to define at a very high level the type of backup or recovery operation desired. The database will utilize all of the above mentioned components to internally locate and access the backup files and move this data into the production database files as needed. ASM-managed backup files are fetched and used to recover ASM-managed data files as needed.

These technologies, in turn, are intended to support the broader goal of *grid-computing*. By essentially relegating database services to a commodity which is easily managed from a logical standpoint, the ability to dynamically provision resources for one database service or another, on demand, is possible.

The Oracle Stack

Briefly review one depiction of the software and hardware layers which comprise the stack of solutions typically configured within a database server.

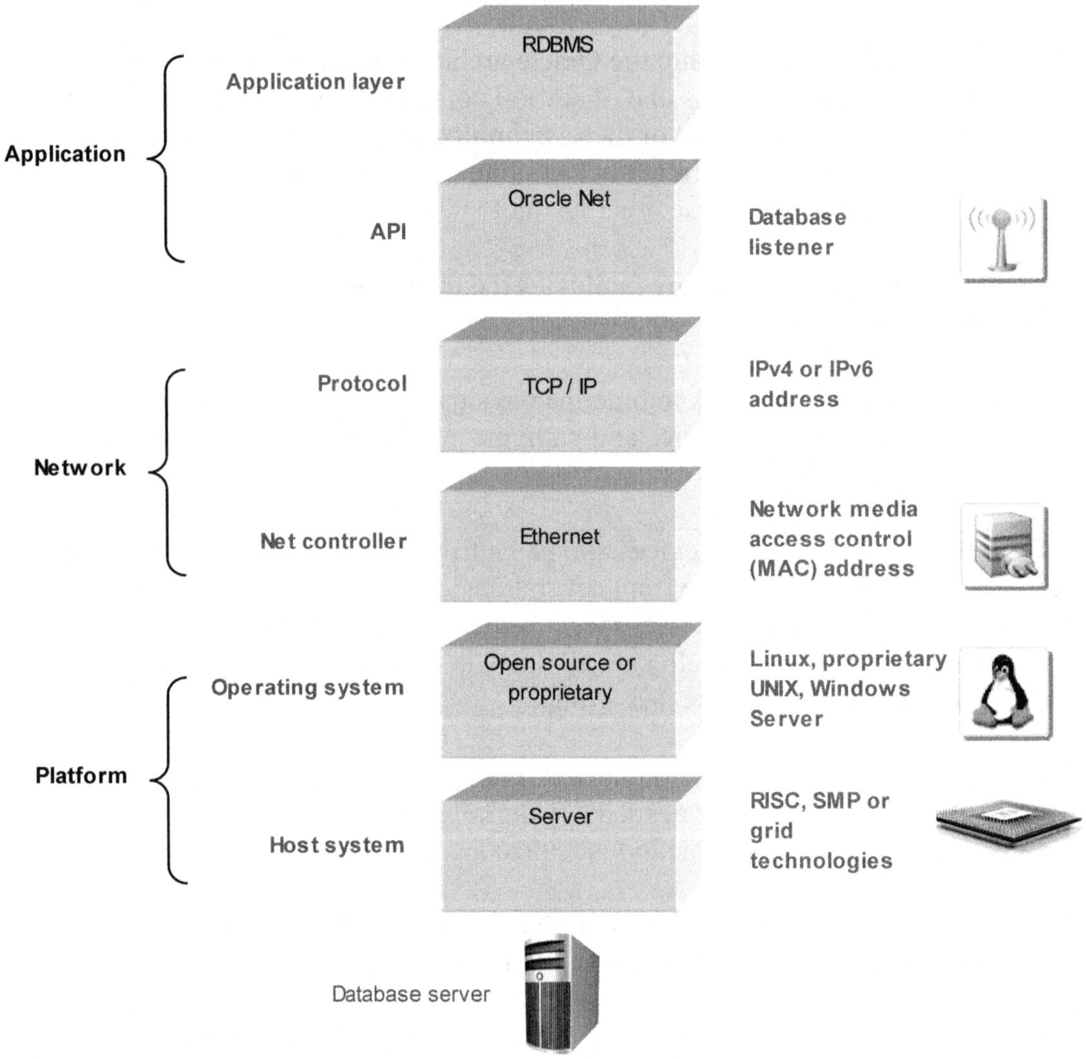

It is the physical storage function of the platform layers which ASM is intended to replace. Since so much of the activity of a database server relates to I/O, being able to remove database storage services from the platform and locate them in a specialized subsystem offers substantial advantages to the database operation.

ASM Storage Virtualization

ASM is a unique software instance created for each database server. It interacts with all other traditional relational database instances running on that same server. ASM provides the services of a *logical volume manager* (LVM) found in some operating and disk subsystems in behalf of all the database instances running on that host system. It is an example of the virtualization of the storage layer of the server stack.

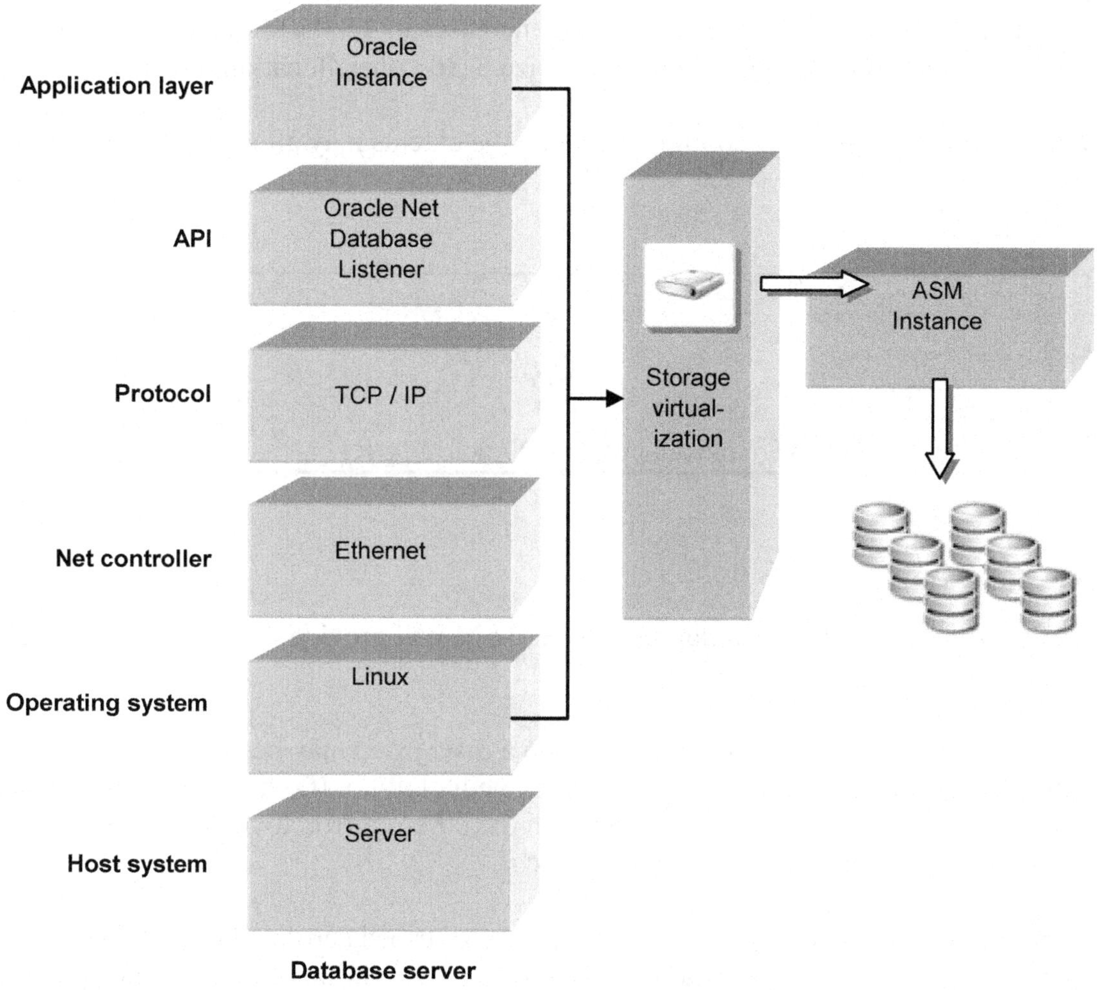

ASM Files

Each data file managed by ASM is divided into pieces known as *extents*, although this should not be confused with the traditional use of the term *extent* within a file system database. Within an extent one will find one or more *allocation units* (AU).

Traditionally an extent and an allocation unit were synonymous, with fixed 1 MB sizes being used. However, recent releases of ASM introduced the concept of *automatic variable size extents* to accommodate very large database (VLDB) and data warehousing environments. With this feature, the variable size of extents automatically increases as the file size increases, based upon the following formula:

- For extents 0 – 19999 the extent size is equal to the allocation unit size.
- For extents 20000 – 39999 the extent size increases to 4 * the allocation unit size.
- For extents 40000 and greater, the extent size is 16 * the allocation unit size.

The storage area within an AU is contiguous, while the extents may allocate AUs from disparate locations.

> ***Note***
>
> Variable size extents were introduced with Oracle 11g R1.

ASM File Services

With this file structure in place, similar to a LVM, ASM will provide the following storage services for the instances:

- Mirroring – database objects created within a disk group may be *mirrored* to provide physical redundancy and protection against media failure. If one member disk crashes, the disk group can continue to operate with the other, mirrored member. A file which is not mirrored is considered to be *unprotected.*

- Striping – database objects will be automatically striped across all devices within the group. In this way a single data segment may have its various extents striped among several devices. *Coarse* striping uses full AU-size chunks and is suitable for larger files such as data files while *fine* striping uses smaller 128 K chunks and is suitable for smaller files such as control file and parameter files.

Why ASM Is So Important

Since most host systems running Oracle instances are dedicated to providing database services, a specialized storage subsystem like ASM which provides these services in a vertical manner highly integrated with the database is superior over generic LVM services implemented horizontally for any service running on the system. For example, the ASM software instance understands the differences and intent of data files versus temp files, control files versus online redo log files, and so on. It will mirror and stripe this data in ways that a generic LVM could never do.

Furthermore, the importance of a storage subsystem like ASM can be demonstrated when looking at the costs associated with storage. While an enterprise may not see a dramatic increase annually in transaction volumes, most organizations are accumulating larger stores of data at a rapid rate. The cost associated with such storage, and the administration of that storage, necessitates an optimal storage management solution, like ASM.

What Does The ASM Instance Do?

The ASM instance manages *disk groups* and communicates the disk metadata to the database instances on the server. Thus, the ASM instance activates whenever a new disk is added to a group, or a device is removed, a new group is defined, and so on. When these actions occur, ASM will *rebalance* all existing data within the disk group according to the latest disk group configuration and the space available.

The latest disk metadata is communicated to the databases instances. These instances then perform the actual reads and writes of data in the normal manner, using the knowledge of the disk groups provided by the ASM instance.

As you can see depicted here, given the limited activities of the ASM instance, its memory consumption is very low with a maximum Shared Global Area (SGA) size of 64 MB and a total instance size of about 100 MB. It processes and buffers no application data.

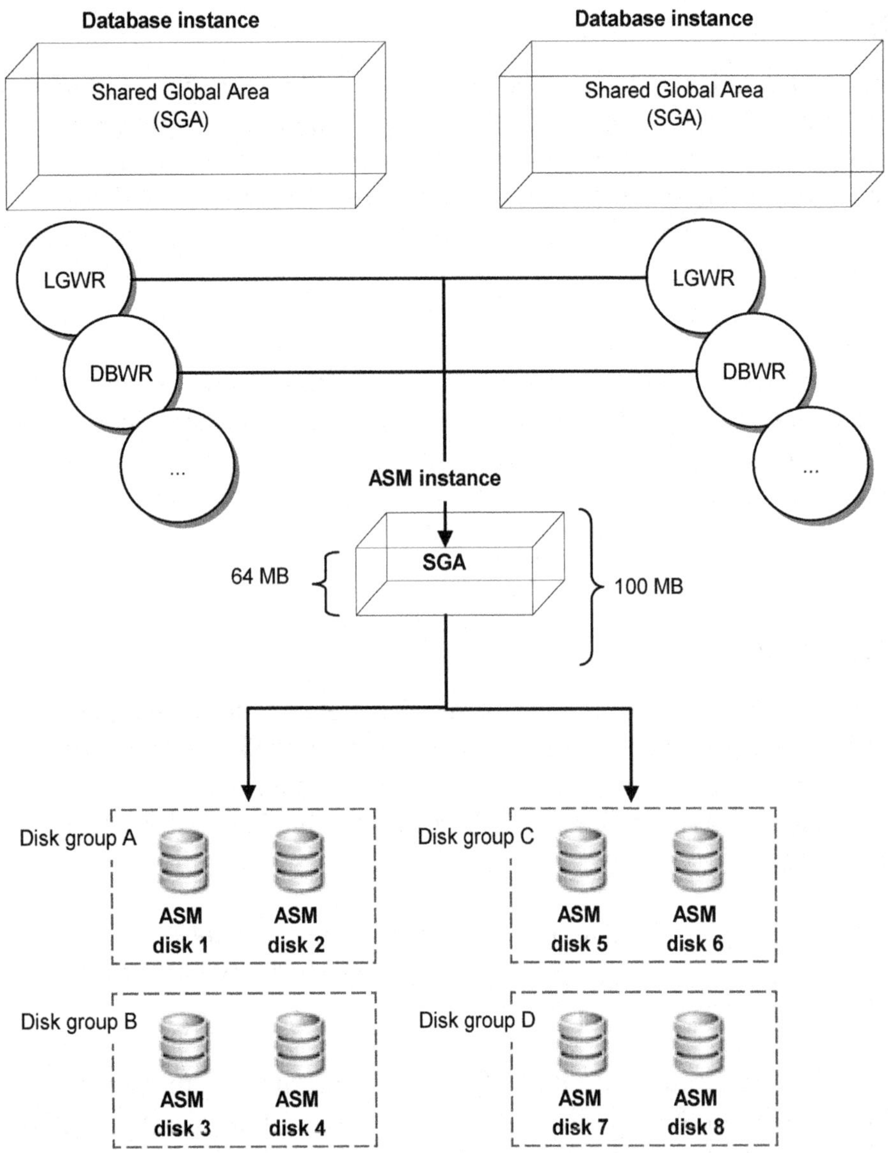

After communicating with the ASM instance, each database then locates its control file and SPFILE in the appropriate disk group, starts up and continues operation in more or less the usual fashion.

The obvious implication for database startup, in this scenario, is that the ASM instance must be started first, and only then may the other instances start. Similarly, the ASM instance would only shutdown after the other instances were shut.

More About ASM Disk Groups

The first level or organization within a *disk group* is the *devices* associated with the group. Next, within a disk group one can define two or more *failure groups* to indicate *redundancy*. For instance, 4 devices within a single disk group could be organized into two distinct failure groups, each with 2 devices. Redundant copies of each allocation unit can then maintained in each of the two failure groups.

The database offers automatic failover capabilities even for the data files in a way that multiplexed control files do in a traditional configuration. The obvious benefit is that media failure may be tolerated and resolved without performing media recovery, so long as a redundant failure group is available. Administrator configuration is limited to specification of the disk groups and the enclosed failure groups.

Moreover, the segments within a data file are spread out across the various devices within the failure group, providing concurrent access to different parts of the file at the same time.

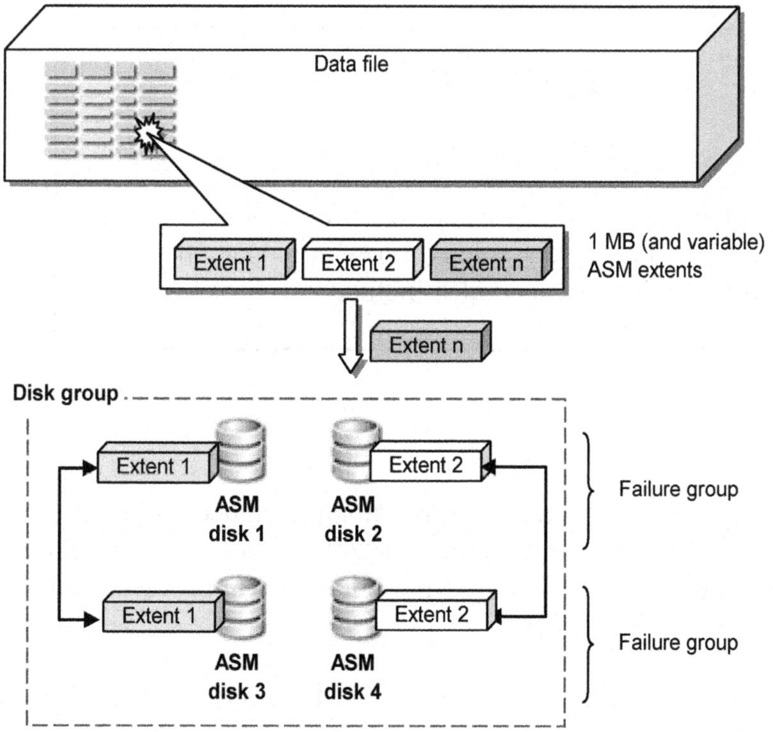

Usual disk configuration guidelines apply when defining such redundancy. For example, each failover group must not only be segregated according to different devices but different disk controllers as well.

Files Outside The ASM Realm

Nearly all database and RMAN backup and recovery files may be managed by ASM. At the same time, one may also choose to integrate individual files in their own traditional devices. Thus some database files may be ASM-administered and others may still be directly administered by the database administrator with the traditional instance.

The following files, though, are always outside the realm of ASM and remain operating system files:

- Diagnostic files within the Automatic Diagnostic Repository (ADR). This would include traditional diagnostic files such as the trace files, alert log file, and so on.
- Password file
- Oracle software binaries

> *Note*
>
> Starting with Oracle 11g R2, an extension to the basic ASM functionality is that of the ASM Cluster File System. With this technology, one can manage the entirety of Oracle database files within ASM and also include non-Oracle database files and even non-database files.

Looking Inside The Instances

The ASM instance has many similarities in architecture to a traditional instance, although its function is clearly very different. The RBAL background process is the coordinator of *balancing* activity within the disk groups. It will invoke one or several individual ORBn processes which actually read and write the individual allocation units.

When the ASM instance is started, each disk group is identified. ASM mounts the disks and then creates an allocation unit map that is communicated to each database instance. The database instances contain a process OSMB which is the communicator with ASM.

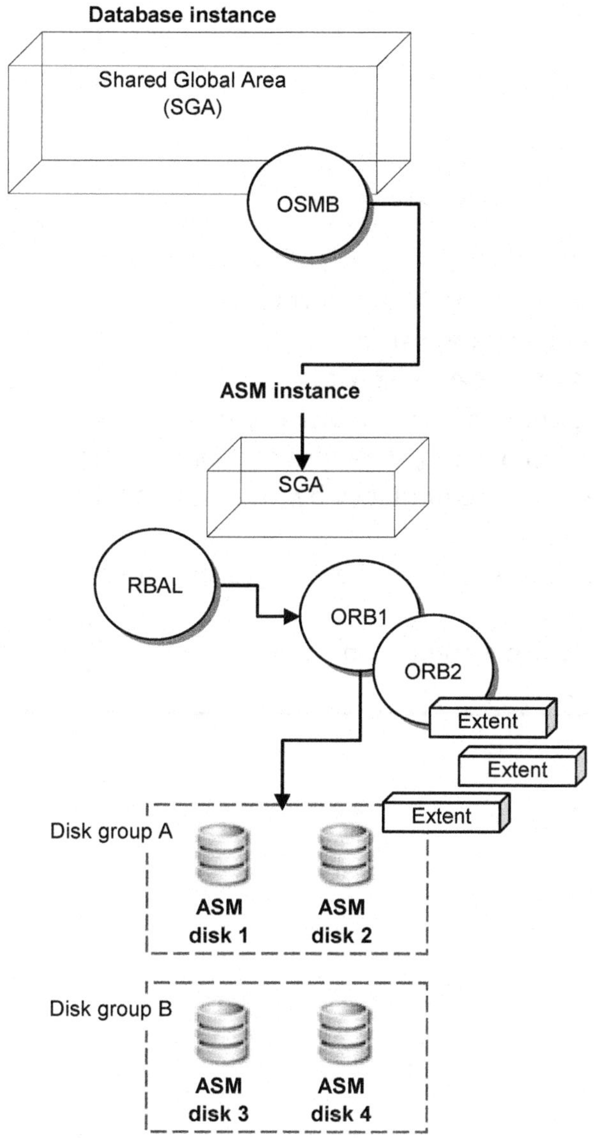
Database instance
Shared Global Area
(SGA)
OSMB
ASM instance
SGA
RBAL
ORB1
ORB2
Extent
Extent
Extent
Disk group A
ASM
disk 1
ASM
disk 2
Disk group B
ASM
disk 3
ASM
disk 4

Section Review

Remember These Points

- ASM is a storage manager specialized for the Oracle database. It represents a virtualization of the storage functions of the operating system.
- ASM is one component within the Oracle database server stack.
- Administrators interact with an abstract structure known as a disk group.
- ASM internally manages storage with disk group devices, data files and allocation units.
- The devices within a disk group allow ASM to offer redundancy by means of failure groups.
- The disbursement of data file extents amongst the devices of a disk group allows concurrent, striped access to a data file.
- Each database server can have one ASM software instance which manages database storage for the server.

Section 5
Using ASM Storage

Objectives

- ✓ File Storage Within ASM
- ✓ ASM Database Storage Via DBCA
- ✓ ASM Database Storage Via DBUA
- ✓ Database Storage Migration Using EM

Section Overview

Once the Grid Infrastructure and one or more databases have been configured on a server, there are a variety of ways in which these databases may then employ ASM for its storage. These are among the options we will discuss in this section:

- Selective storage of files within ASM – a database instance using traditional file system storage could selectively store objects within ASM on a limited basis.
- Database Configuration Assistant (DBCA) – a newly created database may utilize ASM for all database file storage.
- Database Upgrade Assistant (DBUA) – during the software version upgrade of a database instance one could choose to also migrate the storage to ASM.
- ASM Migration Using EM – one may migrate all database file system storage to ASM as part of a single operation launched from an EM wizard.

File Storage Within ASM

For a database which uses traditional file system storage, one can employ ASM for individual database files.

ASM Data Files

For example, when creating a new tablespace one could reference the ASM storage system as part of the DATAFILE clause. In place of the file system path and file name for an object, one could reference an ASM disk group by means of a plus sign (+) symbol.

```
SQL> CREATE TABLESPACE siderisTS1
        DATAFILE '+DATA' SIZE 1M;
Tablespace created.
```

Now notice how the physical data files for this database instance have a combination of file system storage for some tablespaces and ASM disk group storage for others. The ASM file name includes a combination of the administrator-supplied tablespace name and a system-generated identifier.

```
SQL> SELECT file_name
     FROM dba_data_files;

/u01/app/oracle/oradata/test4g/users01.dbf
/u01/app/oracle/oradata/test4g/undotbs01.dbf
/u01/app/oracle/oradata/test4g/sysaux01.dbf
/u01/app/oracle/oradata/test4g/system01.dbf
/u01/app/oracle/oradata/test4g/example01.dbf
+DATA/test4g/datafile/sideristsl.256.723751977
```

Other Database Files

A similar form may be used to refer to an ASM disk group when specifying the file name for redo log files, control files, the flash recovery area path, and so on.

Define Data Files With EM

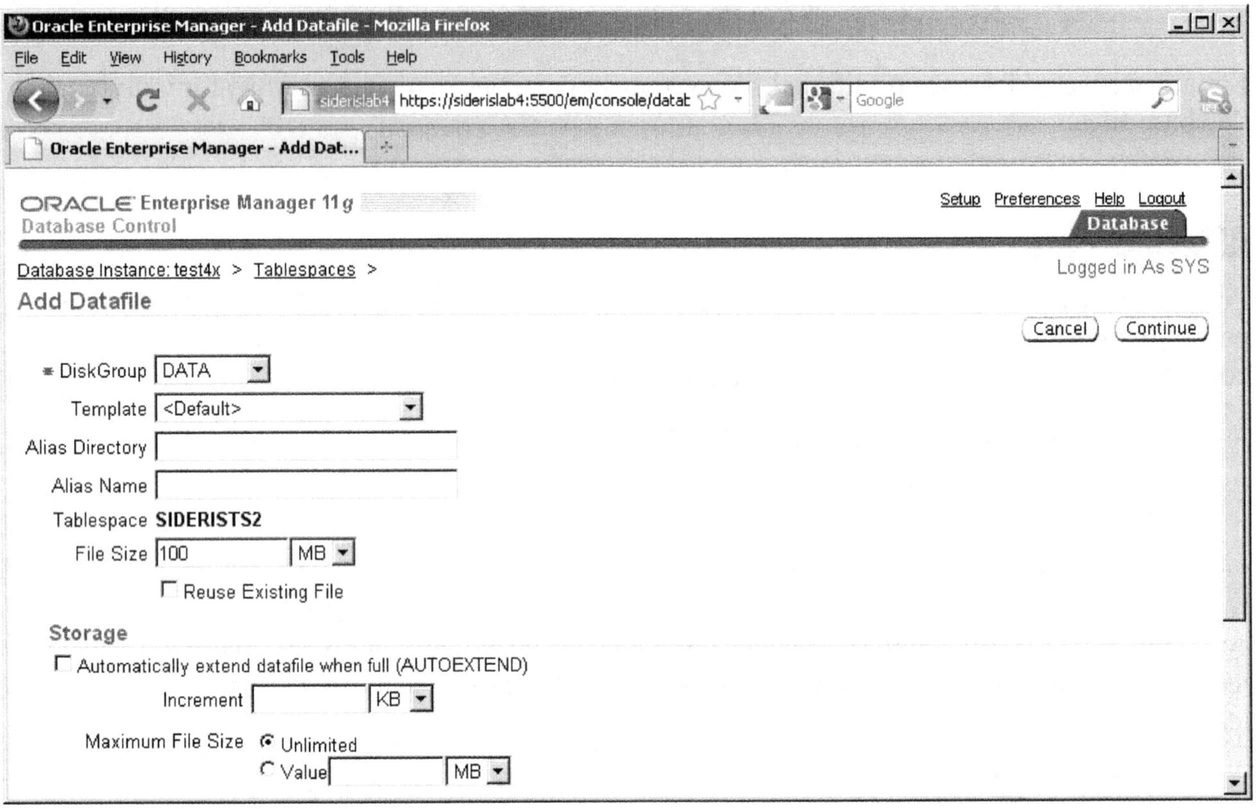

As you probably know one can also create tablespaces and data files from within EM. This is typically done from the Server tab. As you can see from this sample screen, when the data file is stored within an ASM disk group, EM will also present various ASM attributes which may be defined as well. These include Template, Alias Directory and Alias Name. These attributes will be discussed elsewhere within this course.

DBCA

When creating a new database using DBCA, that utility likewise supports integration of the new database with ASM storage. When moving through the steps of the DBCA dialog, one will encounter the Database File Locations screen. The ASM instance is detected and the Storage Type item offers the option Automatic Storage Management (ASM).

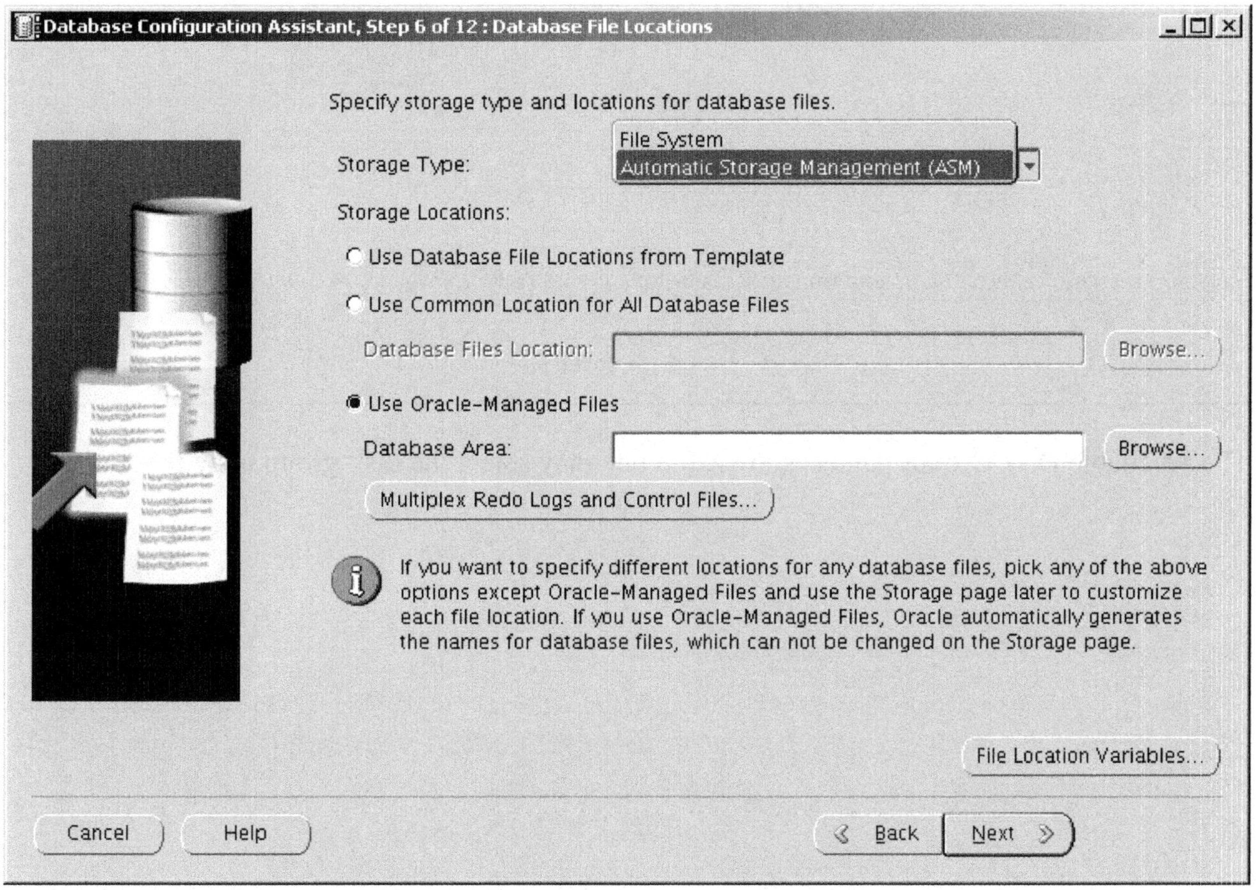

This option will store the entirety of the database files within ASM-managed storage space. By default the Oracle-Managed Files option is selected and one must then click the Browse... button to identify the disk group to be used for storage.

One may be asked to provide super administrator credentials to access the ASM instance. Once one is authenticated, the ASM instance is consulted for available storage, in the form of disk groups.

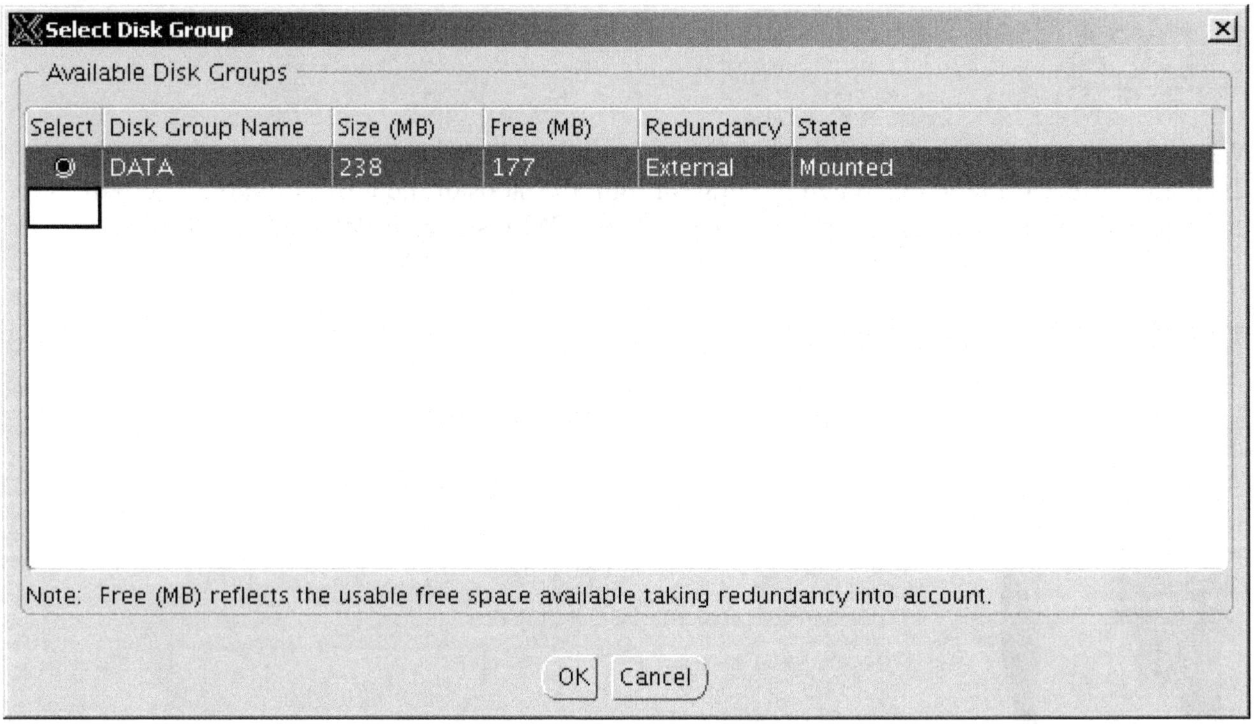

The Available Disk Groups page is shown and one may select the disk group to be used.

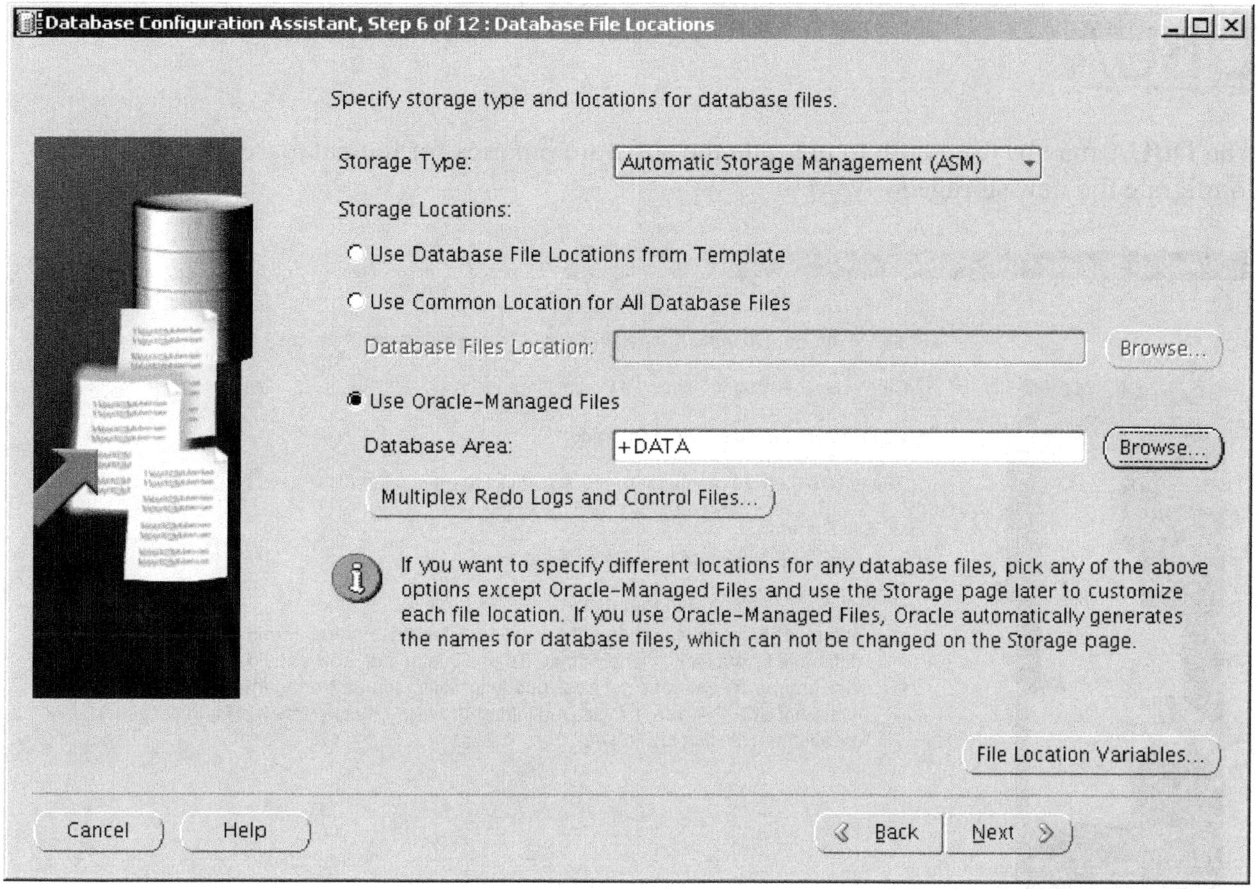

The Database Area now indicates the ASM disk group within which storage for the new database will be created. The remainder of the DBCA dialog is completed in the usual manner.

DBUA

The DBUA may be used both to upgrade the software binaries for the database installation and to migrate the new storage to ASM.

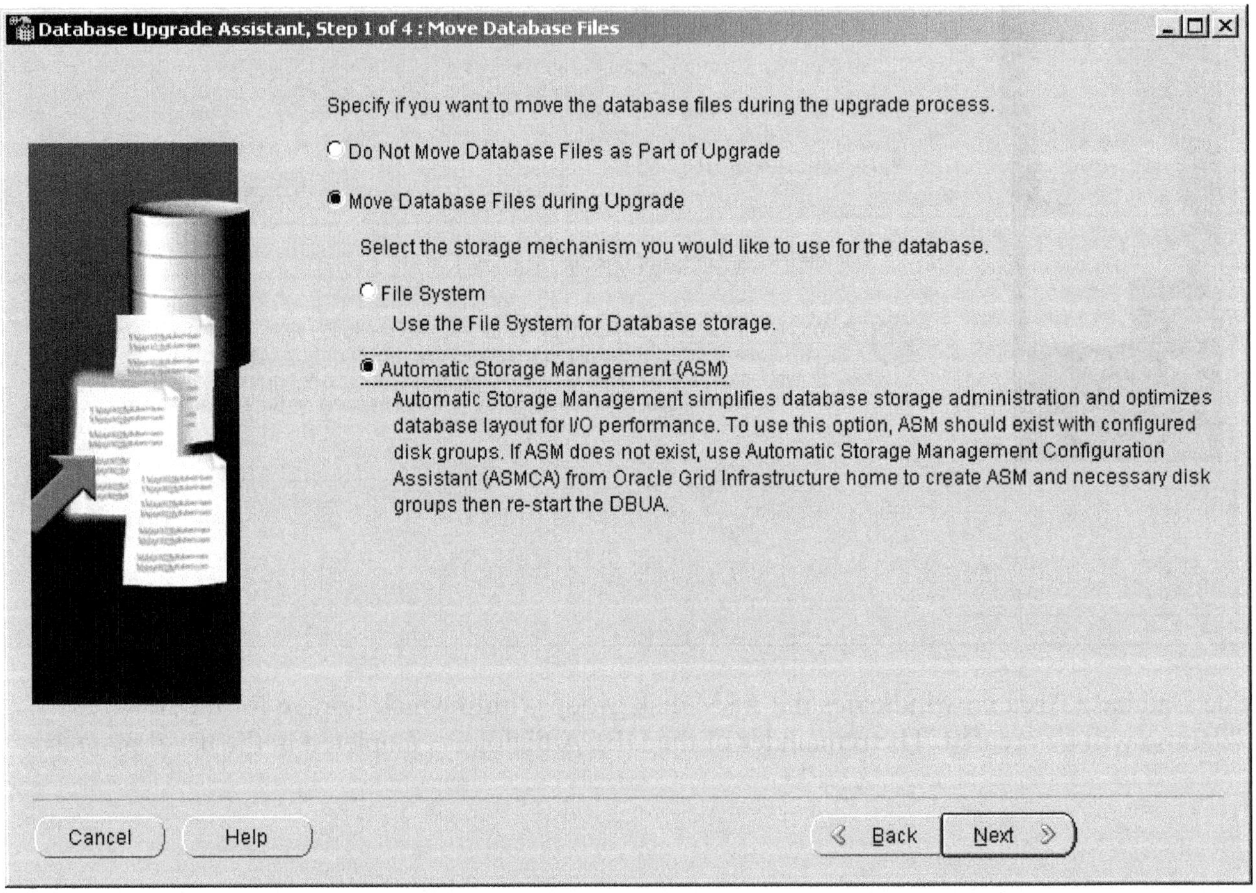

During the upgrade of a selected database instance, DBUA will check if the database currently uses file system storage and if an ASM instance is available. If both of these checks are true, then one has the option to include migration to ASM at the same time that the software version upgrade is performed.

ASM Migration Using EM

Oftentimes one will want to migrate the entirety of database storage to ASM independent of any software upgrade. Such a migration is possible using the EM interface. Additionally, one may use options presented to migrate only selected tablespaces, recovery-related files and other subsets of database storage.

> *Note*
>
> It is important to note that such a migration can be a very lengthy process, directly related to the sum total amount of storage used by the database and which must be migrated to ASM.
>
> Furthermore, if the migration operation fails, one must perform a successful recovery of the database before the database is opened. Otherwise, corruption of the database can easily occur. This in turn, necessitates that a complete, consistent backup of the database is made before embarking on such an endeavor as ASM migration of a production database.

To launch the Migrate Database To ASM wizard available within EM, click on the Server → Migrate To ASM link.

Migrate To ASM Instance Wizard

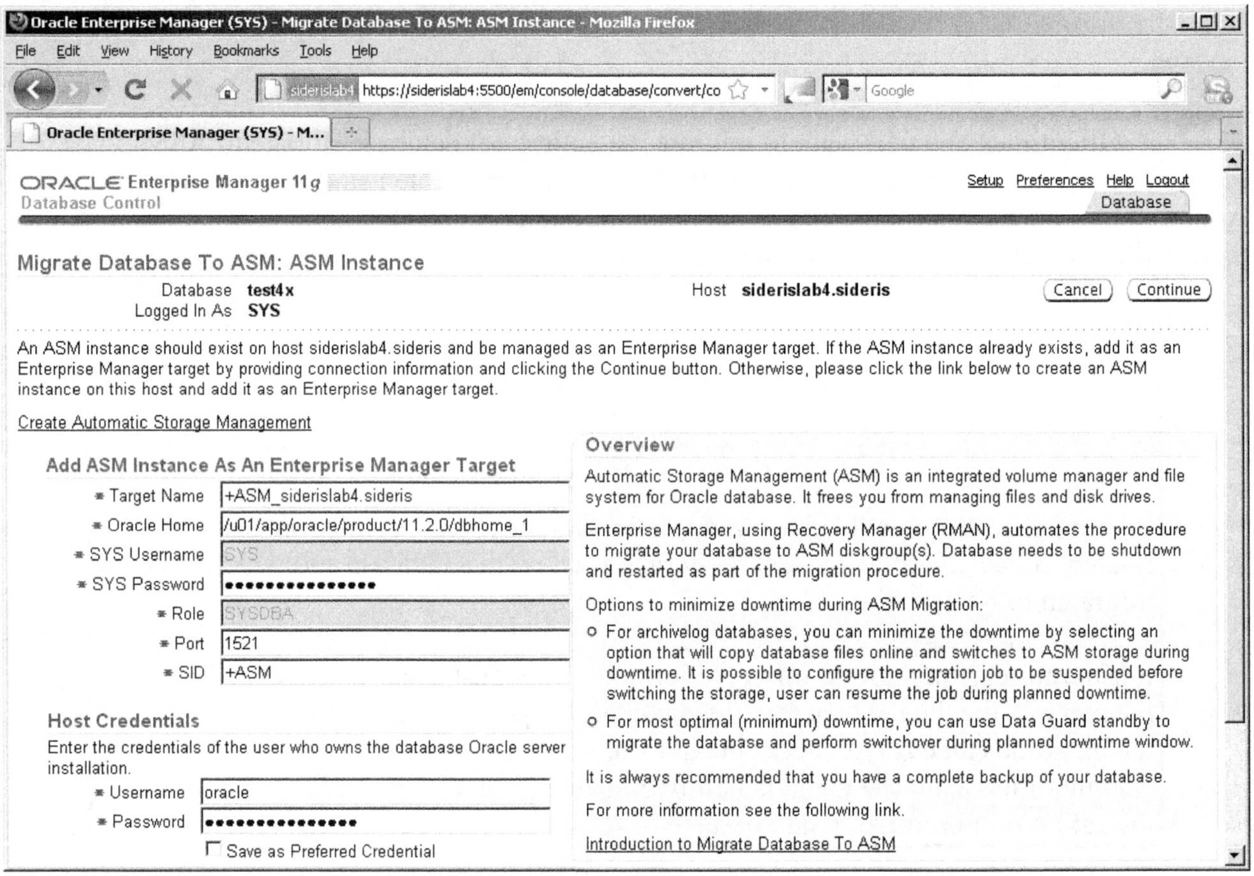

The ASM instance connection information is fetched for the local installation, with the exception of the SYSASM password. One would enter that password along with host system credentials and click the Continue button.

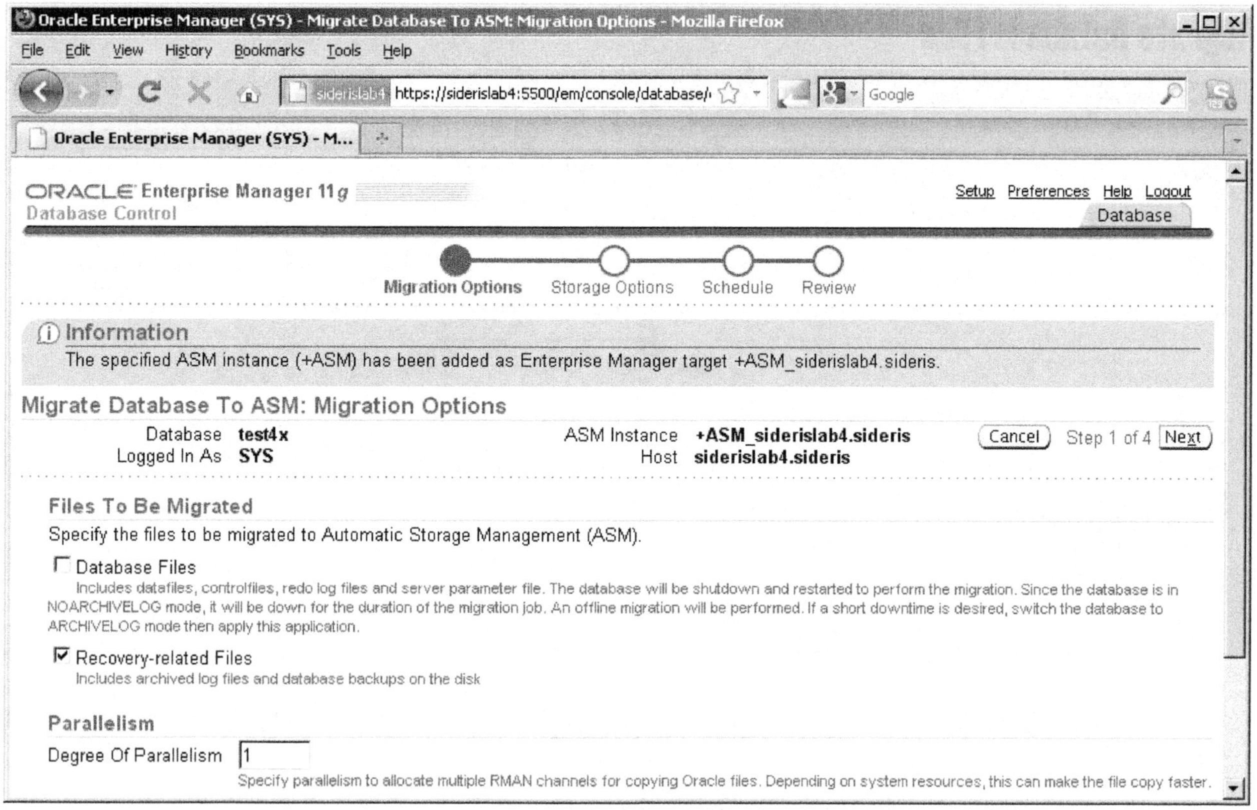

The Migration Options screen offers these choices:

- Database files – When checked this indicates that primary database storage, including data files, temp files and so on, will be migrated from the file system into ASM.

- Recovery-related Files – When checked this indicates that the Fast Recovery Area and all recovery-related files will be migrated into ASM. If the Fast Recovery Area is not in existence for the database, then only the recovery-related files will be migrated.

- Degree Of Parallelism – This option is strongly recommended for reasons of performance as the migration process is substantial. If sufficient CPU resources are available, one should increase the degree beyond the default value of 1, with a value divisible by 2.

Migrate Database Files

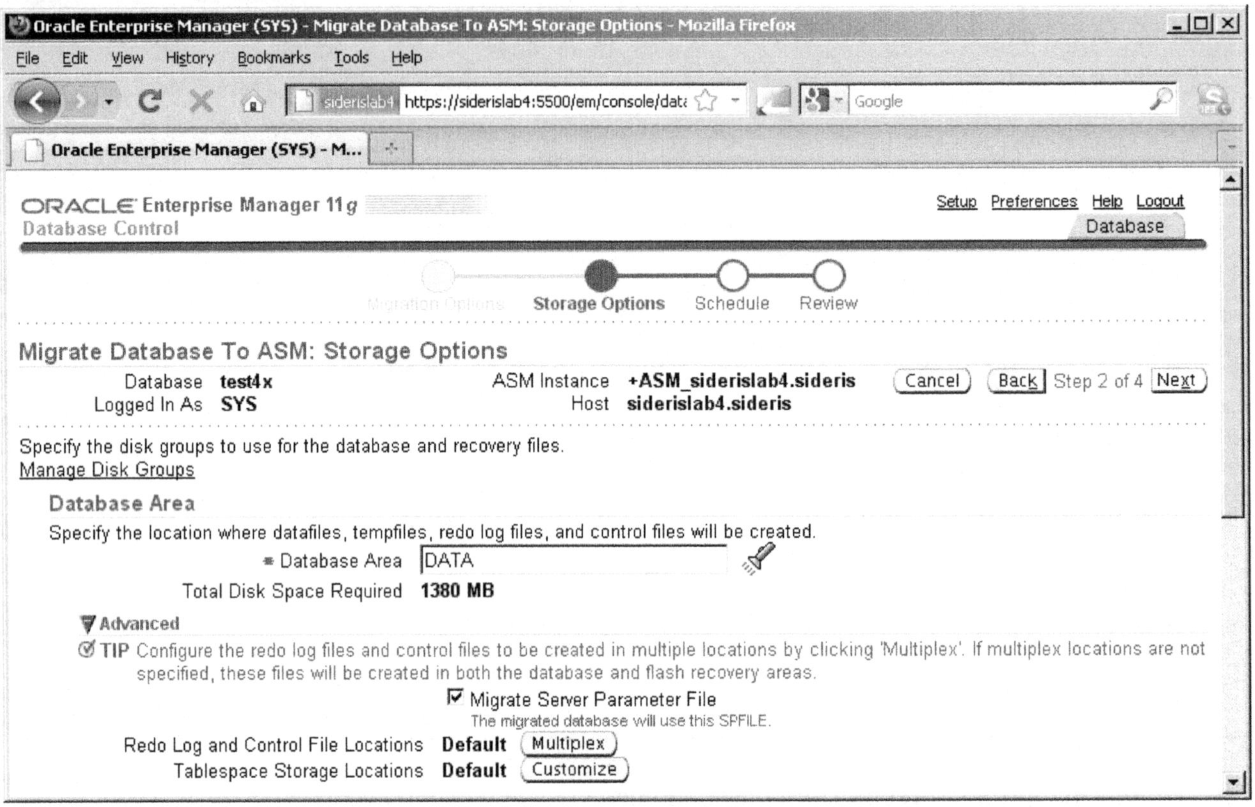

The Storage Options screen is shown next. If one had previously specified migration of the Database Files, then this screen will first display a Database Area section. These options are available:

- Database Area – one may specify the disk group to be used for all database files storage. An estimate of the ASM space required for these files is shown.
- Migrate Server Parameter File – The SPFILE is moved to ASM storage as well if this option is checked.
- Redo Log and Control File Locations – Click on the Multiplex button to choose a disk group for each member of the online redo log file group or each multiplexed copy of the control file. This option is discussed in greater detail below.
- Tablespace Storage Locations – Click on the Customize button to choose a different disk group for one or more tablespaces than that specified by the Database Area item. This option is also discussed in greater detail below.

Multiplex Redo Log & Control Files

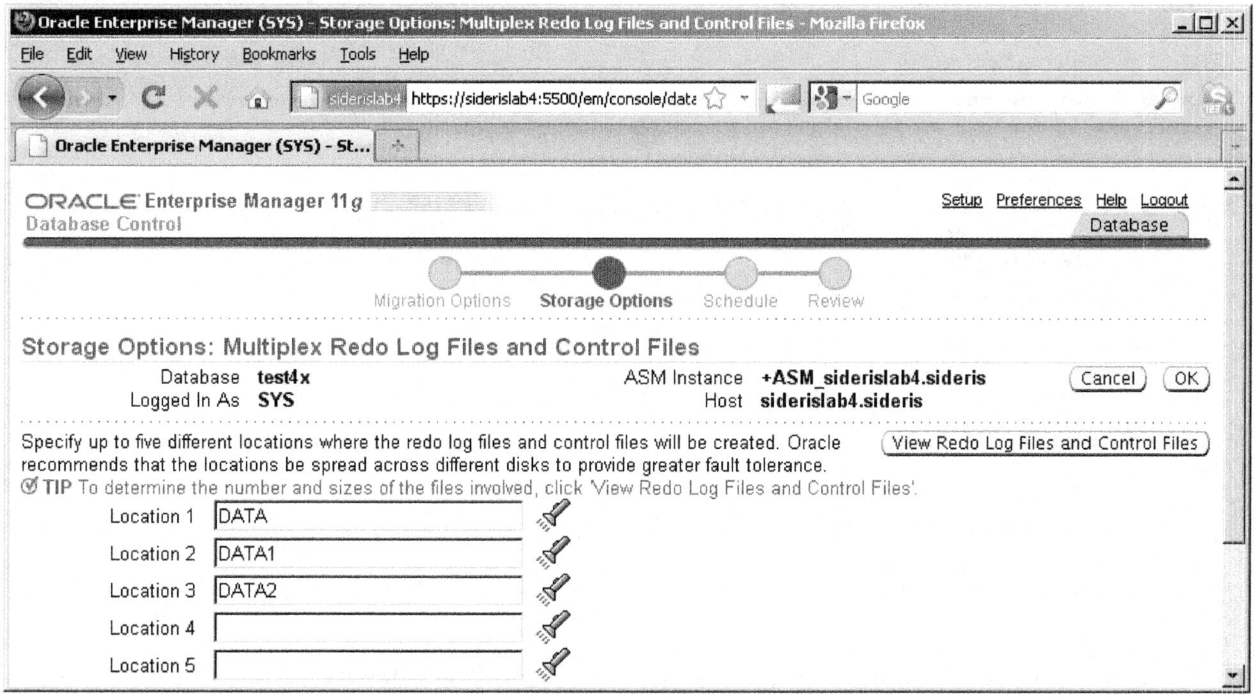

This is an example of the screen which is presented if one clicks on the Multiplex button for redo log and control files. One may specify different disk groups to achieve fault tolerance in the event one disk group fails.

If one wanted to see exactly which redo log and control files currently exist and would be affected by the migration, one can click on the View Redo Log Files And Control Files button.

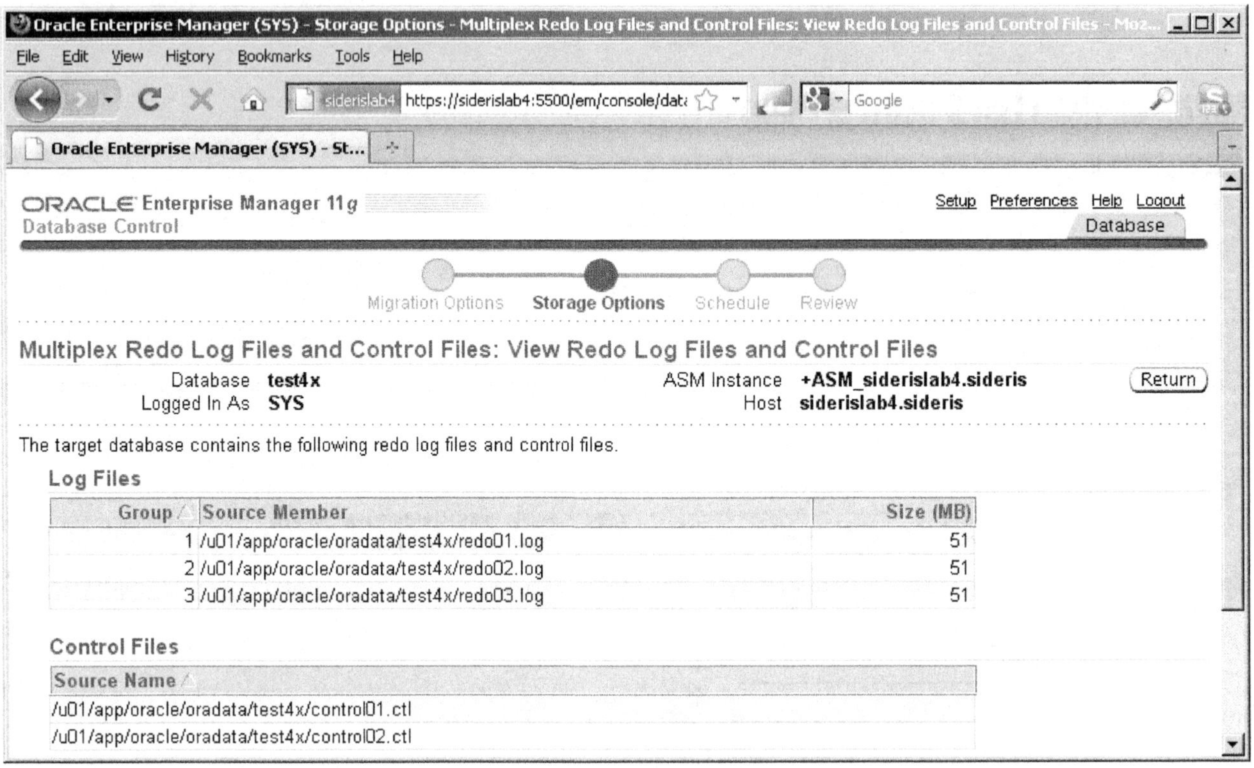

This screen is produced when one clicks on the View Redo Log Files And Control Files button.

Customize Tablespace Storage Locations

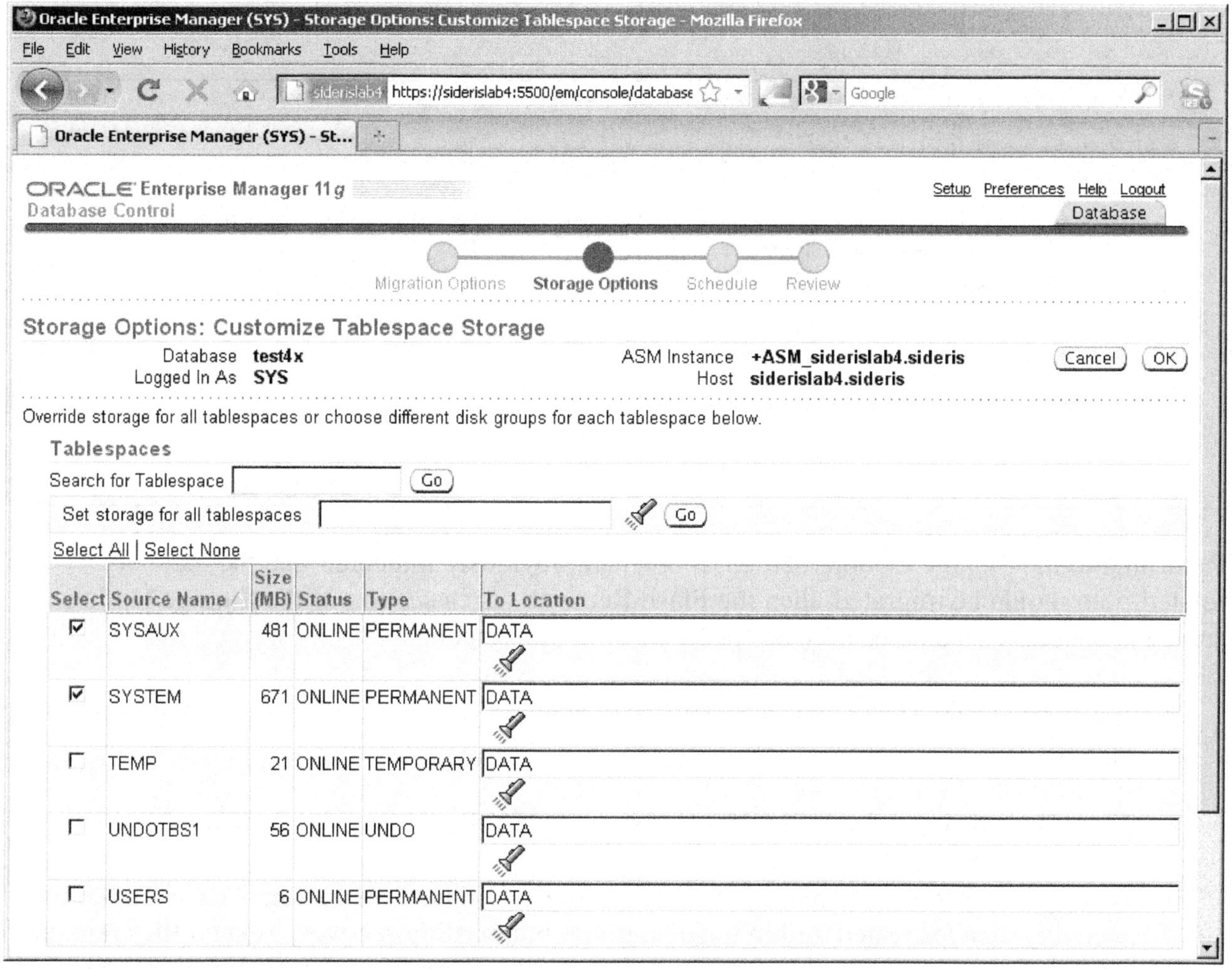

This is an example of the screen which is presented if one clicks on the Customize button for the tablespace storage location. One may specify a different disk group for each tablespace, any may choose to omit one or more tablespaces from the migration process.

Migrate Recovery-related Files

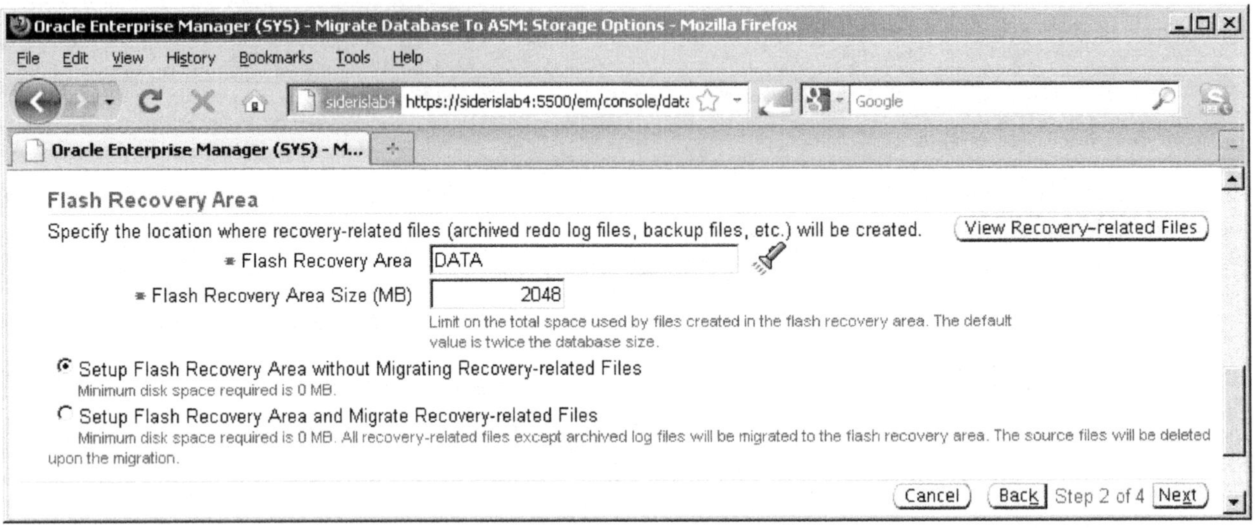

Returning to the Storage Options screen, if one had previously indicated that the recovery-related files should be migrated, then the Flash Recovery Area section of the Storage Options screen is visible. These items may be specified from this screen:

- Flash Recovery Area – This area will be created, or migrated, using the disk group specified.

- Flash Recovery Area Size (MB) – One may specify the size of the flash recovery area.

- Setup Flash Recovery Area Without Migrating ... – When this option is checked the flash recovery area is created within the disk group but existing recovery-related files remain in their original location. New recovery files will be created in the flash recovery area stored within the ASM disk group.

- Setup Flash Recovery Area And Migrate ... – When this option is checked the all existing recovery-related files are deleted from the source location after they are migrated into the ASM disk group.

Note

Remember that the usual guidelines which apply for file system storage likewise apply for ASM-based storage. For example, one will want to isolate database area storage to a different disk group than flash recovery area storage. Further, one would want to employ redundancy for the flash recovery area by selecting a disk group with High or Normal redundancy.

As one is making so many choices regarding the usage of disk groups for the migration, it may be helpful to access the EM management control for ASM. This is possible by clicking on the Manage Disk Groups link, which is accessible from the Storage Options page of the migration wizard.

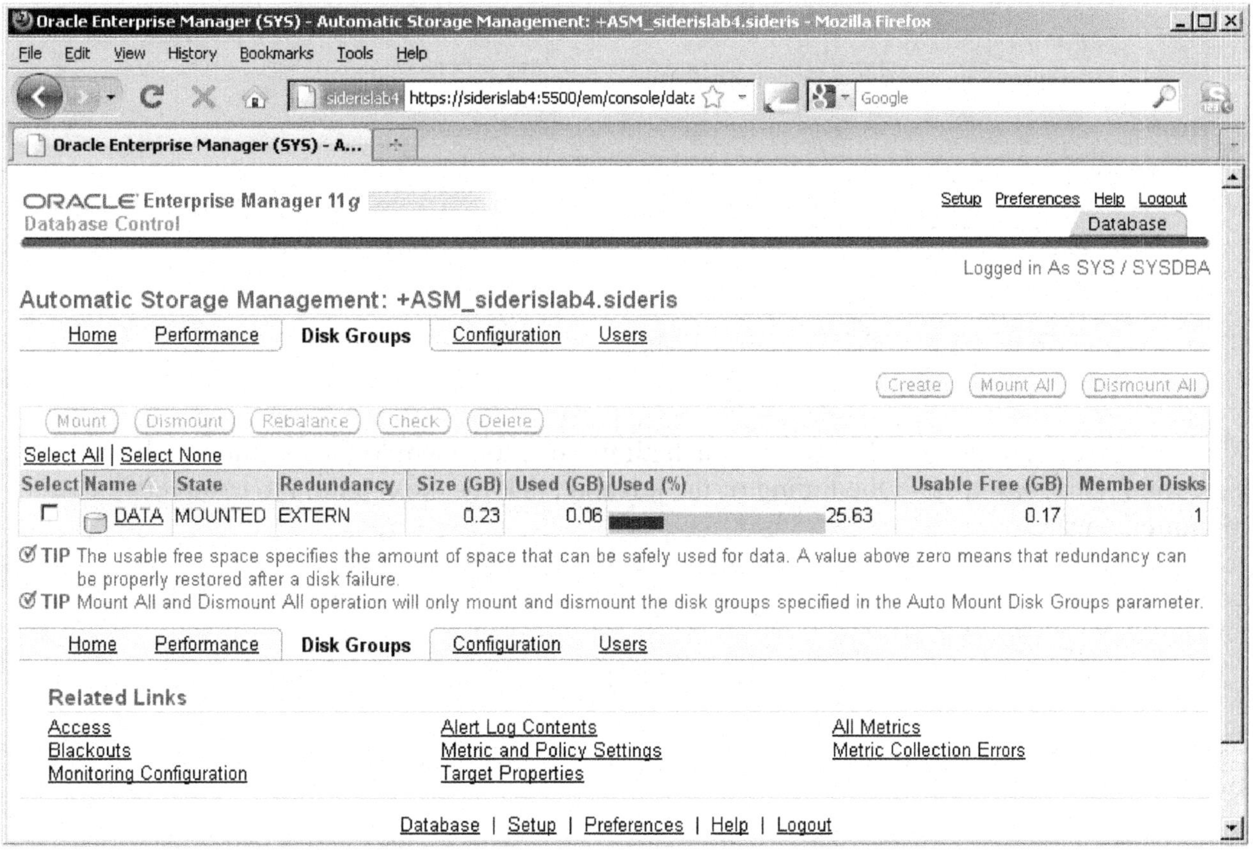

This is an example of the Disk Groups tab and the other tabs available for management of the ASM instance and its disk groups from EM. We will discuss this interface later within this course.

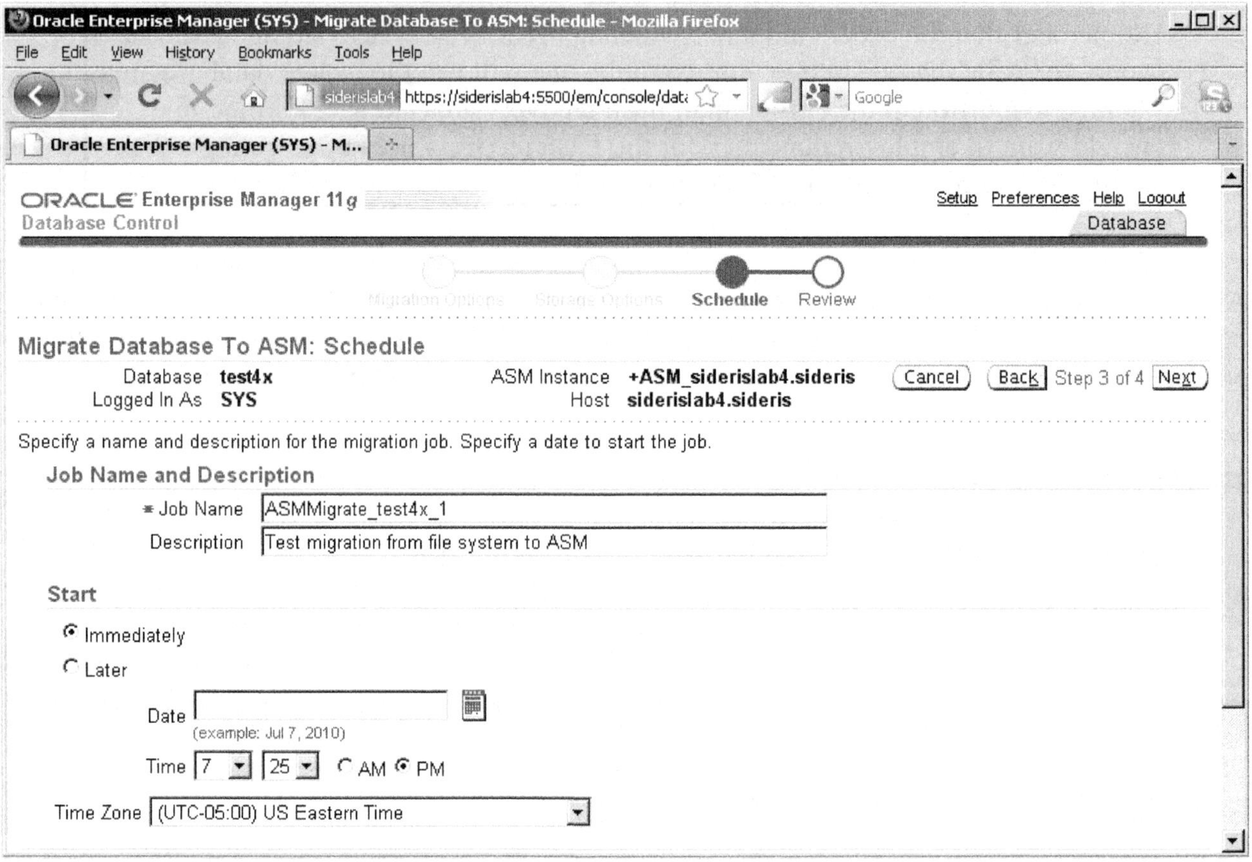

Finally one reaches the Schedule page, which allows one to schedule the migration job for execution. One may specify the timing of the job and click the Next button to complete the migration wizard.

Note

Bear in mind that the migration process will use the EM Job Subsystem running on the host machine and not the database Scheduler or any particular database instance. Given the scope of the job, one should choose the timing carefully in a way that will not interfere with any other processing on the server.

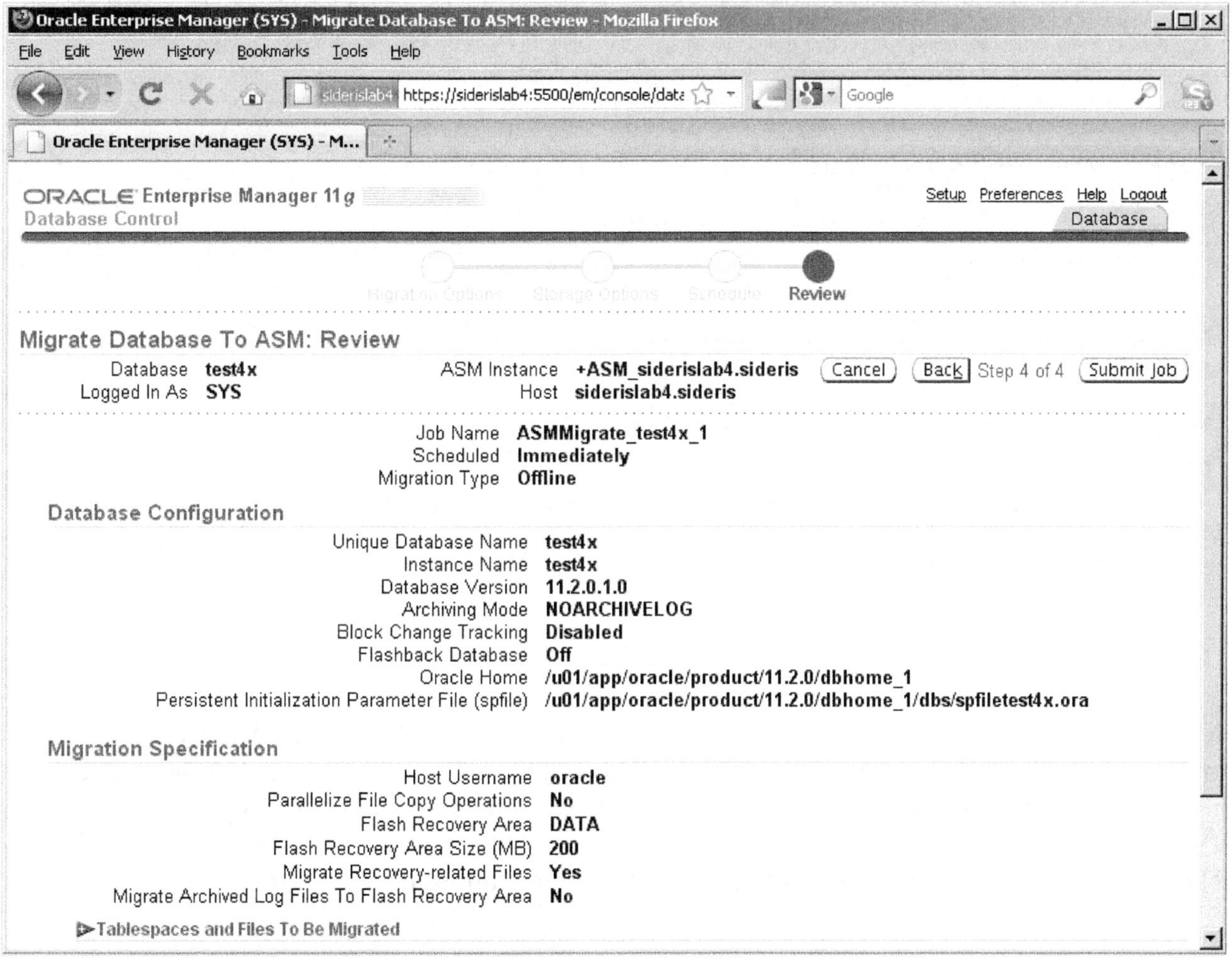

The Review screen is presented displaying all of the options specified within the ASM migration wizard. One can confirm the options selected and click the Submit Job button.

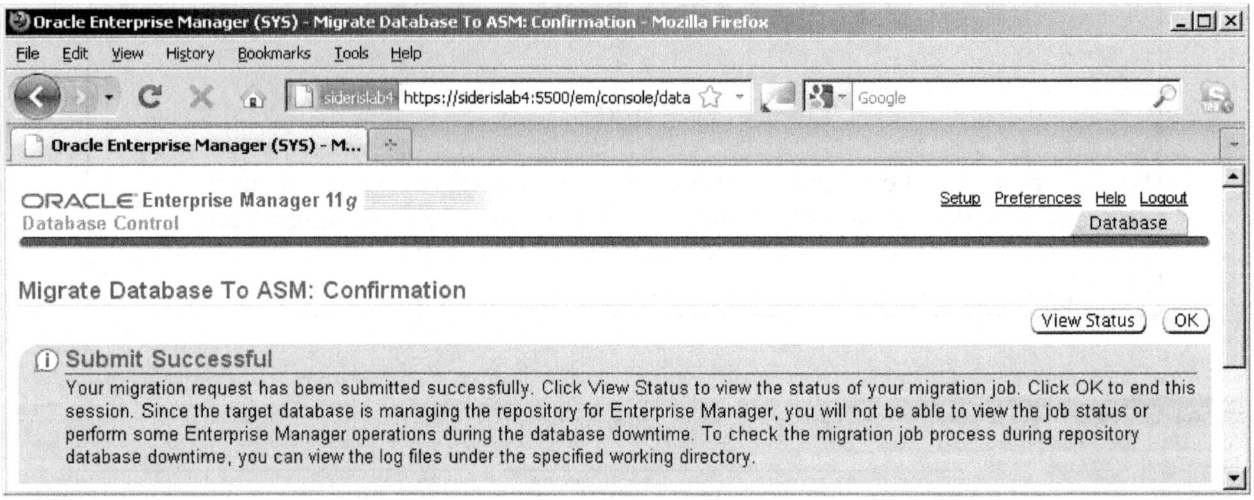

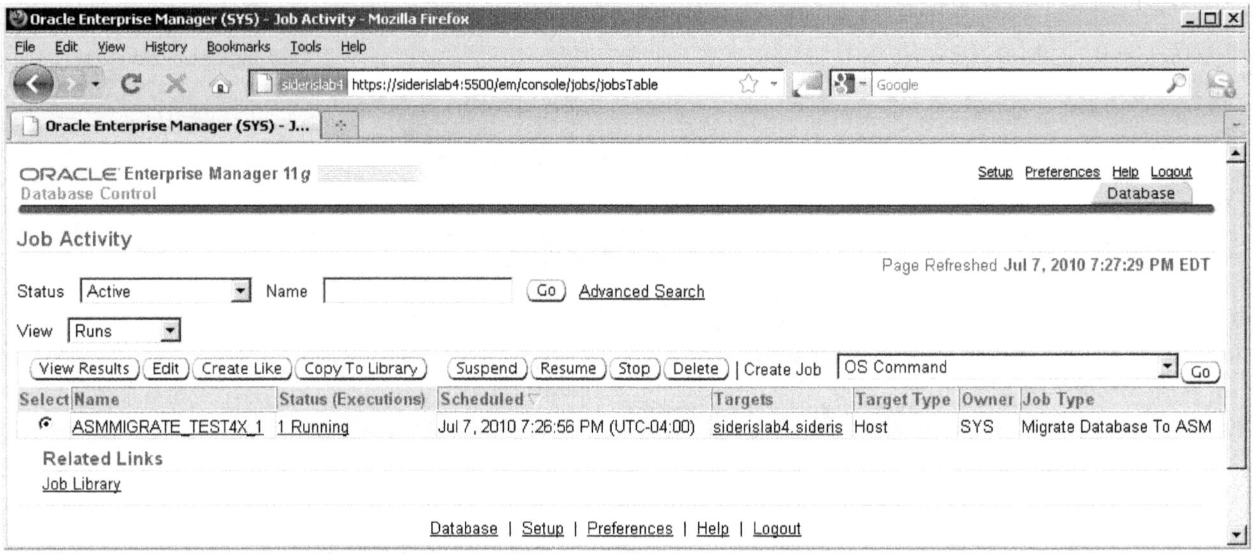

After successful submission of the ASM migration job one may click on the View Status button to navigate to the Job Activity screen. One should find the migration job listed in the queue. One may click on the Name link for the migration job to examine the details of its execution.

The resulting Job Run screen will indicate the success or failure of the migration job.

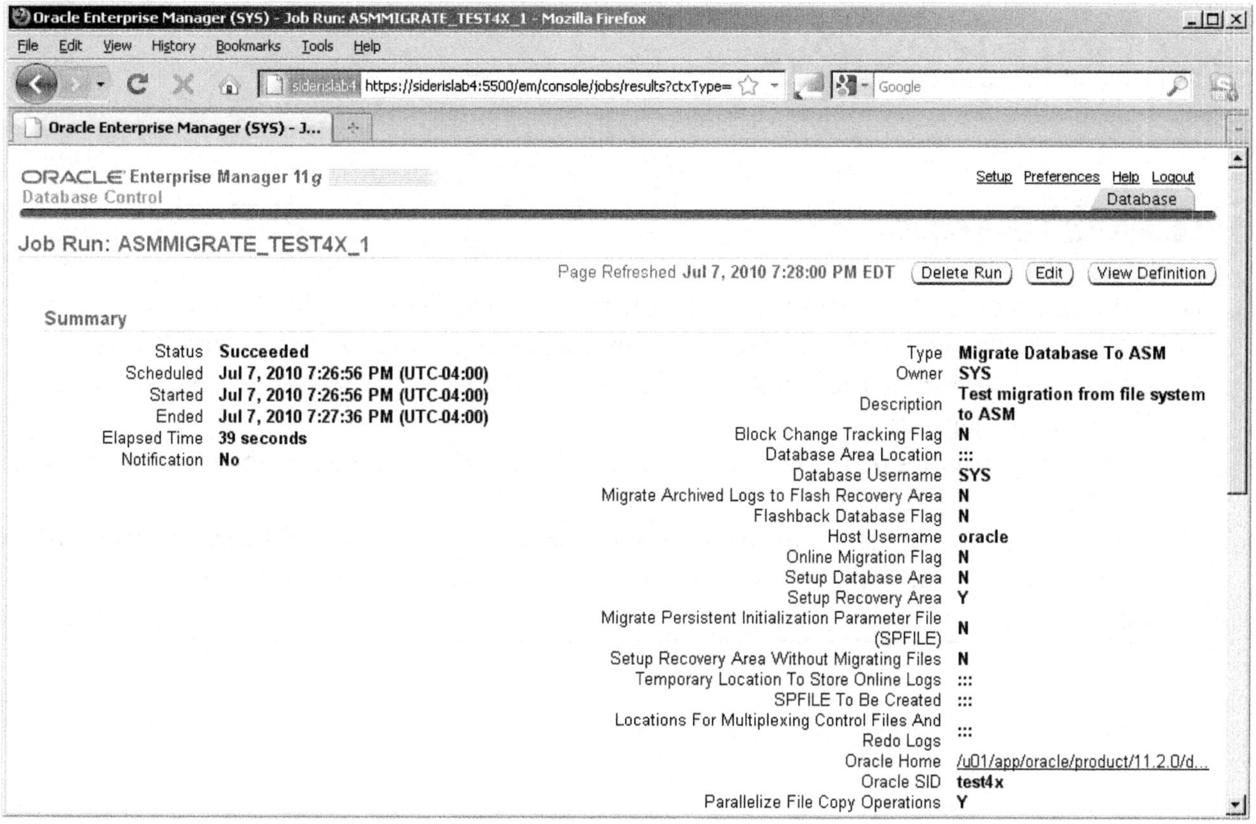

This screen confirms that successful migration of database storage from the file system to ASM has occurred.

Section Review

Remember These Points

- Database files, such as data files, redo log files, control files and the like may be selectively placed in ASM storage by using the file name syntax '+DiskGroupName'.
- Databases created by the DBCA utility may have the entirety of their storage obtained from ASM disk groups.
- During the software upgrade process managed by DBUA one can choose to also migrate database storage to ASM.
- The Enterprise Manager interface offers a Migrate Database To ASM wizard. Using this wizard one may migrate all or some of storage for an existing database into the ASM framework.

Workshop Section
Using ASM Storage

Exercises

What You Will Do in This Workshop

In this workshop, you will:

- Create a new tablespace which uses ASM storage.
- Use the ASM migration wizard accessible from the EM interface to migrate existing file system-based storage to an ASM disk group.

ASM STORAGE-1

❑ In this exercise you will employ ASM for storage of a new tablespace. Using an administrator connection via the SQL interface, create a small tablespace which uses an ASM disk group for storage of the data file. You might query the data file metadata for confirmation of the file which was created.

ASM STORAGE-2

❑ Create another tablespace which places the data file in traditional file system storage. This tablespace will be used in a later exercise for migration to ASM storage using the EM migration wizard.

ASM STORAGE-3

❑ Use the ASM migration wizard within the EM interface to migrate the file system tablespace just created within this workshop to ASM storage.

Solutions

ASM STORAGE-1

It is important to note that the terminal session which launches the SQL interface must be defined for access to the database installation, not the Grid Infrastructure installation. Therefore, the environment variables must be defined for access to the database, as explained earlier in this course.

Once this is done, from the terminal session, launch the SQL*Plus interface and establish a connection to the database instance.

```
SQL> CONNECT system/*****;
Connected.
```

From the database instance the ASM disk groups are accessible. Create a tablespace which locates the data file within an ASM disk group.

```
SQL> CREATE TABLESPACE siderisTS1
        DATAFILE '+DATA' SIZE 1M;
Tablespace created.

SQL> SELECT file_name
     FROM dba_data_files;

/u01/app/oracle/oradata/test4g/users01.dbf
/u01/app/oracle/oradata/test4g/undotbs01.dbf
/u01/app/oracle/oradata/test4g/sysaux01.dbf
/u01/app/oracle/oradata/test4g/system01.dbf
/u01/app/oracle/oradata/test4g/example01.dbf
+DATA/test4g/datafile/sideristsl.256.723751977
```

ASM STORAGE-2

```
SQL> CREATE TABLESPACE siderisTS2
        DATAFILE 'sideristS2a.dbf' SIZE 1M;
Tablespace created.

SQL> SELECT file_name
     FROM dba_data_files;

/u01/app/oracle/oradata/test4g/users01.dbf
/u01/app/oracle/oradata/test4g/undotbs01.dbf
/u01/app/oracle/oradata/test4g/sysaux01.dbf
/u01/app/oracle/oradata/test4g/system01.dbf
/u01/app/oracle/oradata/test4g/example01.dbf
+DATA/test4g/datafile/sideristS1.256.723751977
/u01/app/oracle/product/11.2.0/dbhome_1/dbs/sideristS2a.dbf
```

ASM STORAGE-3

Launch the EM interface using a super administrator SYS connection. Click on the Server → Migrate To ASM link and follow these steps.

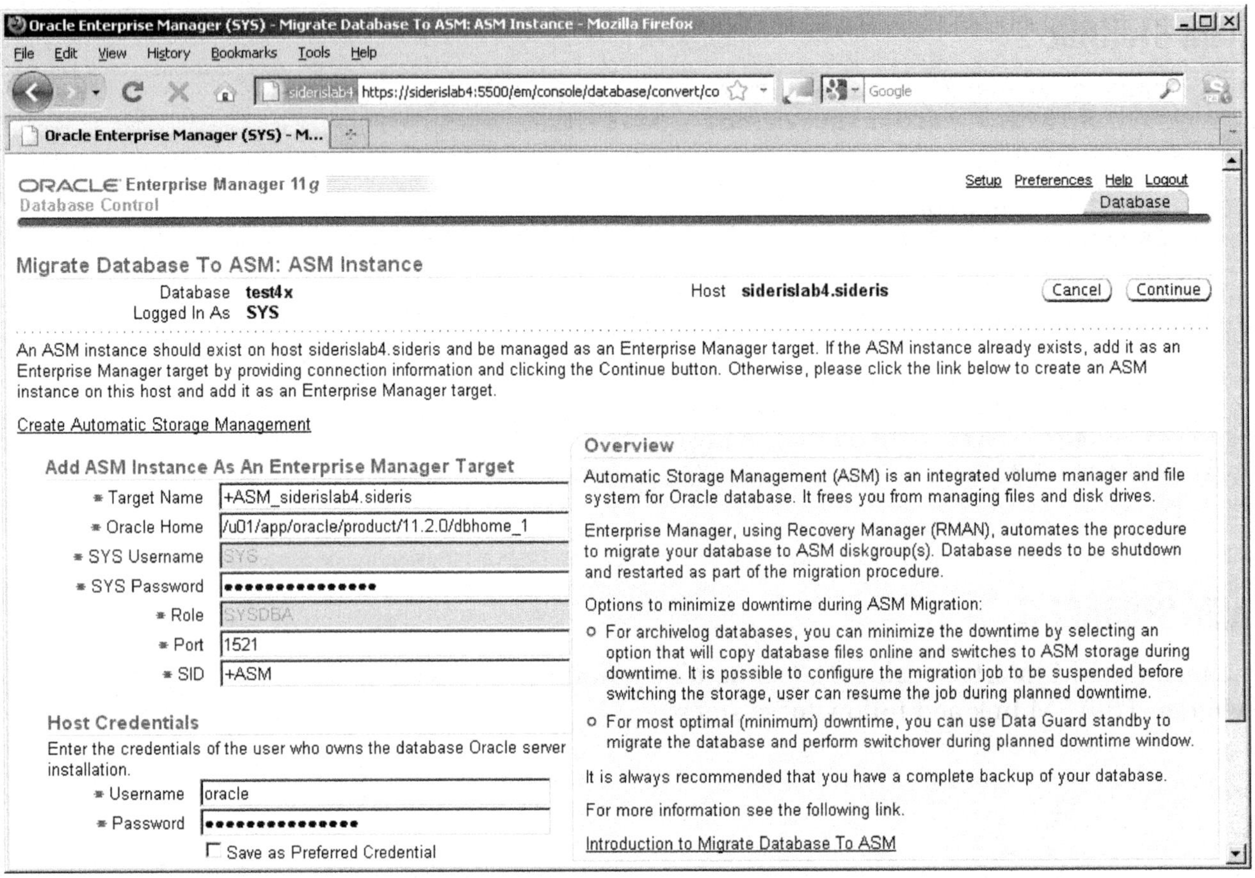

From the ASM Instance page enter the SYSASM super administrator password and the host system credentials and click the Continue button. You should find that the ASM instance details are automatically detected by EM and the migration wizard, as shown here in this sample screen.

Next, complete the migration wizard by means of these steps:

1. From the Migration Options screen select the Database Files option, uncheck the Recovery-related Files option, and click the Next button.
2. From the Storage Options screen click the Advanced icon to expand the display.
3. Click the Customize button for the Tablespace Storage Locations item.
4. Check only the file system-based tablespace just created in the earlier workshop, enter the name of a valid ASM disk group and click the OK button.
5. When you have returned to the Storage Options page, uncheck the Migrate Server Parameter File, and click the Next button.
6. From the Schedule button ensure that the Immediately option is checked and click the Next button.
7. From the Review screen click the Submit Job button.

Once the job has successfully been submitted, follow the progress of the job as follows:

1. From the Submit Successful screen click on the View Status button.
2. From the Job Activity screen click on the Name link for the migration job just submitted and confirm its success.

To conclusively establish that the tablespace is using ASM storage, you might follow this sequence from the EM home page:

1. Click on the Server → Tablespaces link.
2. Click on the Name link which reflects the tablespace migrated to ASM storage.
3. From the resulting View Tablespace page, confirm that the Directory attribute of the Datafiles section of the page does in fact indicate that the data file is stored within the ASM disk group.

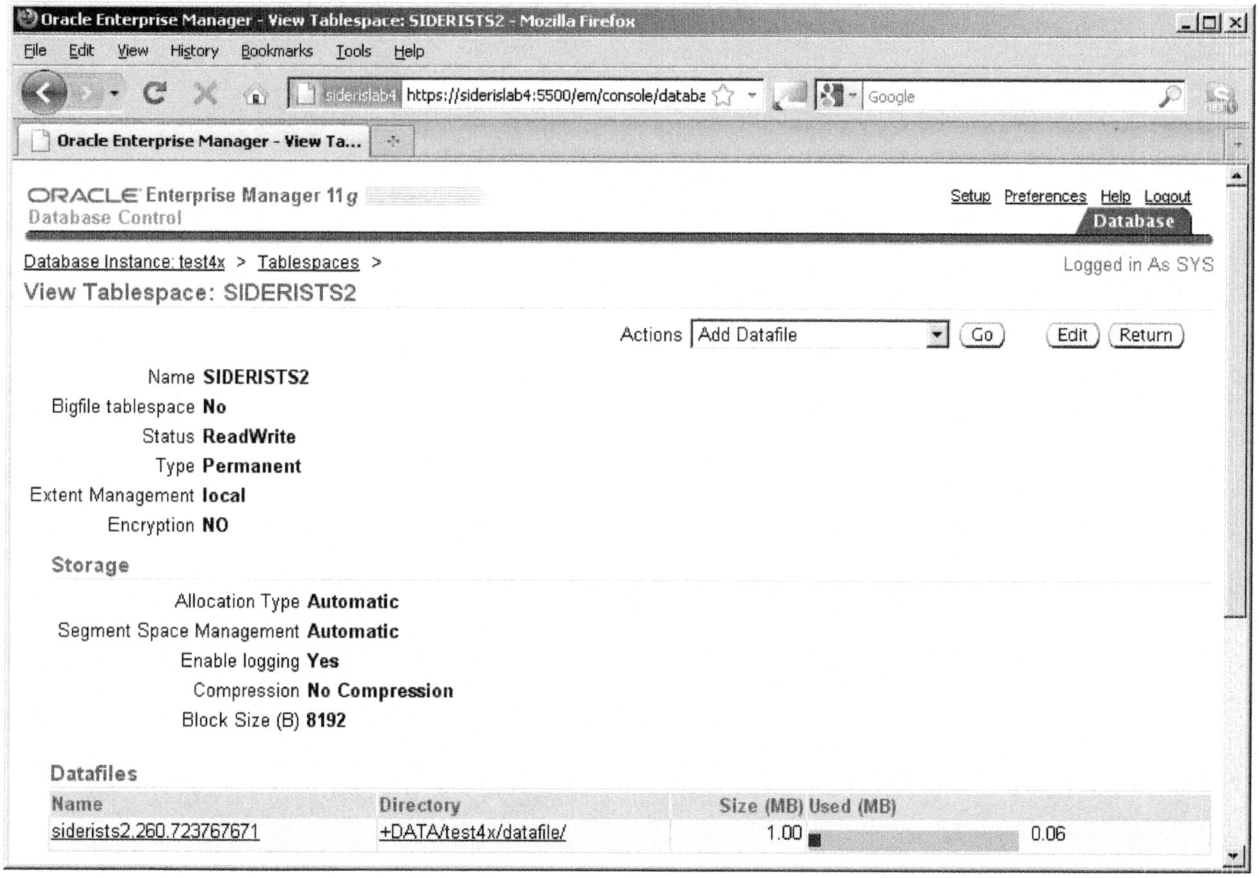

Section 6
ASM Instance Administration

Objectives

- ✓ Administering The ASM Using SQL
- ✓ Administering The ASM Using EM

Section Overview

Like any other Oracle software instance, the ASM instance requires periodic oversight from an administrator. In this section we will discuss how one would perform these administration tasks:

- Acquiring SYSASM super administrator rights
- Managing the initialization file and setting instance parameters
- Manual instance startup and shutdown
- Registering the ASM instance as an EM target
- Using the EM interface to ASM

Administering The ASM Instance

In some ways an ASM instance is administered somewhat similar to the manner in which a database instance is administered. One will configure the instance using initialization parameters, periodically perform manual instance startup and shutdown operations, and so on.

Also similar to database instance administration, one may use the command-line SQL interface or the graphical Enterprise Manager.

SYSASM Super Administrator

In older releases of the database an administrator who acquired the database super administrator right SYSDBA was able to function as a super administrator for the ASM instance as well. However, starting with the Oracle 11g release, SYSASM rights are required for administration of the ASM instance.

By having distinct super administrator rights for an ASM instance, one can segregate the responsibilities for database administration from those for ASM administration. For example, one who is a super administrator for a particular relational database running on a host system does not necessarily have the same super administrator rights to the ASM instance on that same machine. The ASM instance may be servicing any number of other relational databases for which the administrator should have no rights at all.

Conceptually the database group OSASM will acquire SYSASM rights. On a Linux platform, the default group name is "asmadmin". Any users thus placed within the "asmadmin" group will inherit SYSASM instance rights, although they will not necessarily also have SYSDBA rights on the database instances.

Using V$ASM_CLIENT

Once connected to an ASM instance one has access to the V$ASM_* dynamic views. For example, the V$ASM_CLIENT view contains one row for each database instance using a disk group managed by the ASM instance. The database instance is considered as a *client* to the ASM subsystem.

```
SQL> SELECT group_number, instance_name, db_name, status
     FROM v$asm_client;

GROUP_NUMBER INSTANCE_NAME        DB_NAME  STATUS
------------ -------------------- -------- ------------
           1 test4g               test4g   CONNECTED
           1 +ASM                 +ASM     CONNECTED
           1 test4x               test4x   CONNECTED
```

About The SPFILE

By default the ASM instance name is +ASM. For example, the SPFILE may typically be found under the following file name.

```
$ORACLE_HOME/dbs/spfile+asm.ora
```

Since the duties of ASM are limited in comparison with a database instance, there are few parameters defined in the SPFILE. Those you are most likely to use are shown next.

General Instance Parameters

Parameter	*Description*
INSTANCE_TYPE	This value is set to ASM and indicates to the Oracle software that an ASM instance is being configured. While most other parameters have default values which apply, this must be explicitly stated. The default value of RDBMS indicates a traditional database instance.
DB_UNIQUE_NAME	Service provider for which the ASM instance manages disk groups. The default value is +ASM. This value will only need to be modified if you are running multiple ASM instances on the same server, which is a very unlikely scenario since one ASM instance can manage any number of database instances on the host system.

Notice how these parameter values are obtained from the V$PARAMETER view when connected to an ASM instance.

```
SQL> SELECT name, value
     FROM v$parameter
     WHERE name IN ('instance_type', 'db_unique_name');

NAME                                 VALUE
------------------------------------ --------------------
instance_type                        asm
db_unique_name                       +ASM
```

In an ASM instance, some default settings are different than for a database instance. For example, although the MEMORY_TARGET parameter may not be set explicitly, automatic memory management is implemented by default. While this could be disabled by setting MEMORY_TARGET=0, this is certainly not recommended.

Viewing The Parameter Settings

This is an example of a default PFILE for an ASM instance. As you can see, one may also set some common database parameters to non-default values, such as the location of Automatic Diagnostic Repository files using the DIAGNOSTIC_DEST parameter.

```
+ASM.__oracle_base='/u01/app/oracle'#ORACLE_BASE set from in memory value
*.asm_power_limit=1
*.diagnostic_dest='/u01/app/oracle'
*.instance_type='asm'
*.large_pool_size=12M
*.remote_login_passwordfile='EXCLUSIVE'
```

Based upon a combination of the settings within the instance parameter file and default values, the ASM-specific storage parameter values may appear similar to what is shown here for a running ASM instance.

```
SQL> SELECT name, value
     FROM v$parameter
     WHERE LOWER(name) LIKE '%asm%'
     ORDER BY name;

NAME                                 VALUE
------------------------------------ -------
asm_diskgroups
asm_diskstring
asm_power_limit                      1
asm_preferred_read_failure_groups
```

Otherwise, most other parameters applicable to a relational instance will generate an error if these are used for startup of an ASM instance.

ASM-specific Parameters

While there are some parameters which are common to both a database and an ASM instance, the primary configuration of an ASM instance is done with parameters specific to storage management. Consider a summary of some of the most common ones.

Parameter	*Description*
ASM_POWER_LIMIT	This parameter controls the amount of processing resources allocated to a rebalance operation. The default *power limit* value is 1 but one may increase this value to a maximum of 11. A lower value performs rebalancing essentially in the background and with a minimum of disruption to the database instances. A higher value will consume more database resources in order to perform the rebalance faster. One can monitor the EST_MINUTES column of the V$ASM_OPERATION view to determine how long rebalance is taking and whether one wishes to decrease this time with a higher power limit value.
ASM_DISKSTRING	This is a platform-specific format mask which identifies those disks which may be *discovered* or which are accessible to ASM for inclusion in a disk group. Generally the default value will be sufficient, or NULL which makes all disk devices available. In the event that a very large number of devices exist then some operations may be slightly faster if one limits the disks discovered to those specified by this pattern. Disks which contain the host operating system are never discovered even if they are part of the disk string mask. This is essential as absorption of the boot disk into the ASM architecture would corrupt the server software configuration.
ASM_DISKGROUPS	Normally this parameter is automatically maintained by the ASM instance. It defines which disk groups will be mounted by the instance upon startup. If one wanted to explicitly remove a disk group, or manually add one to this process, then one might modify this value but generally it will not be necessary as all disk groups will be automatically mounted, except under maintenance conditions of some sort.

ASM_PREFERRED_READ_FAILURE_GROUPS

This parameter is applicable under rather narrow circumstances where the cluster nodes and the storage systems are connected by a Systems Area Network (SAN) that is somewhat widespread geographically. When this is the case and disk group recovery is occurring after a failure, then one may wish to specify a preferred failure group to be read during recovery. The preferred failure group would be any disk devices directly connected to the ASM node, thereby allowing faster recovery without dependency upon the SAN connection.

Instance Startup & Shutdown

There are a variety of ways in which an ASM instance may be started or shutdown. A summary of the possibilities are shown here:

- Oracle Restart – this is certainly the recommended method considering the advantages offered by Oracle High Availability Services and Oracle Restart. Oracle Restart was considered elsewhere within this course.

- Manually – under rare circumstances, perhaps when troubleshooting system problems which have interfered with Oracle Restart, one may need to perform legacy manual startup and shutdown using the SQL*Plus utility.

We will discuss manual startup and shutdown next.

> ***Note***
>
> A legacy method of automatic instance startup at the time of system reboot involved creating appropriate instance entries within the `/etc/oratab` file on a Linux system. While this option is still possible, it is mutually exclusive with Oracle Restart and this method is no longer recommended.

Startup

One would connect to the instance using the SYSASM rights, and then perform a startup or shutdown in the normal manner.

```
$ sqlplus /nolog
SQL*Plus: Release 11.1.0.6.0 - Production on Thu Jan 31 12:52:14 2008
Copyright (c) 1982, 2007, Oracle.  All rights reserved.

SQL> CONNECT / AS SYSASM;
Connected.

SQL> SHUTDOWN NORMAL
ASM diskgroups dismounted
ASM instance shutdown

SQL> STARTUP
ASM instance started
Total System Global Area   83886080 bytes
Fixed Size                  1247420 bytes
Variable Size              57472836 bytes
ASM Cache                  25165824 bytes
ASM diskgroups mounted
```

These options are available for the STARTUP command.

Option	*Description*
FORCE	Issues a SHUTDOWN ABORT and then restarts the instance.
STARTUP STARTUP MOUNT STARTUP OPEN	Each of these is synonymous and starts the instance and mounts the disk groups. An ASM instance does not really open in the traditional sense, therefore this keyword is synonymous with MOUNT. The database instances may be started next.
NOMOUNT	Starts the ASM instance without mounting any disk groups. ASM instance configuration is possible but the database instances cannot be started.

Shutdown

Bear in mind that the database instances should be shutdown before the ASM instance. If this is not done, then the following error message will be produced if one attempts a normal shutdown of ASM.

```
ORA-15097: cannot SHUTDOWN ASM instance with connected RDBMS instance
```

When shutting the ASM instance these SHUTDOWN options exist.

Option	*Description*
NORMAL IMMEDIATE TRANSACTIONAL	These are all synonymous and perform an orderly shutdown of the ASM instance and its connections to the database instances. If any of the database instances are running and thereby connected to the ASM instance, an error is returned.
ABORT	Crashes the ASM instance and instance recovery is required upon startup. If any database instances are active, then these crash and instance recovery of those instances is also required.

Caution

One should not crash the ASM instance by means of SHUTDOWN ABORT without first shutting down the individual database instances which might be referencing ASM for storage information.

ASM Instance Administration With EM

In our discussion next we will conduct a brief tour of how one may administer the ASM instance using EM. However, before one may use the EM tool for ASM administration, it is necessary for one to *register* the ASM instance with ASM.

Recognizing Registration

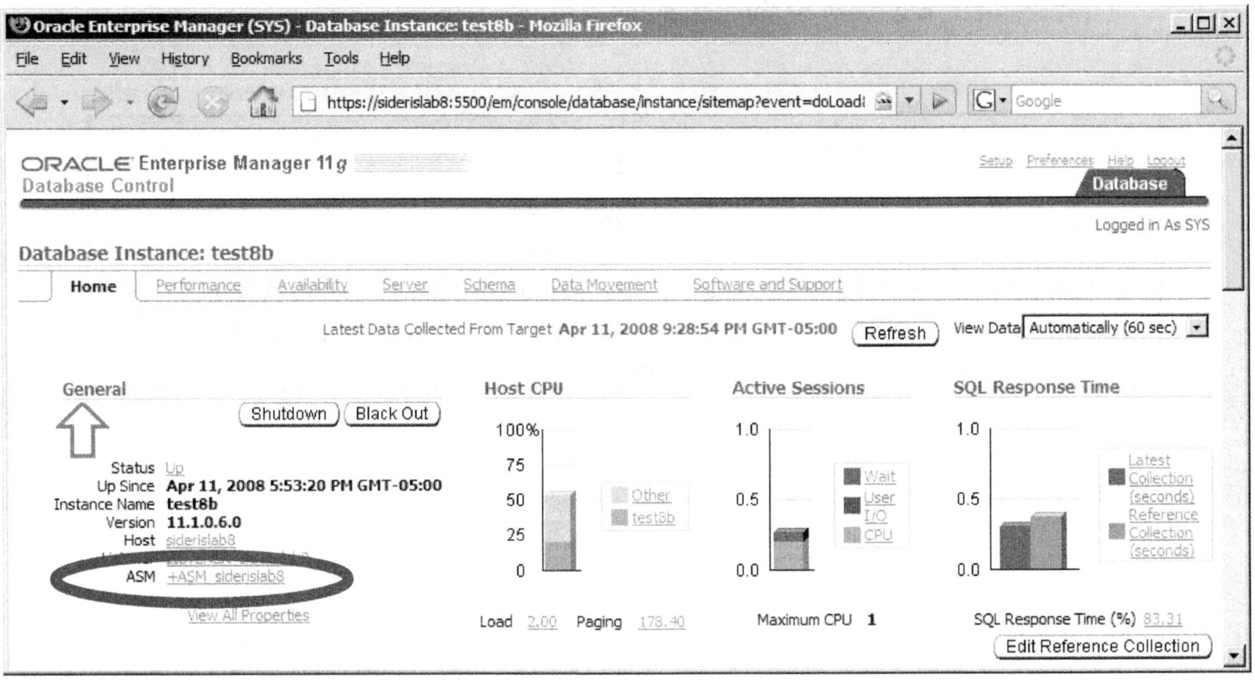

If the ASM instance has been registered with EM, this may be recognized from the database home page and the ASM link. From this location one may click on the ASM link to access the *ASM instance home page*.

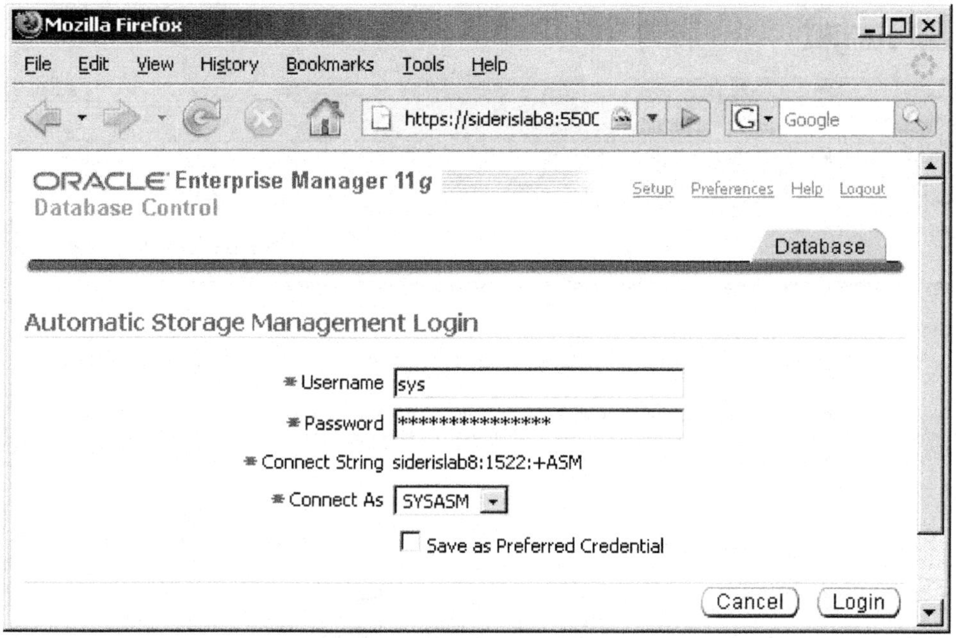

Bear in mind that the super administrator rights for an ASM instance are different from that of a relational database instance. Hence, if one were connected via EM to a relational database instance with SYSDBA connection rights, the EM interface will challenge the administrator for SYSASM credentials when attempting to access the disk groups.

Once SYSASM rights are acquired, then one can use the EM interface to ASM without restriction.

Register ASM As An EM Target

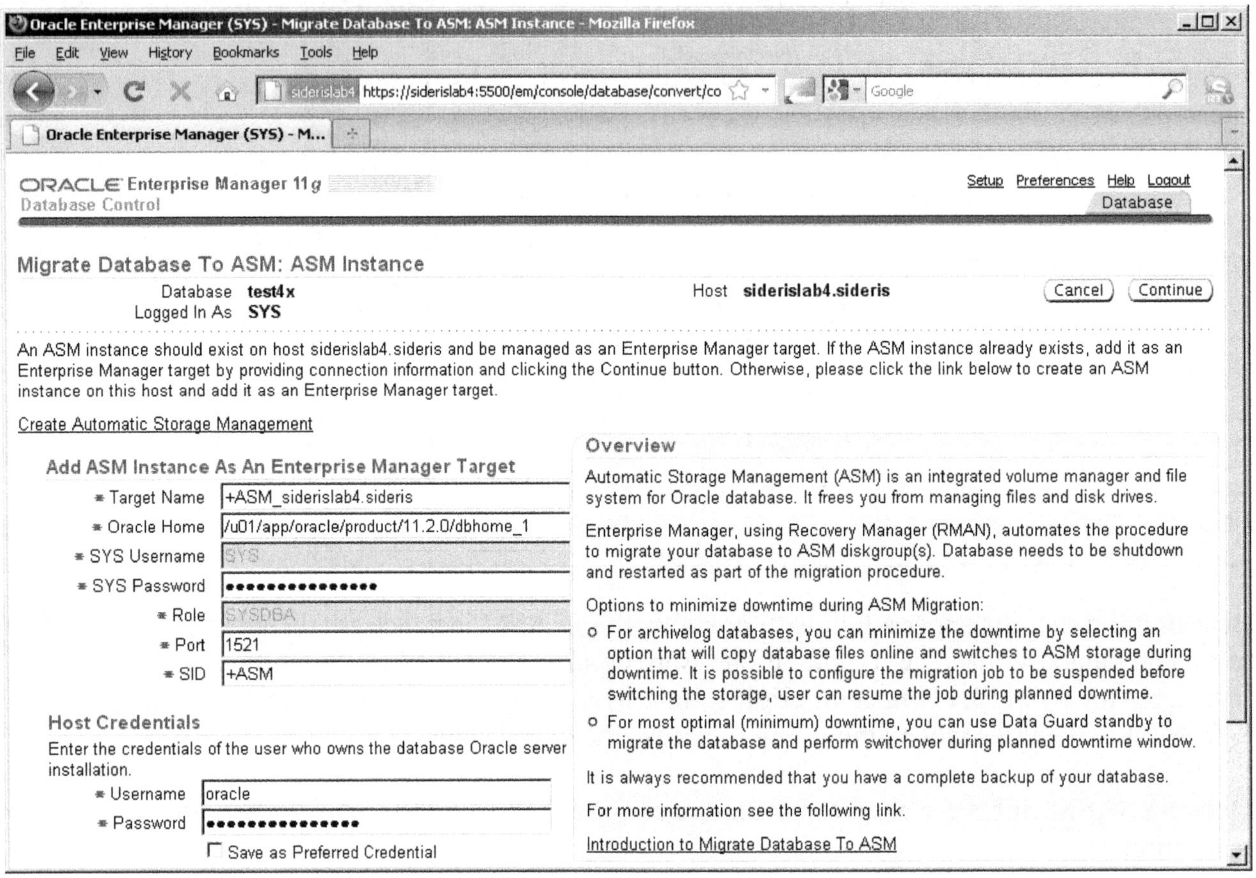

Of course, such is not possible if a given ASM instance has not been registered with EM. One simple way in which such registration may be done is by means of the Migrate To ASM wizard. One can use this wizard for registration, even if no subsequent migration is desired.

To initiate the wizard, click the Server → Migrate To ASM link from the database control. The instance connection information is fetched for ASM, with the exception of the SYSASM password. One would enter that password along with host system credentials and click the Continue button.

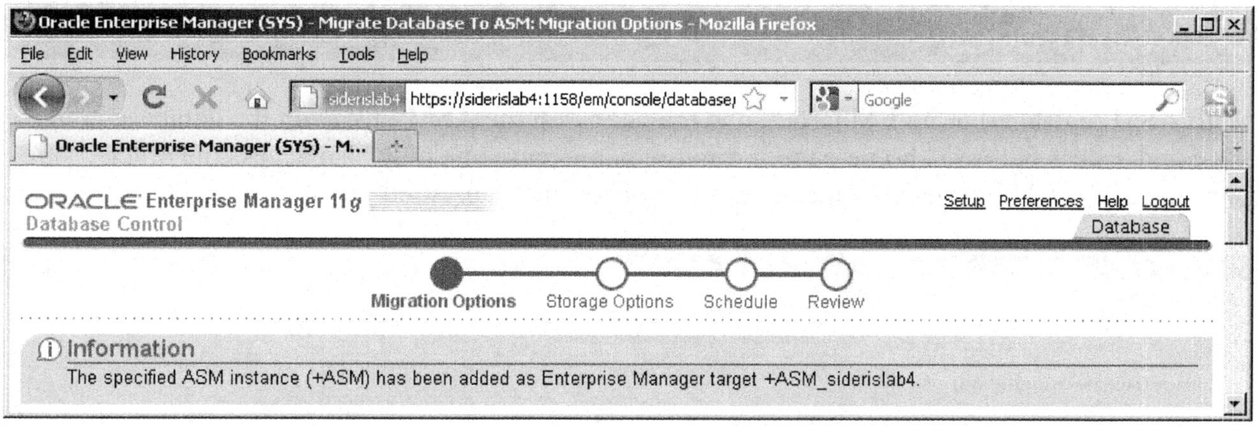

The next screen presented from the wizard will indicate that the ASM instance has now been registered with EM as one of its targets. One could continue with the wizard if migration to ASM was also desired at this time, but one could also just accept this registration result and cancel from the wizard.

EM ASM Pages

With ASM registered as an EM target, one may click on the ASM link from the database home page and access the ASM home page. From the home page one may also access the other portions of the EM interface by means of the tabbed links presented.

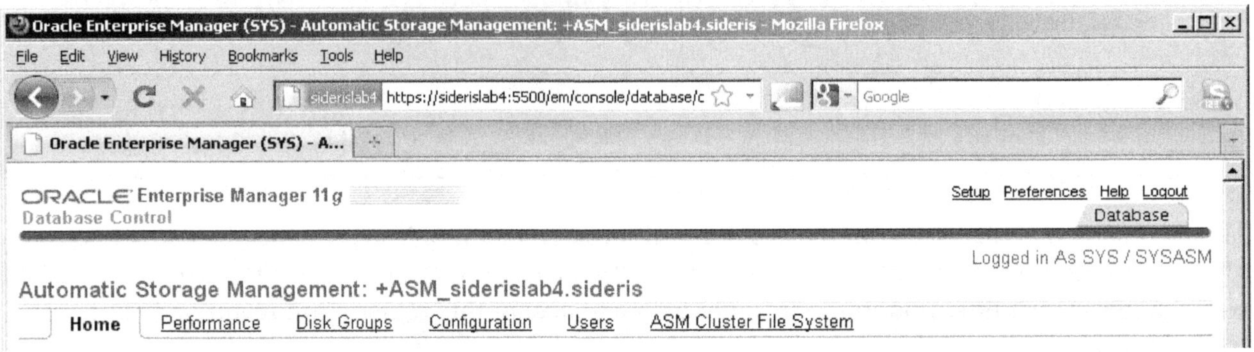

We will briefly explore the pages which relate specifically to the ASM instance next.

Home

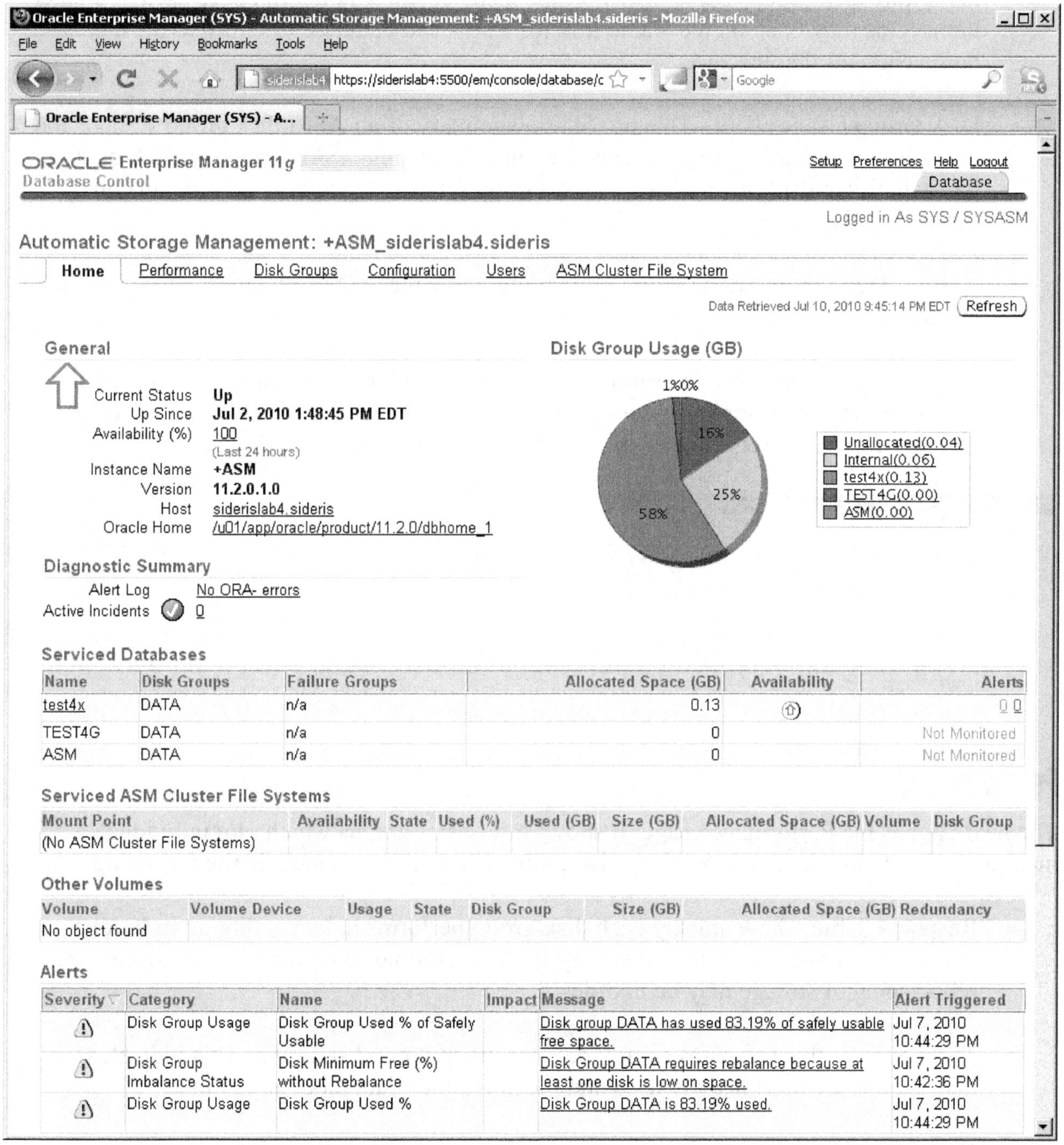

There are several significant pieces of information available from the home page:

- Serviced Databases – This provides a summary of the instances using ASM. Included are the failure disk groups associated with the instance, the amount of space used and other items. One may click on the Name link for a serviced database to return to the database home page for that instance.

- Disk Group Usage chart – This provides a summary of all ASM disk group storage and how this is allocated among the database instances using ASM. One may click on any of the statistics to drill-down into the Disk Group set of EM pages to view details on individual disk groups.

- Alerts – these are metric violations encountered by the ASM instance or one of its disk groups.

- Host Alerts – these put ASM information in context by reporting host system metric violations. In the example shown next host memory utilization constraints will have an indirect impact on performance of the ASM instance and overall throughput.

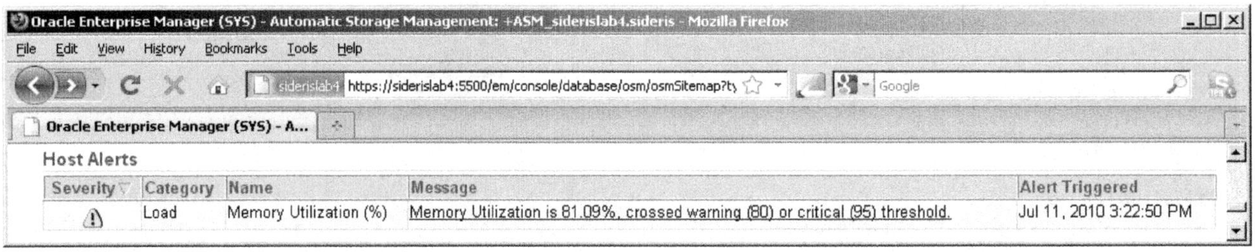

Performance

The next page is the Performance page. It shows a series of graphs which plot individual measurements within the graph for each disk group. Measurements include the following:

- Response Time – how quickly each disk group performs in responding to individual operations. If one sees a great disparity in the performance of various disk groups then rebalancing of storage may be in order.

- Throughput – this measures overall data throughput per disk group. This indicates which disk groups are most heavily used and the amount of data input and output.

- Operations Per Second – this provides a different measurement of disk group load. Rather than measuring activity in terms of data volumes, this measures operations. A relatively small amount of overall throughput may be occurring while a very heavy number of operations are being performed.

- Operation Size – whereas Throughput measures the data volumes for each second, Size measures the data volumes for each operation.

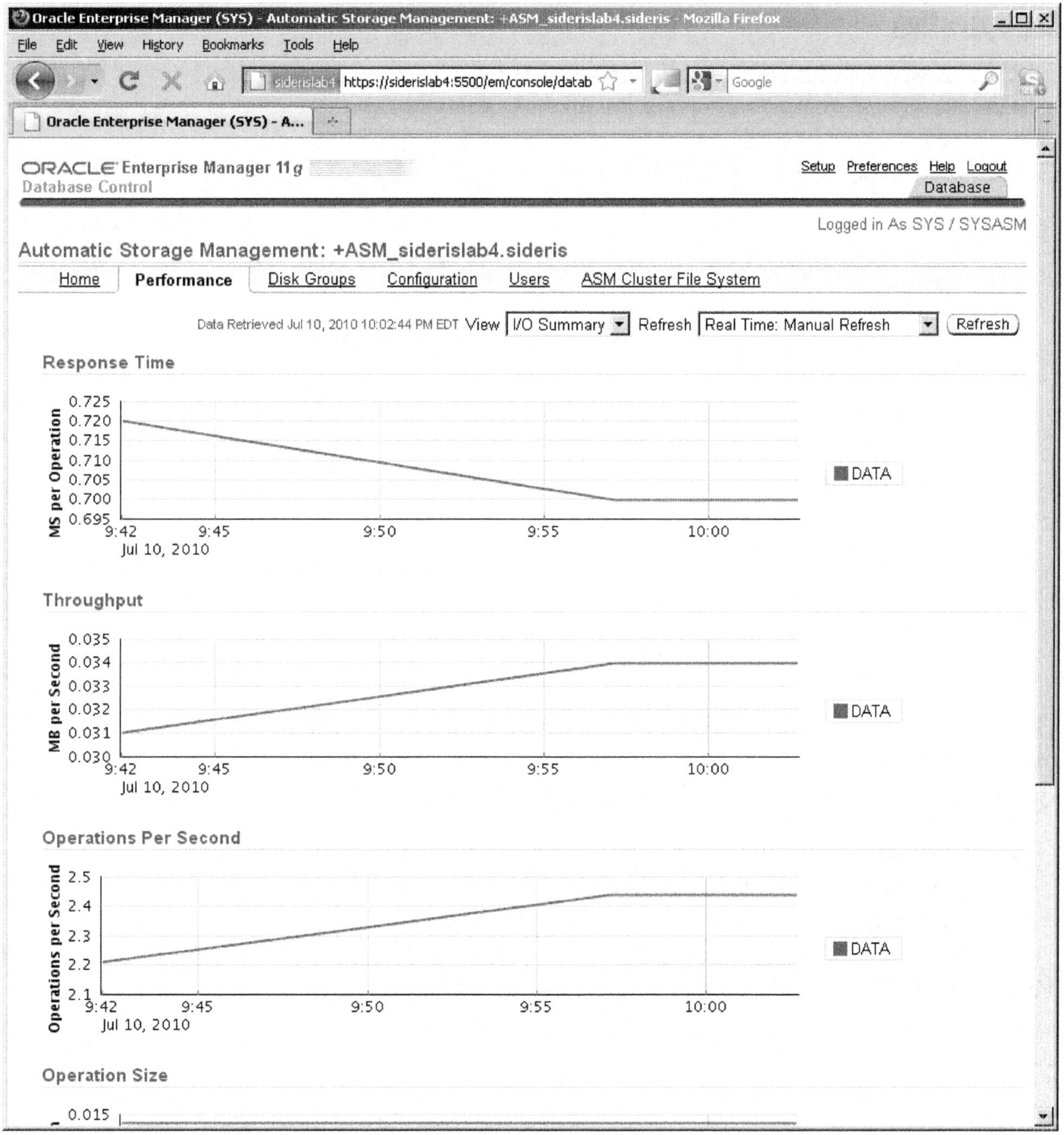

The View drop-list allows one to produce these graphs for Reads, Writes or both (e.g. I/O Summary), while the Refresh drop-list defines the time period to be monitored.

Configuration

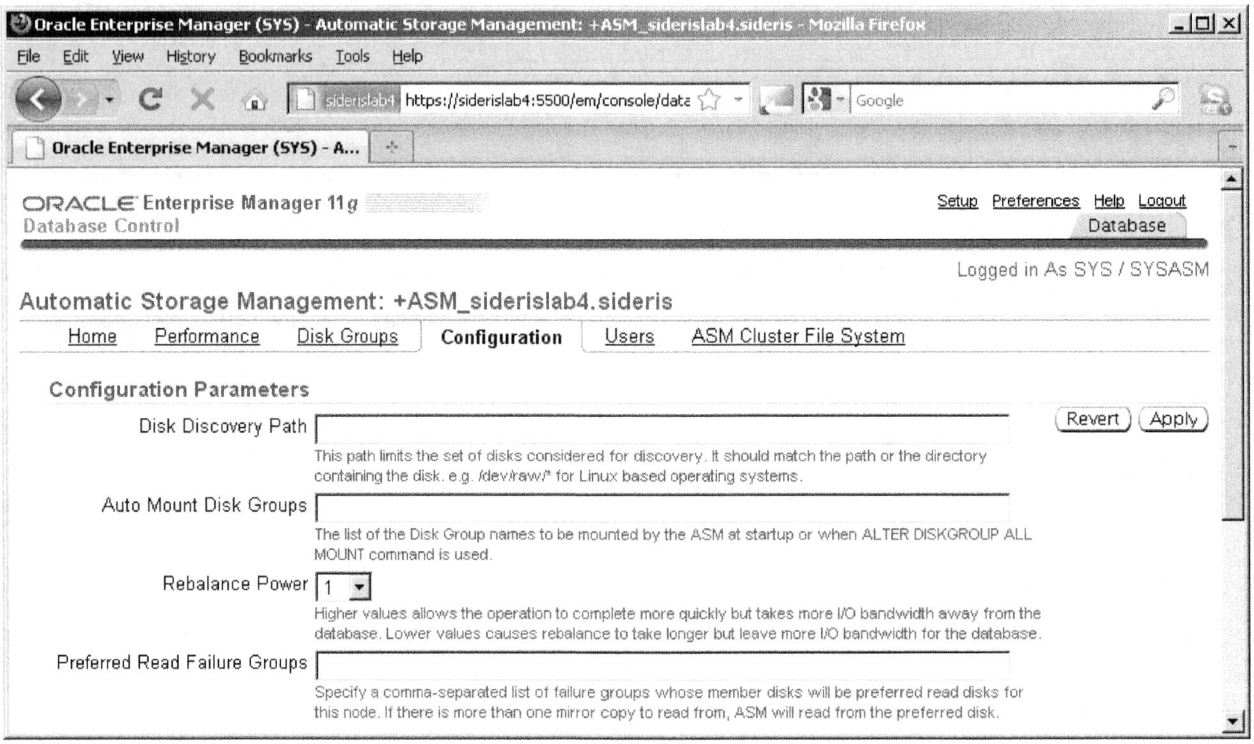

The ASM instance parameters may be modified from this screen. The parameters which are set from this screen, in the order in which they are presented, are as follows.

- ASM_DISKSTRING
- ASM_DISKGROUPS
- ASM_POWER_LIMIT
- ASM_PREFERRED_READ_FAILURE_GROUPS

The impact of these parameters was discussed earlier in this course.

Users

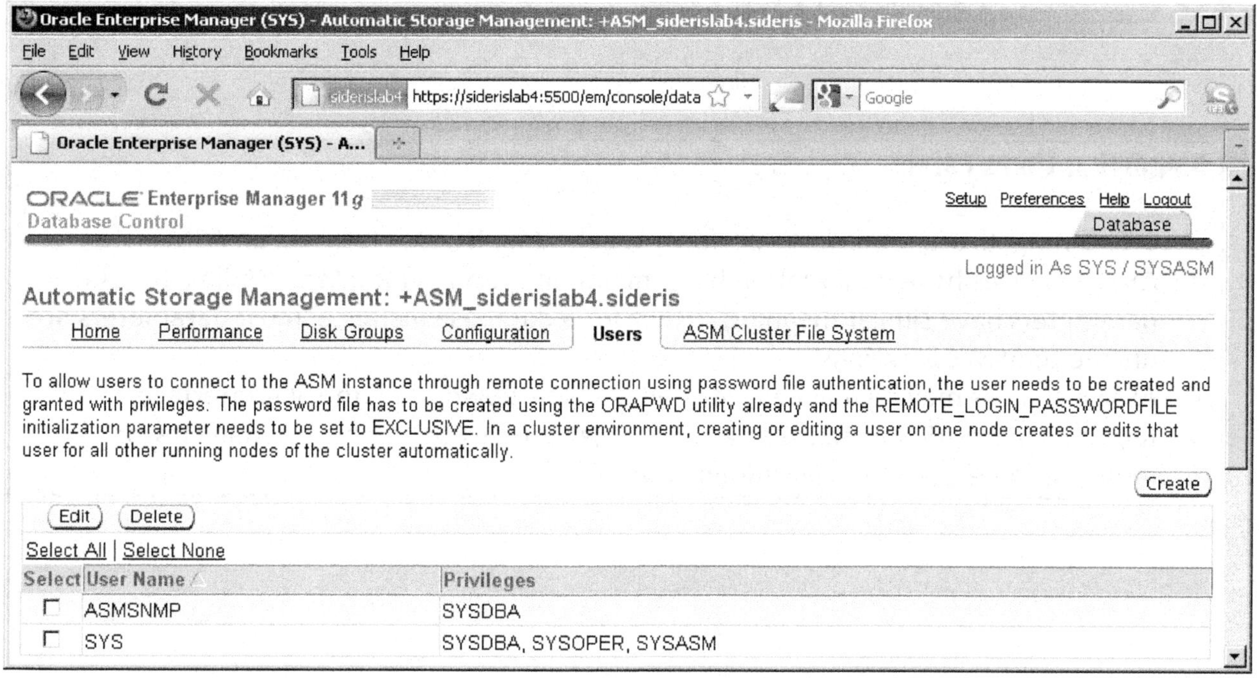

The Users page modifies the password file for the ASM instance to determine which database accounts may acquire the SYSASM connect privilege. By default only the super administrator account SYS may obtain the SYSASM privilege, but other database accounts may be added from this screen.

Section Review

Remember These Points

- SYSASM rights are required to perform super administrator tasks on an ASM instance.
- ASM instances have initialization files and initialization parameters. While a few such parameters have similar meaning as that for a database instance, most parameters are unique to ASM operations.
- ASM instances may be manually started and shutdown using the SQL interface.
- Registering the ASM instance as an EM target allows the graphical administrator interface to be used for ASM administration.

Workshop Section
ASM Instance Administration

Exercises

What You Will Do in This Workshop

In this workshop, you will:

- Configure various terminal sessions which access the ASM instance or the database instance.
- Examine parameter settings as they currently exist within the ASM instance.
- Examine the initialization parameter file for the ASM instance.
- Register the ASM instance as a target for the EM interface and use EM to administer the instance.
- Create a scenario which simulates heavy usage of files stored within an ASM disk group and use the EM performance monitors to observe disk group activity in real-time.

INSTANCE ADMINISTRATION-1

❑ Configure a terminal session with access to the ASM instance and launch the SQL*Plus interface. Connect as a SYSASM super administrator and examine the settings of the instance parameters.

INSTANCE ADMINISTRATION-2

❑ Of course, a far more preferable administration interface is Enterprise Manager. Connect to the database instance via the EM interface by means of a SYSDBA connection. Using that connection, register the ASM instance as an EM target.

INSTANCE ADMINISTRATION-3

❑ From the database home page, look for the link to the ASM instance within the General section of the page. Click on the link and confirm that you can access the ASM home page.

INSTANCE ADMINISTRATION-4

❑ Briefly peruse the pages of the EM interface to ASM which were discussed in this section. See if you can relate the concepts discussed to what you see in your local installation.

INSTANCE ADMINISTRATION-5

❑ In this exercise we will create the circumstances in which a data file within the disk group is heavily accessed, and then we will use the EM performance monitors to examine its performance.

Presently you should have a tablespace stored within the disk group which was created during an earlier workshop. Modify the ElectronicsDefine.sql script to re-create the Customers table using this tablespace.

Once that is done, execute the script CustomersAddDeleteLoop.sql to simulate heavy application usage of the tablespace.

As this script is executing, using the disk group performance monitors within EM to observe the performance measurement which is being performed.

Solutions

INSTANCE ADMINISTRATION-1

As discussed throughout this course, one must define appropriate environment variables in order to access the ASM instance or one of the database instances. In this case, we will define environment variables for access to the ASM instance.

```
export ORACLE_BASE=/u01/app/oracle
export ORACLE_HOME=/u01/app/oracle/product/11.2.0/grid
export ORACLE_SID=+ASM
export ORACLE_HOSTNAME=siderislab4.sideris
export ORACLE_PATH=/u01/app/oracle/product/11.2.0/grid/bin:.
export PATH=$PATH:/u01/app/oracle/product/11.2.0/grid/bin:.
```

Establish a terminal session with these settings in effect. By means of the account which owns the Grid Infrastructure installation, one can be assured that SYSASM rights are available. Launch the SQL*Plus interface and connect to the ASM instance.

```
[oracle@siderislab4 bin]$ sqlplus /nolog
SQL*Plus: Release 11.2.0.1.0 Production on Mon May 10 15:49:43 2010
Copyright (c) 1982, 2009, Oracle.  All rights reserved.

SQL> CONNECT sys/***** AS SYSASM;
Connected.
```

Examine the instance parameter settings which indicate that this is in fact an ASM software instance.

```
SQL> SELECT name, value
     FROM v$parameter
     WHERE name IN ('instance_type', 'db_unique_name');

NAME                                 VALUE
------------------------------------ --------------------
instance_type                        asm
db_unique_name                       +ASM
```

Examine the ASM-specific parameter settings.

```
SQL> SELECT name, value
     FROM v$parameter
     WHERE LOWER(name) LIKE '%asm%'
     ORDER BY name;

NAME                                    VALUE
-------------------------------------- -------
asm_diskgroups
asm_diskstring
asm_power_limit                          1
asm_preferred_read_failure_groups
```

Finally, you could examine the actual text of the instance SPFILE by means of these steps:

```
SQL> CREATE PFILE = '$ORACLE_HOME/dbs/classroom.ora'
        FROM SPFILE;
File created.

SQL> exit
Disconnected from Oracle Database 11g Enterprise Edition Release 11.2.0.1.0 -
Production
With the Automatic Storage Management option

[oracle@siderislab4 ~]$ cat $ORACLE_HOME/dbs/classroom.ora

+ASM.__oracle_base='/u01/app/oracle'#ORACLE_BASE set from in memory value
*.asm_power_limit=1
*.diagnostic_dest='/u01/app/oracle'
*.instance_type='asm'
*.large_pool_size=12M
*.remote_login_passwordfile='EXCLUSIVE'

[oracle@siderislab4 ~]$
```

INSTANCE ADMINISTRATION-2

Using the URL for EM announced during the installation of your database, launch a browser and enter the URL. After making a SYSDBA connection, perform these steps starting from the EM database home page:

1. Examine the General section of the database home page and confirm that the ASM instance is not currently registered.
2. Click on the Server → Migrate To ASM link.
3. From the ASM Instance page enter the SYS password for the ASM instance, enter the host credentials and click the Continue button.

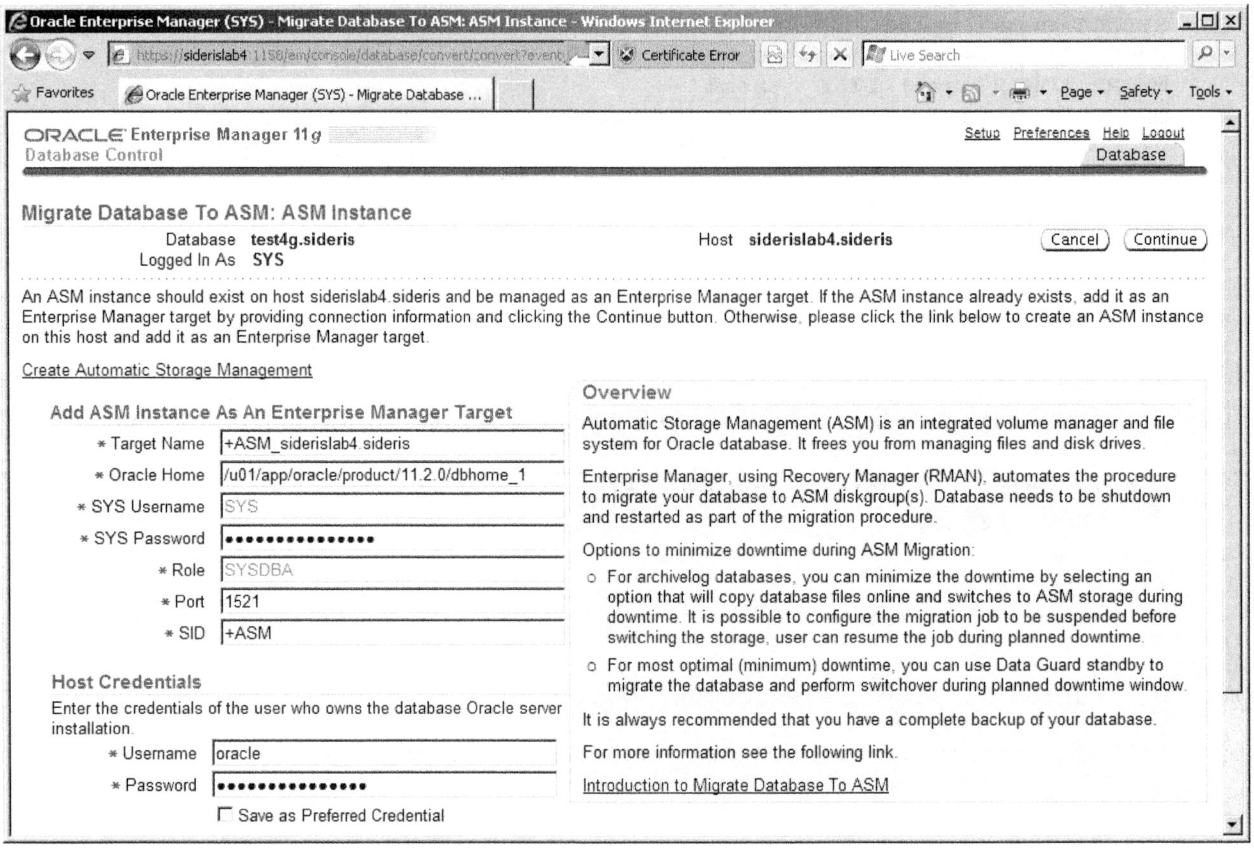

This is an example of what the ASM Instance page might look like when completed. As mentioned, click the Continue button.

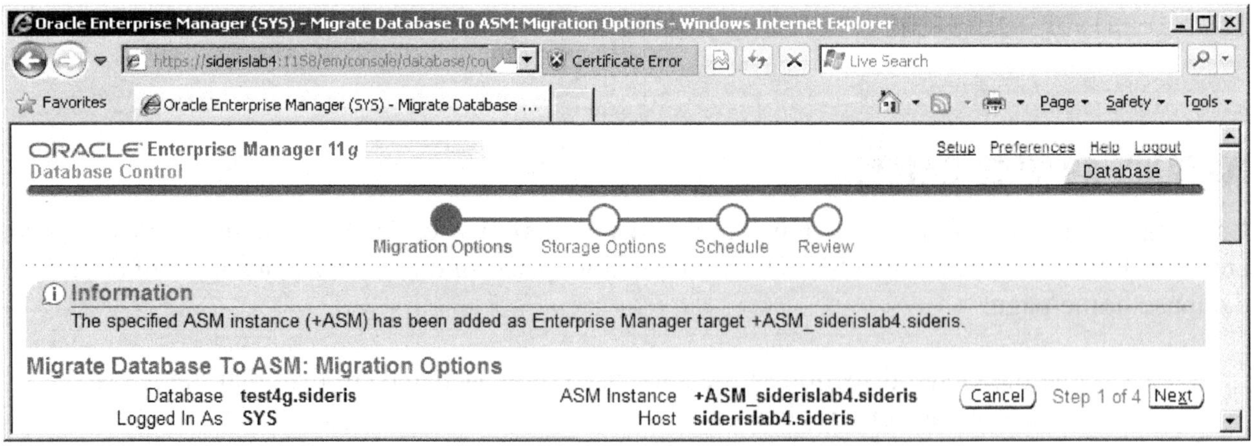

At the top of the Migration Options screen you should see confirmation that ASM has been registered as a target with EM. Click the Cancel button and do not proceed with an actual migration.

INSTANCE ADMINISTRATION-3

In order to reach the newly accessible ASM instance link from the database home page, follow these steps:

1. Close your browser session and wait a few minutes.
2. Re-launch your browser and connect to the database instance as a SYSDBA user.

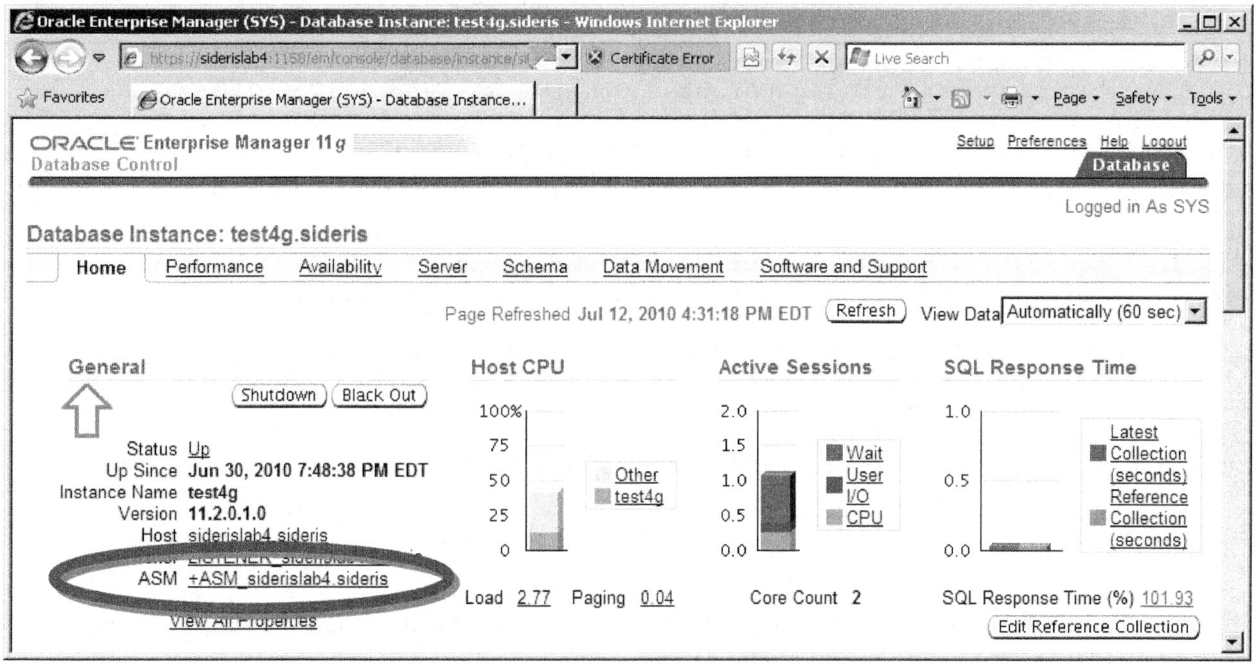

You should now see the ASM instance link in the General section of the database home page.

In the event that this does not occur in a reasonable time frame, you could follow the procedure outlined next.

First, close the terminal session with which you made a connection to the ASM instance. Next, create a new terminal session connected as the owner of the database installation and which is configured for accessing the database instance. The following is a reminder of the environment variable settings on the Sideris lab that you may use a reference.

```
export ORACLE_BASE=/u01/app/oracle
export ORACLE_HOME=/u01/app/oracle/product/11.2.0/dbhome_1
export ORACLE_SID=test4g
export ORACLE_UNQNAME=test4g
export ORACLE_HOSTNAME=siderislab4.sideris
export ORACLE_PATH=/u01/app/oracle/product/11.2.0/dbhome_1/bin:.
export PATH=$PATH:/u01/app/oracle/product/11.2.0/dbhome_1/bin:.
export HOME=/u01/app/oracle
export JAVA_HOME=$ORACLE_HOME/jdk
```

Finally, stop and restart the `dbconsole` process which manages the Database Control.

```
[oracle@siderislab4 oracle]$ emctl stop dbconsole
Oracle Enterprise Manager 11g Database Control Release 11.2.0.1.0
Copyright (c) 1996, 2009 Oracle Corporation.  All rights reserved.
https://siderislab4.sideris:1158/em/console/aboutApplication
Stopping Oracle Enterprise Manager 11g Database Control ...
 ...  Stopped.

[oracle@siderislab4 oracle]$ emctl start dbconsole
Oracle Enterprise Manager 11g Database Control Release 11.2.0.1.0
Copyright (c) 1996, 2009 Oracle Corporation.  All rights reserved.
https://siderislab4.sideris:1158/em/console/aboutApplication
Starting Oracle Enterprise Manager 11g Database Control .......... started.
------------------------------------------------------------------
Logs are generated in directory
/u01/app/oracle/product/11.2.0/dbhome_1/siderislab4.sideris_test4g/sysman/log

[oracle@siderislab4 oracle]$
```

If you re-launch the browser and connect to the database home page, then the ASM link should now be available.

INSTANCE ADMINISTRATION-4

No specific solution required.

INSTANCE ADMINISTRATION-5

After creating a terminal session with appropriately defined environment variables for access to the database instance, launch the SQL*Plus utility and create the Customers table within the appropriate tablespace.

```
[oracle@siderislab4 bin]$ sqlplus /nolog
SQL*Plus: Release 11.2.0.1.0 Production on Mon May 10 15:49:43 2010
Copyright (c) 1982, 2009, Oracle.  All rights reserved.

SQL> CONNECT student1/student1;
Connected.

SQL> CREATE TABLE customers ( CustomerID         NUMBER(4),
                              Name               VARCHAR2(20),
                              Address            VARCHAR2(30),
                              Telephone          CHAR(10),
                              Type               VARCHAR2(15)
                            )
     TABLESPACE SiderisTS1;
Table created.
```

Now execute the CustomersAddDeleteLoop.sql script.

```
SQL> @ CustomersAddDeleteLoop.sql
PL/SQL procedure successfully completed.
```

You should now be able to see the activity in the disk group as it is measured by the EM performance monitors. From the ASM home page, perform these steps:

1. Click on the Performance link
2. Set the monitoring period to Last 24 Hours using the Refresh drop-list.
3. Observe the various performance charts for the I/O Summary view and modify the View drop-list to observe measurements taken for Reads and Writes

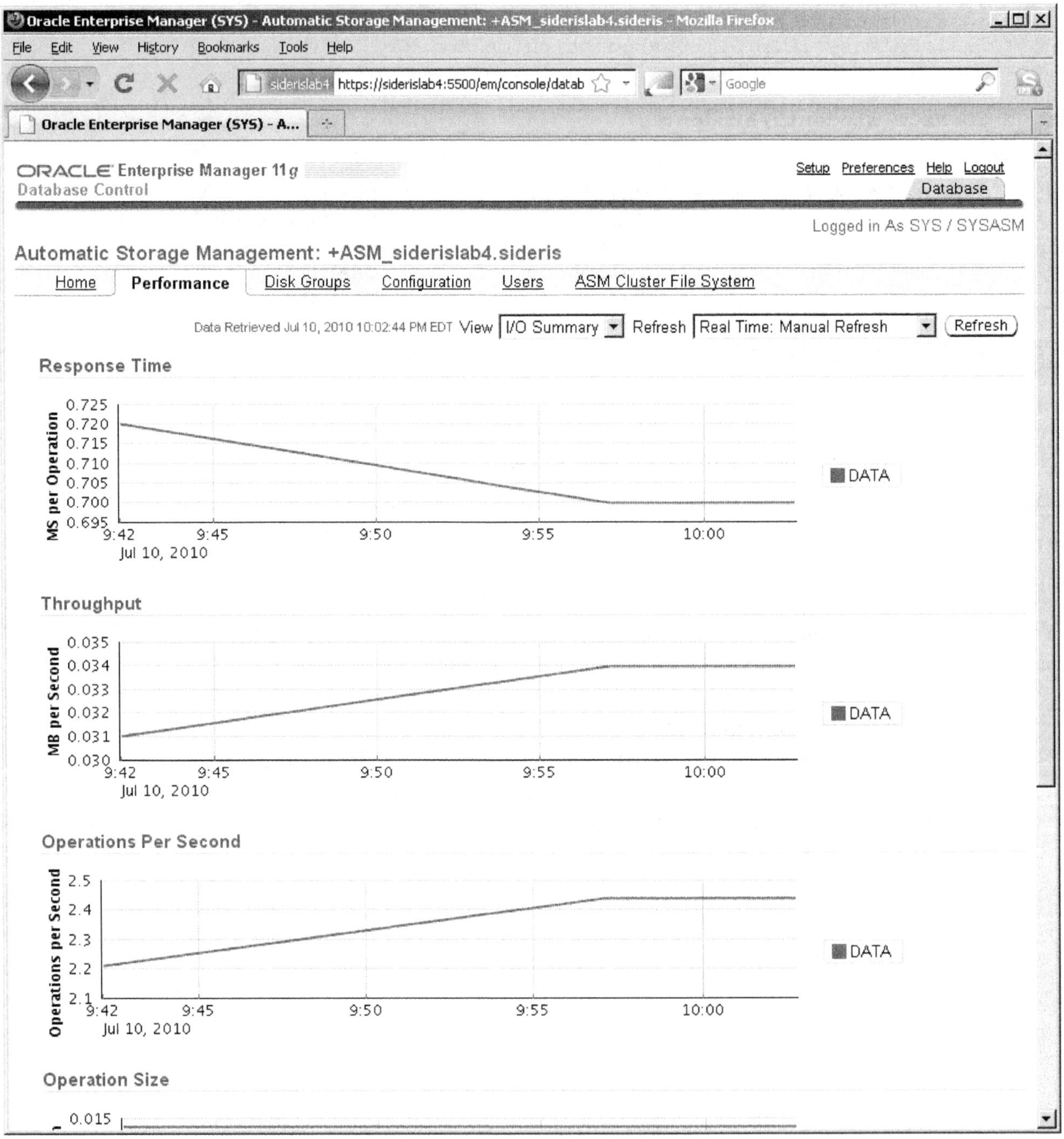

If you do not see meaningful information you may execute the script several times and you may modify the script to increase the number of iterations within the loop.

Ultimately of course, the performance measurement is based upon a contrived scenario, but hopefully this does demonstrate how one would monitor in real-time the overall performance of the ASM instance using the metrics Response Time, Throughput, and so on.

Section 7
ASM Storage Administration

Objectives

- ✓ Create & Manage Disk Groups
- ✓ Intelligent Data Placement
- ✓ Using High-Capacity Disks
- ✓ Using Disk Group Templates
- ✓ Managing Storage Using EM
- ✓ Managing Storage Using ASMCA
- ✓ Managing Storage Using ASMCA
- ✓ Managing Storage Using ASMCMD

Section Overview

The primary purpose of an ASM instance is to provide access to storage. Therefore, administrators must also be concerned about storage administration within the ASM framework, in addition to administration of the software instance. Within this section we will explore these topics:

- Create and configure additional disk groups
- Manage existing disk group configurations
- Setting disk group software version compatibility
- Implementing access control and managing privileges
- Managing individual disk group files
- Implementing intelligent data placement
- Using 4K sector high-capacity disks
- Using disk group templates to achieve consistency and enforce storage standards
- Manage storage using the EM, ASMCA, ASMCMD and SQL interfaces

Create & Manage Disk Groups

During the creation of the ASM instance one had the opportunity to define initial disk groups. These definitions must thereafter be managed, with the option to create, drop, or otherwise modify disk group definitions. New disk groups may also be created after the installation.

All of these tasks are possible using the SQL interface to the ASM instance.

Create Disk Groups

One might first query the list of disks currently mounted and in use by means of the view V$ASM_DISK.

```
SQL> SELECT group_number, disk_number, mount_status, header_status,
            mode_status, state, redundancy, name, failgroup, path
     FROM v$asm_disk
     WHERE mode_status = 'ONLINE';

GROUP_NUMBER DISK_NUMBER MOUNT_S HEADER_STATU MODE_ST STATE  REDUNDA NAME   FAILGROUP  PATH
------------ ----------- ------- ------------ ------- ------ ------- ------ ---------- ----------
           1           0 CACHED  MEMBER       ONLINE  NORMAL UNKNOWN DATA1  DATA1      ORCL:DATA1
...
```

This view contains one row for every disk *discovered.* Discovery simply means that the disk is accessible to the ASM instance. The HEADER_STATUS column indicates the use of the disk and may contain one of the following values:

- MEMBER – This disk is assigned to a disk group.

- PROVISIONED – The disk has been stamped with ASM data thereby prepared for assigned to a disk group and use by ASM. At present though, the disk is not being used.

- CANDIDATE – The disk has been discovered and is potentially usable by ASM, but otherwise no actions have been taken to utilize the device.

One could next see which candidate disks are available by querying this same view.

```
SQL> SELECT disk_number, label
     FROM v$asm_disk
     WHERE header_status = 'PROVISIONED';

DISK_NUMBER    LABEL
-----------    -----
          1    DATA2
          2    DATA3
...
```

The CREATE DISKGROUP command is then used to create the disk groups using those available devices. The disks are specified as one or more operating system dependent format masks. This command creates a disk group which includes two failure groups.

```
SQL> CREATE DISKGROUP sidDG1 NORMAL REDUNDANCY
       FAILGROUP sidDB1FGa DISK
         '/dev/data2',
         '/dev/disk3'
       FAILGROUP sidDB1FGb DISK
         '/dev/data2a',
         '/dev/data3a';
Diskgroup created.
```

It is important that all devices within a disk group have the same size and characteristics. Otherwise, balancing among unevenly configured devices would be counterproductive.

Manage Disk Groups

Disk groups may be dropped. This command drops the group and all files included in the group. Obviously the INCLUDING CONTENTS clause should be used only with an understanding of the data begin dropped, as redo log flies, control files, data files and so on could be using this storage space.

```
SQL> DROP DISKGROUP sidDG1 INCLUDING CONTENTS;
Diskgroup dropped.
```

Individual devices may be added to a disk group. In this case one device is added to each of the failure groups within the disk group. While one could have an uneven number of devices within a failure group, again this is counterproductive in many cases and not recommended.

```
SQL> ALTER DISKGROUP sidDG1 ADD
       FAILGROUP sidDB1FGa
          DISK '/dev/data4'
       FAILGROUP sidDB1FGb
          DISK '/dev/data4a';
Diskgroup altered.
```

Or one can drop disks from a disk group.

```
SQL> ALTER DISKGROUP sidDG1 DROP DISK '/dev/data4';
Diskgroup altered.
```

One can override the default rebalancing power limit defined in the ASM_POWER_LIMIT attribute for any disk group.

```
SQL> ALTER DISKGROUP sidDG1 REBALANCE POWER 5;
Diskgroup altered.
```

Mount / Dismount Disk Groups

While a disk group can remain defined and its storage objects in tact, it can be dismounted, or later manually mounted.

```
SQL> ALTER DISKGROUP sidDG1 DISMOUNT;
Diskgroup altered.
```

```
SQL> ALTER DISKGROUP sidDG1 MOUNT;
Diskgroup altered.
```

The objects stored within a disk group must be offline before the disk group may be dismounted. For example, a tablespace must be placed offline by the database instance before the ASM instance may dismount the disk group in which the tablespace is located.

Viewing Basic Disk Group Metadata

The V$ASM_* views provide helpful information about the current configuration of the disk groups and their member disks. The V$ASM_DISKGROUP view indicates the current state and basic configuration of the disk groups.

```
SQL> SELECT name, allocation_unit_size, state, type, offline_disks
     FROM v$asm_diskgroup;

NAME                 ALLOCATION_UNIT_SIZE STATE       TYPE   OFFLINE_DISKS
-------------------- -------------------- ----------- ------ -------------
sidDG1                            1048576 MOUNTED     EXTERN             0
sidDG2                            1048576 CONNECTED   EXTERN             0
```

One can drill into individual disks within a group to view their attributes using V$ASM_DISK.

```
SQL> SELECT group_number, disk_number, mount_status, state, redundancy
     FROM v$asm_disk;

GROUP_NUMBER DISK_NUMBER MOUNT_S STATE    REDUNDA
------------ ----------- ------- -------- -------
           1           0 CACHED  NORMAL   UNKNOWN
           1           1 CACHED  NORMAL   UNKNOWN
           2           0 CACHED  NORMAL   UNKNOWN
           2           1 CACHED  NORMAL   UNKNOWN
```

Internal Metadata Consistency Check

Although rare, at times there may be inconsistencies between the internal metadata maintained for disk group files and the actual storage of those files. Other internal errors could occur as well. One can perform a check and request that needed repairs to the metadata be performed using the ALTER DISKGROUP ... CHECK command.

```
SQL> ALTER DISKGROUP data CHECK REPAIR;
Diskgroup altered.
```

Resize Operations

Based upon the storage usage of the devices within a disk group one may wish to resize the space used for ASM. Sometimes additional free space on the disk which had not been allocated to ASM is now needed for ASM storage. Or, one may wish to release space from ASM for other uses.

The ALTER DISKGROUP ... RESIZE operation will allow one to modify the size of storage and to perform a rebalance operation as well.

```
SQL> ALTER DISKGROUP data
       RESIZE DISK data1
       SIZE 300 G
       REBALANCE POWER 2;
Diskgroup altered.
```

About Fast Mirror Resync

One can more quickly bring a disk within a disk group back online after a crash by means of the *fast mirror resync* capability.

Consider the following scenario: an individual disk within a disk group crashes and for a period of two hours is offline from its disk group. Each update to a different extent creates a stale extent, although these are relatively few since updates during this period are concentrated on a few specific extents.

Once the disk comes online, re-synchronizing it with the other members of the disk group can be very time consuming. For this reason one can bring the disk online individually with the following command.

```
SQL> ALTER DISKGROUP sidDG1 ONLINE DISK d1_0001;
Diskgroup altered.
```

This immediately allows new writes to be included on this disk, avoiding any further backlog of stale extents. Then, as processing permits, extents which became stale during the disk outage are copied to the device. This enhancement provides a dramatic reduction in disk group failure repair time.

COMPATIBLE.ASM & COMPATIBLE.RDBMS

You may be familiar with the database parameter COMPATIBLE, which allows one to ensure backward compatibility with an older release of the database. Note the setting of this parameter within a relational database instance.

```
SQL> SELECT name, value
     FROM v$parameter
     WHERE name = 'compatible';

NAME                 VALUE
-------------------- ---------------
compatible           11.1.0.0.0
```

This value indicates that the database is running at compatibility level 11g Release 1. Features greater than this level are not supported and the instance is compatible with the features as they existed at that point.

Disk Group Version Compatibility

In a similar way, compatible attribute settings at the disk group level can allow older relational databases to coexist with newer ones in the same ASM environment. This attribute also determines whether or not newer ASM features are enabled.

Setting	*Description*
COMPATIBLE.ASM	Determines the compatibility level of the ASM instance.
COMPATIBLE.RDBMS	Determines the compatibility level of all RDBMS instances using the ASM disk group.

To illustrate, suppose that an Oracle 11g R2 ASM instance needed to support Oracle 10g R1 database instances, and that one wanted to ensure that no ASM features beyond Oracle 10g were used within the disk groups. One would set the compatibility attributes for both properties to 10.1. This is the case in the disk group listed next within the V$ASM_DISKGROUP view.

```
SQL> SELECT name, compatibility, database_compatibility
     FROM v$asm_diskgroup;

NAME       COMPATIBIL DATABASE_C
---------- ---------- ----------
DATA       10.1.0.0.0 10.1.0.0.0
```

Modifying Disk Group Compatibility

Now suppose that one wanted to use this same ASM instance to take advantage of the new features within Oracle 11g. One could create a different disk group named "sidDG1" using the same ASM instance. Next, within this new disk group one might enable the new features by a higher setting for COMPATIBLE.ASM.

```
SQL> ALTER DISKGROUP sidDG1
       SET ATTRIBUTE 'compatible.asm' = '11.2';
Diskgroup altered.
```

One would also require that the disk group be restricted to compatible database instances by means of setting the COMPATIBLE.RDBMS attribute for this same disk group as follows:

```
SQL> ALTER DISKGROUP sidDG1
       SET ATTRIBUTE 'compatible.rdbms' = '11.2';
Diskgroup altered.
```

Note

Once these attributes have been moved forward for a particular disk group, they cannot revert to their earlier or lesser values.

Disk Group Access Control

One of the strengths of the ASM framework is that it can support all the database storage requirements for multiple database instances. At the same time, one must be able to isolate access to ASM data for one instance from another database instance which may have distinct security authorizations. Otherwise, any user with SYSDBA rights would be able to access any ASM disk group or file for any instance using the ASM installation.

With access control, a user with SYSDBA rights is selectively granted SYSASM rights on the disk group or file to which access control has been granted.

Note

This feature is available starting with Oracle 11g R2.

Access Control Privileges

The following privileges may be assigned to a disk group or to an individual file within a disk group.

Privilege	*Description*
owner	This is the user which created the disk group or file for which access control privileges are assigned.
group	This is a list of users assembled into an ASM group and for which access control privileges will be assigned.
other	These are the access control privileges for any SYSDBA user who is not the owner or an authorized group.

Implementing Access Control

In order to implement access control, each database installation must be owned by a distinct system account. Thereafter, one may implement access control in the following manner:

1. One connects to the database instance using SYSDBA rights.

2. A new disk group is created for that database instance or an existing disk group is modified. Default access control privileges are assigned to the disk group at this same time and all subsequent files created within the disk group will inherit these privilege settings.

3. Individual files whose default access control privileges were inherited from the disk group may be overridden with file-specific privileges.

Access Control Details

The specific access control privileges for a disk group are assigned in this manner:

1. One enables access control for the disk group.

2. One specifies the rights for the owner, access control user group and other users in the form of a 3-digit *user mask*, with each digit indicating the rights for the respective user accounts.

3. One adds system accounts as authorized users for the disk group.

4. One adds users from the list of authorized users to the list of user groups for the disk group.

The 3-digit mask may be understood as follows, with each of the 3 positions in the mask indicating the privilege assigned to the owner, user group and other users respectively.

Privilege	*Description*
0	Read-write privileges
2	Read-only privileges
6	No privileges

With this in mind, consider the following examples of masks and how they are interpreted by ASM disk group access control.

Mask	*Description*
000	Read-write privilege for the owner, user group and other users.
026	Read-write privilege for the owner, read-only privilege for the user group, no privileges for other users.

066	This is the default setting and indicates read-write privilege for the owner, no privileges for the user group, no privileges for other users.

Default Access Control For A Disk Group

Notice in this example how this would be implemented for a disk group. The access control mask indicates that read-write privileges are granted to owner and the access control group, while read-only privileges are granted to other SYSDBA users.

```
SQL> ALTER DISKGROUP data
        SET ATTRIBUTE 'access_control.enabled' = 'true';
Diskgroup altered.

SQL> ALTER DISKGROUP data
        SET ATTRIBUTE 'access_control.umask' = '002';
Diskgroup altered.
```

Managing Disk Group Access Control Groups

With the access control privileges in effect for a disk group, one can then define which system accounts will belong to the user group(s) associated with the disk group. First, one must define one or more system accounts as users for the disk group. The owner is always considered to have access to the disk group.

```
SQL> ALTER DISKGROUP data
        ADD USER 'oracle1', 'administrator';
Diskgroup altered.
```

Next, these users may be associated with an access control group by means of the ALTER DISK GROUP ... ADD USERGROUP statement. These users will now obtain the user group privileges assigned to the disk group earlier in this discussion.

```
SQL> ALTER DISKGROUP data
         ADD USERGROUP 'test4x_storageadmin'
         WITH MEMBER 'oracle1', 'administrator';
Diskgroup altered.
```

One can list the system accounts associated with the disk group user groups by querying V$ASM_USER.

```
SQL> SELECT group_number, user_number, os_name
     FROM v$asm_user;

GROUP_NUMBER USER_NUMBER OS_NAME
------------ ----------- --------------------
           1           1 oracle
           1           2 administrator
           1           3 oracle1
```

A new member to the user group may be added.

```
SQL> ALTER DISKGROUP data
         MODIFY USERGROUP 'test4x_storageadmin'
         ADD MEMBER 'oracle2';
Diskgroup altered.
```

Or a member may be dropped from the user group, thereafter obtaining its privileges from the other users position in the mask.

```
SQL> ALTER DISKGROUP data
         MODIFY USERGROUP 'test4x_storageadmin'
         DROP MEMBER 'oracle2';
Diskgroup altered.
```

Finally a user group may be dropped altogether.

```
SQL> ALTER DISKGROUP data
         DROP USERGROUP 'test4x_storageadmin';
Diskgroup altered.
```

Additional Disk Group Attributes

DISK_REPAIR_TIME

Individual disks within a group for which redundancy is enabled can fail while the others remain operational. Until such time as the failed device is repaired and brought back online, extents updated on the other online disks of the group become *stale* and must be eventually copied to the failed disk once it is back online. As long as the failed disk is part of the group and the stale extents are tracked, the disk group may be *repaired* once the device is online again.

The disk group attribute DISK_REPAIR_TIME indicates the time period for which stale extent tracking should occur. If the offline disk is brought online during this period, then it will be resynchronized using fast mirror resync, discussed later in this section. If the offline disk is not brought online during this time period, then it will be dropped from the disk group permanently. At a later point in time a device can be added to the group and it may be either resynchronized or rebalanced with the other disk group members as needed.

The default value for DISK_REPAIR_TIME is 3.6 hours, but it may be modified using the following command.

```
SQL> ALTER DISKGROUP sidDG1
       SET ATTRIBUTE 'disk_repair_time' = '4h';
Diskgroup altered.
```

AU_SIZE

Earlier in our discussion we considered the capability of *automatic variable size extents*. As you might recall, this allowed ASM to dynamically respond to fast-growing files by increasing the size of the extents to include more allocation units.

By default an allocation unit is 1 MB in size. However, if one knows in advance that very large files will be used in a disk group, then one can modify the allocation unit size at the time the disk group is created using the AU_SIZE attribute. The larger sizes permitted are 2, 4, 8, 16, 32 and 64 MB. With variable size extents the same formula in obtaining allocation units is used, but the size of the extents is much larger based upon the larger size allocation unit.

In this example a 2 MB allocation unit is specified for the disk group.

```
SQL> CREATE DISKGROUP sidDG1 NORMAL REDUNDANCY
       FAILGROUP sidDB1FGa DISK
         '/dev/data2',
         '/dev/disk3'
       FAILGROUP sidDB1FGb DISK
         '/dev/data2a',
         '/dev/data3a'
     ATTRIBUTE 'au_size' = '2M';
Diskgroup created.
```

Disk Group File Attributes

One may also manage individual files within the disk groups on a limited basis. Some of these file management features available are discussed next.

File Permissions

As mentioned, all files created within the disk group will inherit the access control privileges associated with the disk group. However, each file may have its own unique set of access control privileges by means of the ALTER DISKGROUP ... SET PERMISSION statement.

```
SQL> ALTER DISKGROUP data
        SET PERMISSION OWNER=Read write, GROUP=Read write, OTHER=Read only
        FOR FILE '+DATA/TEST4G/DATAFILE/SIDERISTS1.256.723751977';
Diskgroup altered.
```

Note

This feature is available starting with Oracle 11g R2.

File Name Aliases

When managing disk group files, it may be advantageous to assign an alias name. One may thereafter reference the file by its alias name rather than its system-assigned name.

```
SQL> ALTER DISKGROUP data
        ADD ALIAS '+DATA/TEST4G/DATAFILE/SiderisIndex' FOR
                  '+DATA/TEST4G/DATAFILE/SIDERISIDX1.263.723912065';
Diskgroup altered.
```

Obtaining File Metadata

Useful metadata for the ASM files is available from the V$ASM_FILE view. Consider one example of a query to this view.

```
SQL> SELECT group_number, file_number, bytes, type, permissions
     FROM v$asm_file;

GROUP_NUMBER FILE_NUMBER      BYTES TYPE                 PERMISSIONS
------------ ----------- ---------- -------------------- ----------------
           1         253       1536 ASMPARAMETERFILE     rw-rw-rw-
           1         256     114688 DATAFILE             rw-rw-rw-
           1         257    9748480 CONTROLFILE          rw-rw-rw-
           1         258    9748480 CONTROLFILE          rw-rw-rw-
           1         259       3584 PARAMETERFILE        rw-rw-rw-
           1         260    1056768 DATAFILE             rw-rw-rw-
           1         261   52429312 ONLINELOG            rw-rw-rw-
           1         262   52429312 ONLINELOG            rw-rw-rw-
           1         263    1056768 DATAFILE             rw-rw-rw-
           1         264     212992 DATAFILE             rw-rw-r--
```

Intelligent Data Placement

To understand how data is placed on mechanical storage devices, and therefore how ASM Intelligent Data Placement is helpful, one must first consider a brief discussion about disk drive mechanisms.

> **Note**
>
> ASM Intelligent Data Placement is available starting with Oracle 11g R2.

Disk Drive Technology

Most mechanical storage devices follow a basic arrangement whereby *platters* are stacked upon each other, with each having the ability to store data. These platters spin around a central *spindle* to position the platter and expose a particular vector of data known as *sectors*. The read/write arms then move inward and outward to access those sectors on a particular *track*.

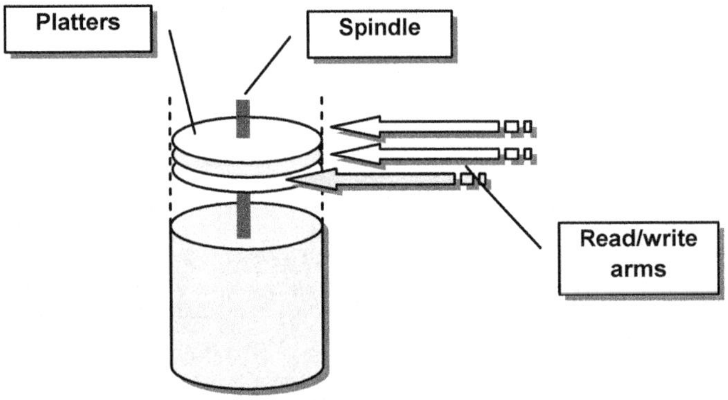

Taking one platter of the stack and examining it in isolation offers greater insight into the actual placement of data storage.

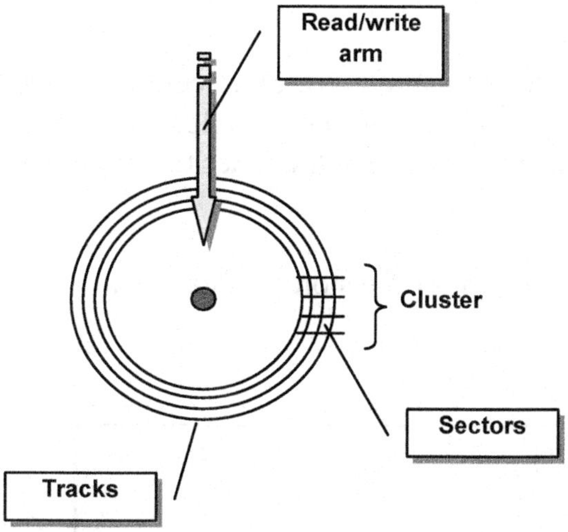

A band on the platter is known as a *track*. Each track is segmented into *sectors*, with each sector containing a chunk of available storage. Typically sectors are 512 bytes in size, with high-density disk drives having 4K sector sizes. To efficiently manage the many sectors on a track these are sometimes organized into groups called *clusters*.

Disk Drive Metrics

Based upon this fundamental function of a disk drive, I/O performance is largely subject to the performance of these mechanical elements. Disk drive performance is often measured using these metrics.

Parameter	*Description*
Latency	The time required for a disk platter to spin one complete revolution. The average latency is one half of a rotation.
Seek time	The time required for a read/write head to move inwards or outwards to position itself over a particular track. The average seek time is half the distance across the platter.
Access time	Latency + Seek Time. The combination of these activities causes the read/write head to be positioned over a particular sector.
Transfer rate	The speed at which data accessed by the read/write head is moved in and out of the disk drive buffer.

About Data Placement

This basic understand of disk drive mechanics yields some critical information. Sectors located on the outermost tracks are the fastest to access, since the read/write arm has the least distance to travel. Furthermore, storage space in the outermost tracks is denser than the inner tracks, since there are more sectors located within the track band.

For this reason, the outermost tracks are considered to be *hot* or prime storage areas, while the innermost tracks represent the *cold* portion of a platter.

Note

Some operating systems utilize the hot portion of platters for storage first, and then use the cold areas as the disk fills. This is one of the reasons why disk performance tends to degrade over the course of time.

Intelligent Data Placement Scenario

With the administrator knowledge of database storage, one can often identify data which should be placed in the host area of disks. We will demonstrate a hypothetical scenario in which this might be done, along with the steps necessary to implement intelligent data placement.

Suppose that one had two tablespaces, one which was used for table storage which contains data segments while the other which is used to store index segments. In this hypothetical scenario, the index tablespace is judged to be a priority over the data segment tablespace.

Notice how one might create these tablespaces and thereafter identify the data files stored within the ASM disk group.

```
SQL> CREATE TABLESPACE siderisTS1
       DATAFILE '+DATA' SIZE 1M;
Tablespace created.

SQL> CREATE TABLESPACE siderisIDX1
       DATAFILE '+DATA' SIZE 1M;
Tablespace created.
```

```
SQL> SELECT file_name
     FROM dba_data_files;

/u01/app/oracle/oradata/test4g/users01.dbf
/u01/app/oracle/oradata/test4g/undotbs01.dbf
/u01/app/oracle/oradata/test4g/sysaux01.dbf
/u01/app/oracle/oradata/test4g/system01.dbf
/u01/app/oracle/oradata/test4g/example01.dbf
+DATA/test4g/datafile/sideristsl.256.723751977
+DATA/test4g/datafile/siderisidx1.263.723912065
```

ASM Intelligent Data Placement

One would implement appropriate data placement of the data files using a few basic steps. First, one must ensure that the compatible.rdbms disk group attribute is set to the appropriate release.

```
SQL> ALTER DISKGROUP data
       SET ATTRIBUTE 'compatible.rdbms' = '11.2';
Diskgroup altered.
```

Next, using the ALTER DISKGROUP...MODIFY FILE command within the ASM instance, one can move the data files to the appropriate region of the disk.

```
SQL> ALTER DISKGROUP data
       MODIFY FILE
       '+DATA/test4g/datafile/sideristsl.256.723751977'
       ATTRIBUTE (COLD);
Diskgroup altered.
```

```
SQL> ALTER DISKGROUP data
       MODIFY FILE
       '+DATA/test4g/datafile/siderisidx1.263.723912065'
       ATTRIBUTE (HOT);
Diskgroup altered.
```

Note

Initially this operation will only affect the placement of new file extensions. Should a rebalance operation occur, then all file extents will be placed according to the instructions given here.

In addition to the primary region of a file, one could also specify the placement of mirror regions using the MIRRORHOT and MIRRORCOLD attributes as well. Of course, the disk group must support mirroring in order for this option to succeed.

```
SQL> ALTER DISKGROUP data
       MODIFY FILE
       '+DATA/test4g/datafile/siderisidx1.263.723912065'
       ATTRIBUTE (HOT
                  MIRRORCOLD);
Diskgroup altered.
```

The EM interface offers an excellent graphical view of these attributes across all files within a disk group.

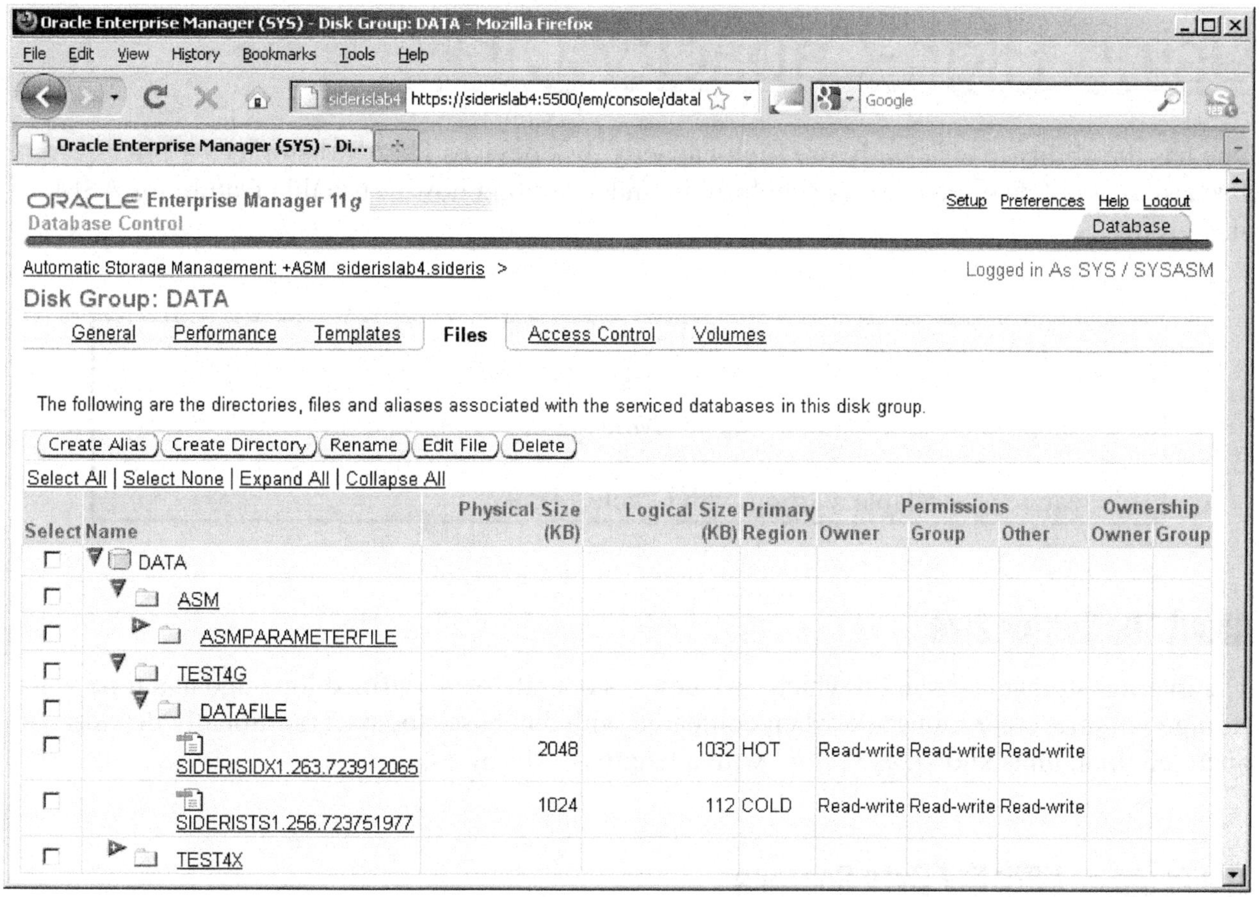

Notice how the Files tab of the Disk Group screen as shown within EM indicates the track placement of the data files.

Using High-Capacity Disks

One has the ability to efficiently use high-capacity disk devices for ASM storage. A brief discussion about disk sector sizes is helpful in understanding how to use this feature for ASM disk groups.

> **Note**
>
> This feature is available starting with Oracle 11g R2.

About The Sector Size

The internal storage units upon which disk devices operate were defined long ago at a time when storage volumes were miniscule when compared with databases today. Traditionally disk drives operated upon units known as *sectors* with a length of 512 bytes.

The Problem With 512 Byte Sectors

Newer high-density devices now have sector sizes of 1024 and 4096. This is one of the main reasons why high-capacity, low-cost storage has been made available. Necessary inter-sector gaps required for the mechanical seek operations to synchronize with the sectors are minimized with the more efficient and dense larger sectors.

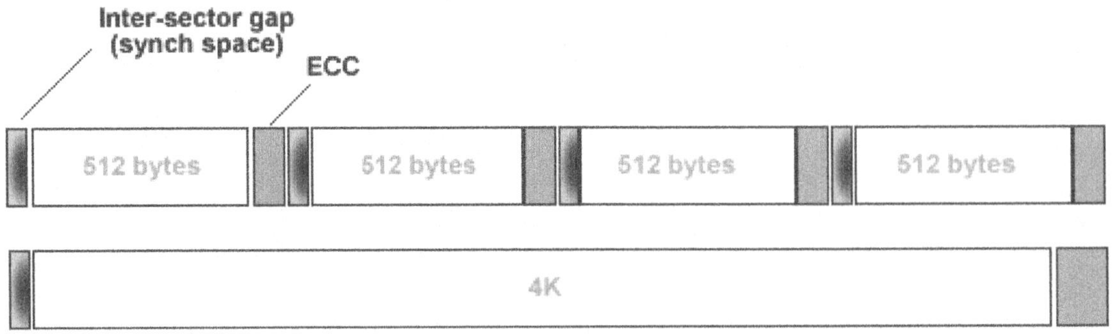

This should be a beneficial development. It is inefficient to read and write small 512-byte units of storage when facilities such as databases move such large volumes of data. It is for this reason that the database block size has for some time supported sizes of 2K to 32K, with the corresponding database buffers matching that size.

There is another problem which has driven the development of 4K sector disks. Since disk devices are more dense, the error rates reading and writing to such media increases. The disks handle this with sector *error correcting code* (ECC), stored in a few bytes at the end of each sector. But increasing density means increased error rates. Thus, the size of the ECC is inadequate. For this reason 4K sectors also include larger, 400 byte ECC. The rate of errors is not different from 512 byte sectors, but the ability of the devices to correct these does increase with a 4K sector. That increased error correction allows the development of high-density devices to continue.

The Problem With 4K Sectors

However, most components of computer systems have yet to fully utilize the new sector sizes. The sector size is such an elemental part of processing that the task is enormous. 4K sectors that are used by systems still functioning on a 512 byte basis results in much wasted space.

As a result, newer high-capacity disks often operate in *emulation mode*, writing four 512 byte chunks into a sector. This allows greater density, the necessary ECC, and is still compatible with existing architectures. But the performance can be degraded.

> ***Note***
>
> Windows 7, the later versions of the Mac OS and recent versions of the Linux kernel are all now 4K sector aware.

ASM Disk Group Sector Size

Having said all that, now consider the impact when such devices are used to store ASM files. Disk groups include an attribute known as SECTOR_SIZE. A substantial degradation in performance will occur if the SECTOR_SIZE setting is 512 while 4K sector disk devices are used. Therefore, one can use this setting to ensure that the operation of the disk group is consistent with the disk devices contained within the group.

```
SQL> CREATE DISKGROUP sidDG1 NORMAL REDUNDANCY
       FAILGROUP sidDB1FGa DISK
         '/dev/data2',
         '/dev/disk3'
       FAILGROUP sidDB1FGb DISK
         '/dev/data2a',
         '/dev/data3a'
       ATTRIBUTE 'sector_size' = '4096';
Diskgroup created.

SQL> SELECT group_number, sector_size
     FROM v$asm_diskgroup;

GROUP_NUMBER SECTOR_SIZE
------------ -----------
           1        4096
```

All devices within a disk group must have the same SECTOR_SIZE setting.

Disk Group Templates

A disk group *template* is a set of attributes which define such things as redundancy mirroring and striping characteristics, intelligent data placement and access control settings for files stored within the disk group.

A system-defined set of templates exists for the different categories of files or file types managed by ASM. By means of such templates, files created within the disk group inherit a consistent set of storage attributes appropriate for their file type.

Each disk group may have its own templates with their own unique attributes appropriate for that disk group.

Examining Template Attributes

The V$ASM_TEMPLATE view will indicate the current set of templates associated with a disk group when the disk group is created. The view will also indicate the default attribute settings for the templates.

```
SQL> SELECT * FROM v$asm_template;

GROUP_NUMBER ENTRY_NUMBER REDUND STRIPE S NAME                      PRIM MIRR
------------ ------------ ------ ------ - ------------------------- ---- ----
           1           60 UNPROT COARSE Y PARAMETERFILE             COLD COLD
           1           61 UNPROT COARSE Y ASMPARAMETERFILE          COLD COLD
           1           62 UNPROT COARSE Y ASMPARAMETERBAKFILE       COLD COLD
           1           63 UNPROT COARSE Y DUMPSET                   COLD COLD
           1           64 UNPROT FINE   Y CONTROLFILE               COLD COLD
           1           65 UNPROT COARSE Y FLASHFILE                 COLD COLD
           1           66 UNPROT COARSE Y ARCHIVELOG                COLD COLD
           1           67 UNPROT COARSE Y ONLINELOG                 COLD COLD
           1           68 UNPROT COARSE Y DATAFILE                  COLD COLD
           1           69 UNPROT COARSE Y TEMPFILE                  COLD COLD
           1          170 UNPROT COARSE Y BACKUPSET                 COLD COLD
           1          171 UNPROT COARSE Y AUTOBACKUP                COLD COLD
           1          172 UNPROT COARSE Y XTRANSPORT                COLD COLD
           1          173 UNPROT COARSE Y CHANGETRACKING            COLD COLD
           1          174 UNPROT COARSE Y FLASHBACK                 COLD COLD
           1          175 UNPROT COARSE Y DATAGUARDCONFIG           COLD COLD
           1          176 UNPROT COARSE Y OCRFILE                   COLD COLD
           1          177 UNPROT COARSE Y OCRBACKUP                 COLD COLD
           1          178 UNPROT COARSE Y ASM_STALE                 COLD COLD
```

One will be able to modify these attributes, as well as the templates themselves, for each disk group.

Using A Template

Consider how a template may be used in a practical example. Suppose that one wanted by default to place all data files within the hot region of the disk for a particular disk group. One could modify the attributes of the system-supplied template named DATAFILE in this manner.

```
SQL> ALTER DISKGROUP data
        ALTER TEMPLATE "DATAFILE"
        ATTRIBUTES (UNPROTECTED COARSE HOT);
Diskgroup altered.
```

Thereafter, if one wanted to create a new data file using this template to ensure that the file was created according to the policies of the disk group, one would reference both the disk group and the template using the syntax '+DiskGroup(TemplateName)'. Note this example.

```
SQL> ALTER TABLESPACE SiderisTS2
       ADD DATAFILE '+DATA(DATAFILE)' SIZE 100M;
Tablespace altered.
```

Managing ASM Storage Using EM

From the ASM home page within EM one can click on the Disk Groups link to manage disk groups and their attributes.

Disk Groups

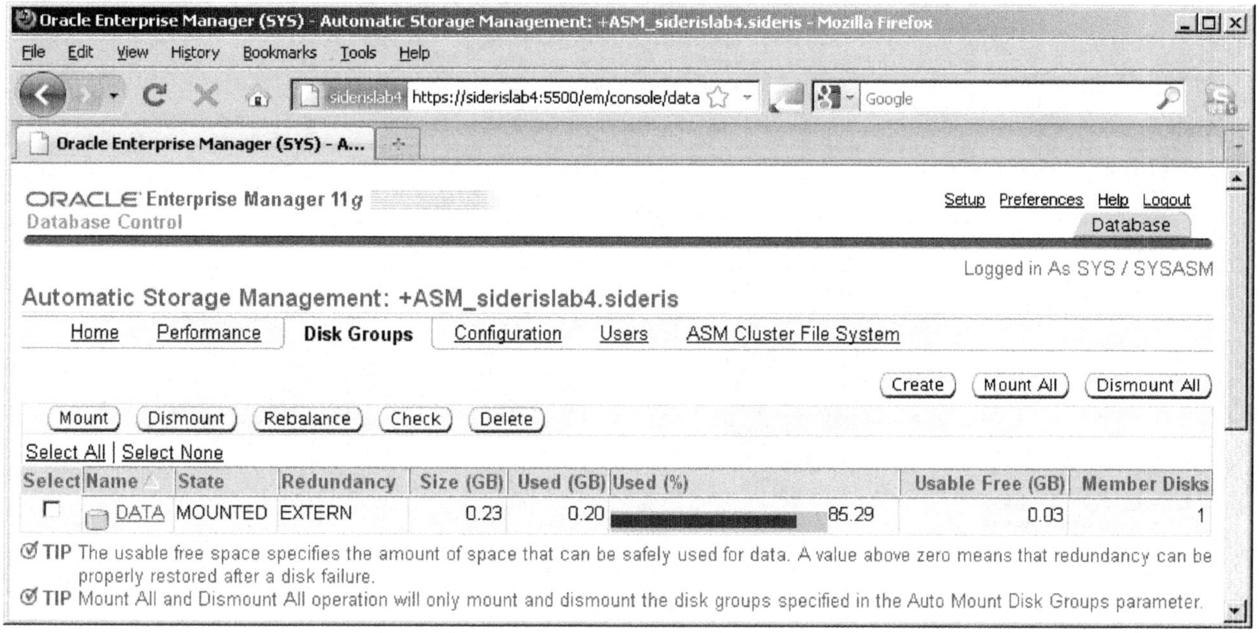

The Disk Groups page lists the individual disk groups managed by the ASM instance in behalf of the database instances. One may drill into the details of any given disk group by clicking on the Name link.

From this page, one may create new disk groups, mount or dismount existing disk groups, launch an immediate rebalance operation, and perform other standard maintenance operations.

Managing An Individual Disk Group

From the Disk Groups page one may drill into the details of an individual disk group by clicking on the Name link for an individual disk group.

General

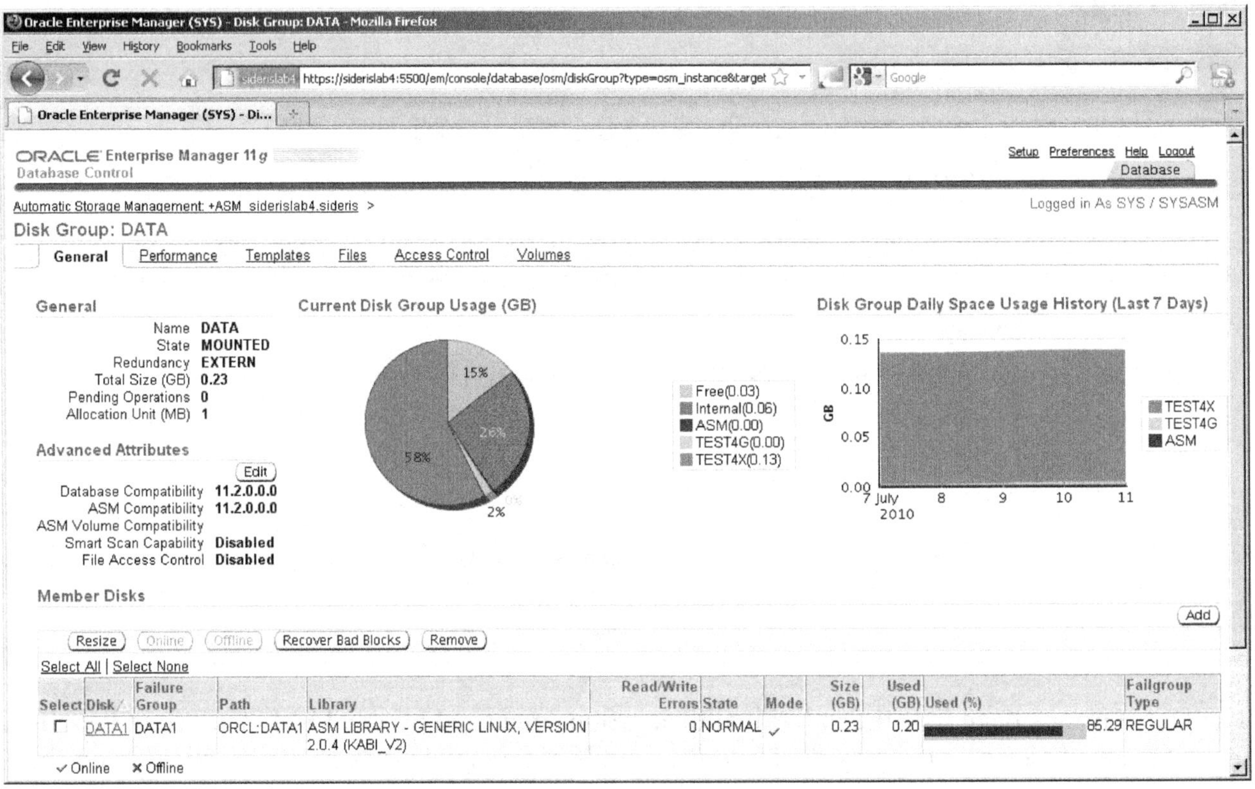

The General page shows the individual devices within a disk group, and how their space is utilized among the relational database instances. Trends for disk group space consumption are shown in the graph, allowing one to see how quickly remaining space is being used.

The Advanced Attributes page allows one to modify the attribute settings for a disk group, as discussed earlier in this section.

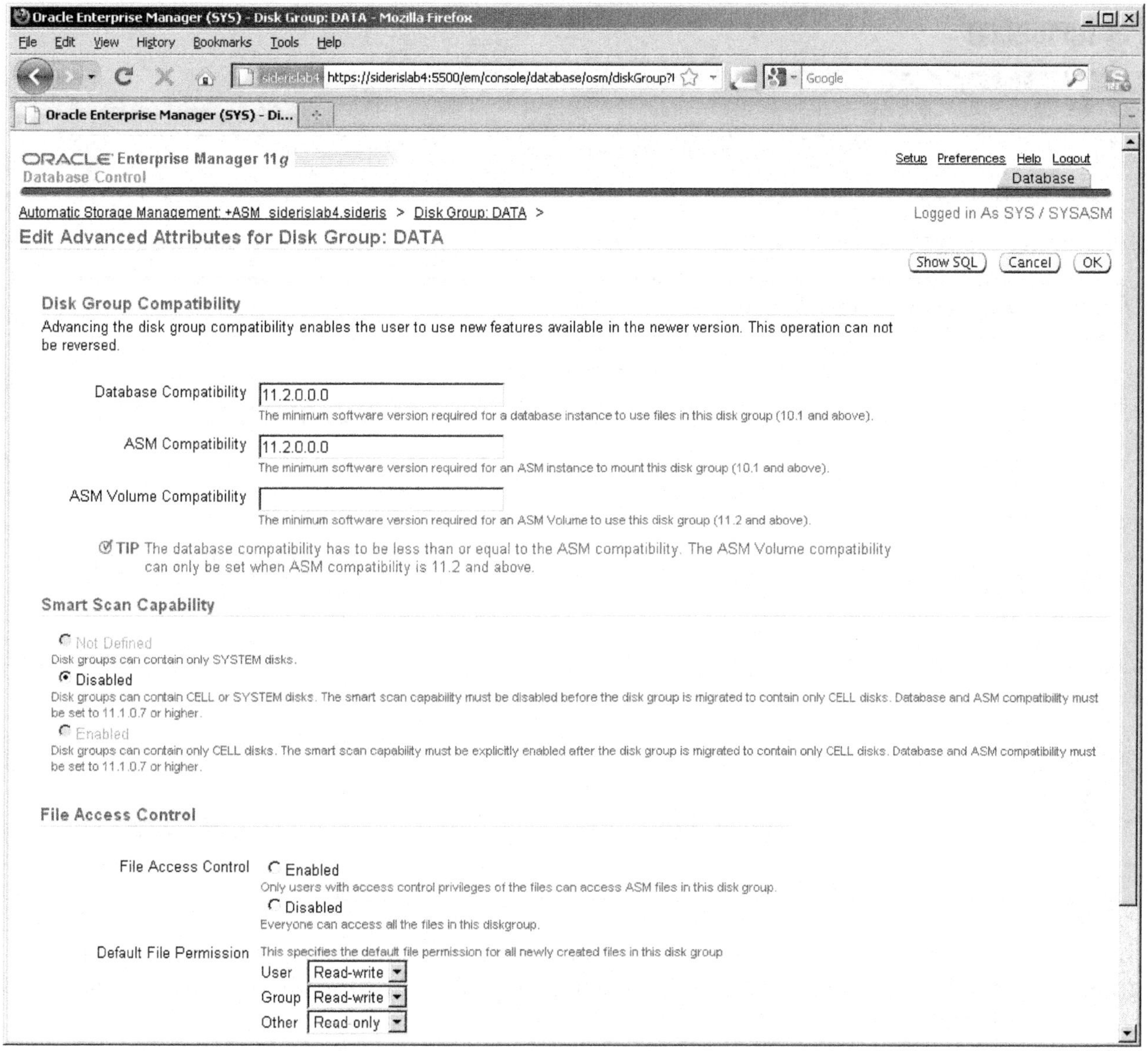

For instance, if one clicked the Edit button, then the disk group compatibility attributes could be modified, or the File Access Control settings could be changed.

Performance

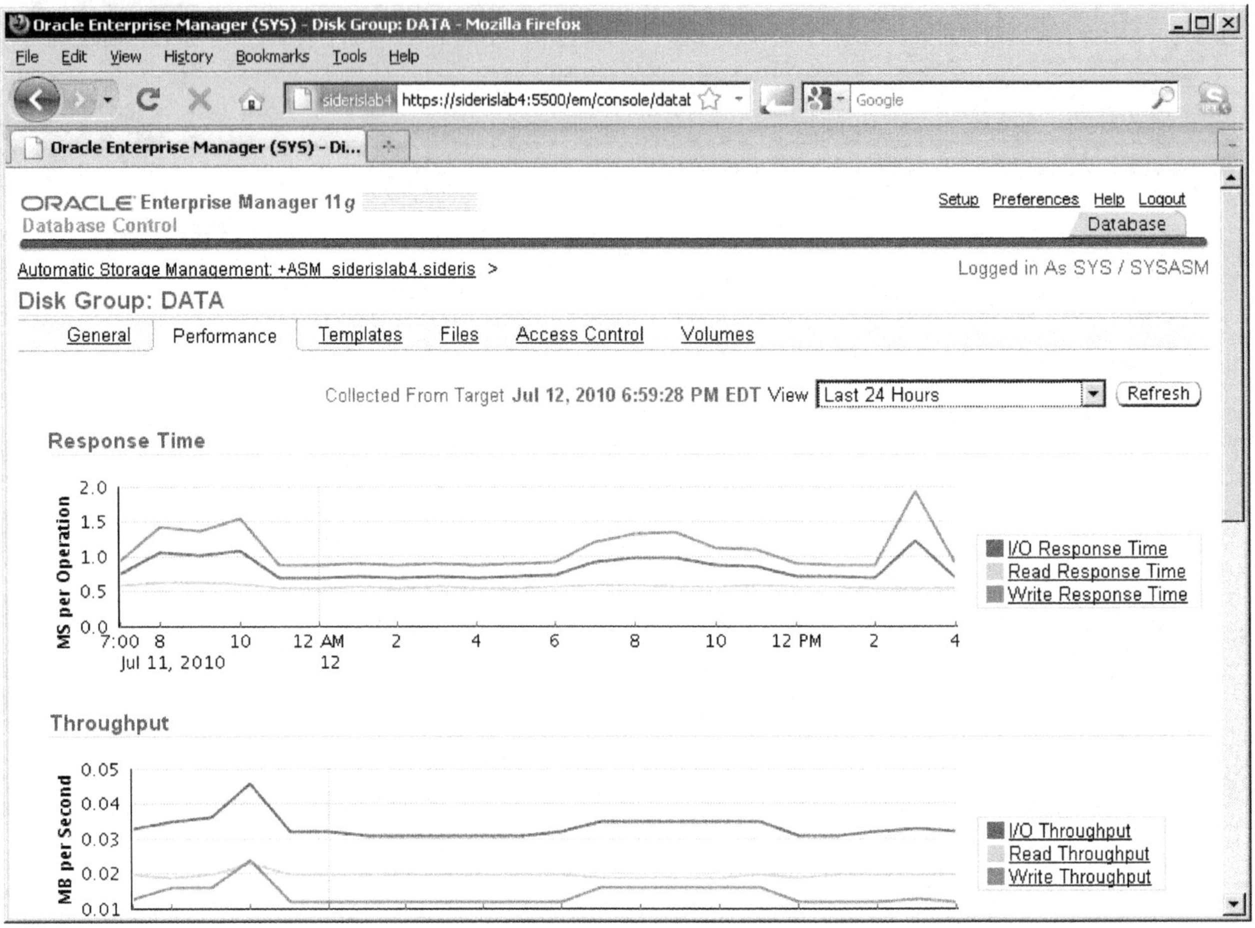

Similar performance metrics discussed earlier for all disk groups are available for individual groups. By modifying the View item one can examine activity historically over the past 24 hours, 7 days, etc.

Templates

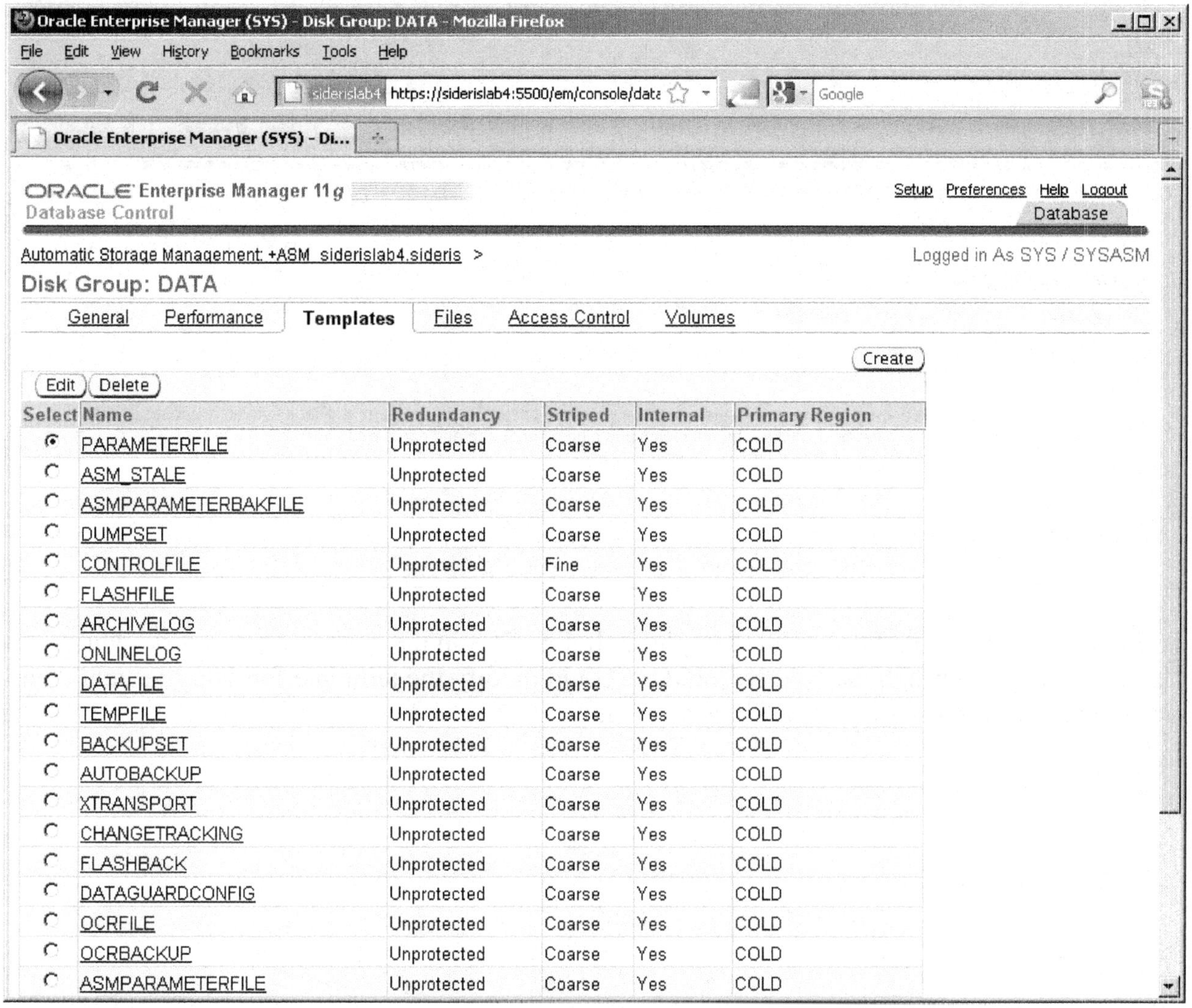

Select	Name	Redundancy	Striped	Internal	Primary Region
●	PARAMETERFILE	Unprotected	Coarse	Yes	COLD
○	ASM_STALE	Unprotected	Coarse	Yes	COLD
○	ASMPARAMETERBAKFILE	Unprotected	Coarse	Yes	COLD
○	DUMPSET	Unprotected	Coarse	Yes	COLD
○	CONTROLFILE	Unprotected	Fine	Yes	COLD
○	FLASHFILE	Unprotected	Coarse	Yes	COLD
○	ARCHIVELOG	Unprotected	Coarse	Yes	COLD
○	ONLINELOG	Unprotected	Coarse	Yes	COLD
○	DATAFILE	Unprotected	Coarse	Yes	COLD
○	TEMPFILE	Unprotected	Coarse	Yes	COLD
○	BACKUPSET	Unprotected	Coarse	Yes	COLD
○	AUTOBACKUP	Unprotected	Coarse	Yes	COLD
○	XTRANSPORT	Unprotected	Coarse	Yes	COLD
○	CHANGETRACKING	Unprotected	Coarse	Yes	COLD
○	FLASHBACK	Unprotected	Coarse	Yes	COLD
○	DATAGUARDCONFIG	Unprotected	Coarse	Yes	COLD
○	OCRFILE	Unprotected	Coarse	Yes	COLD
○	OCRBACKUP	Unprotected	Coarse	Yes	COLD
○	ASMPARAMETERFILE	Unprotected	Coarse	Yes	COLD

From the Templates page one may view the templates currently in effect for the disk group, deleting or editing existing templates or creating new ones.

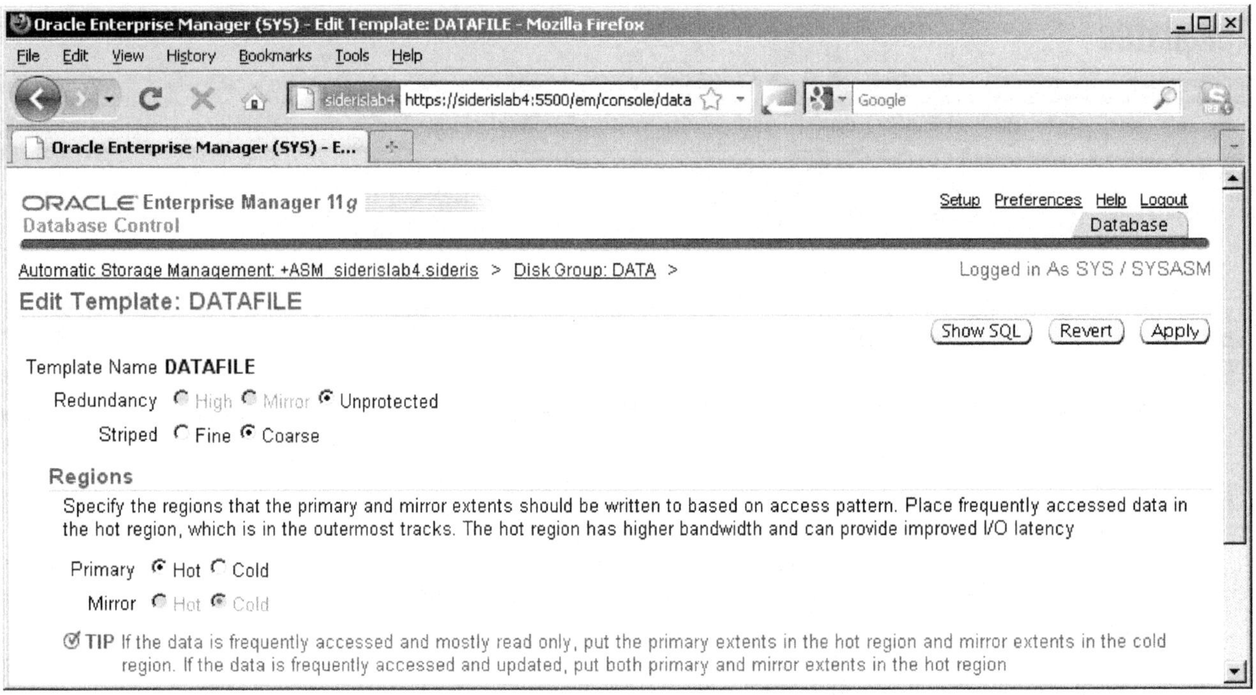

To illustrate, suppose that one wanted to place all data files in the hot region of a disk, while placing other file types in the cold region. One could modify the template for data files and then use that template whenever a data file is created.

Files

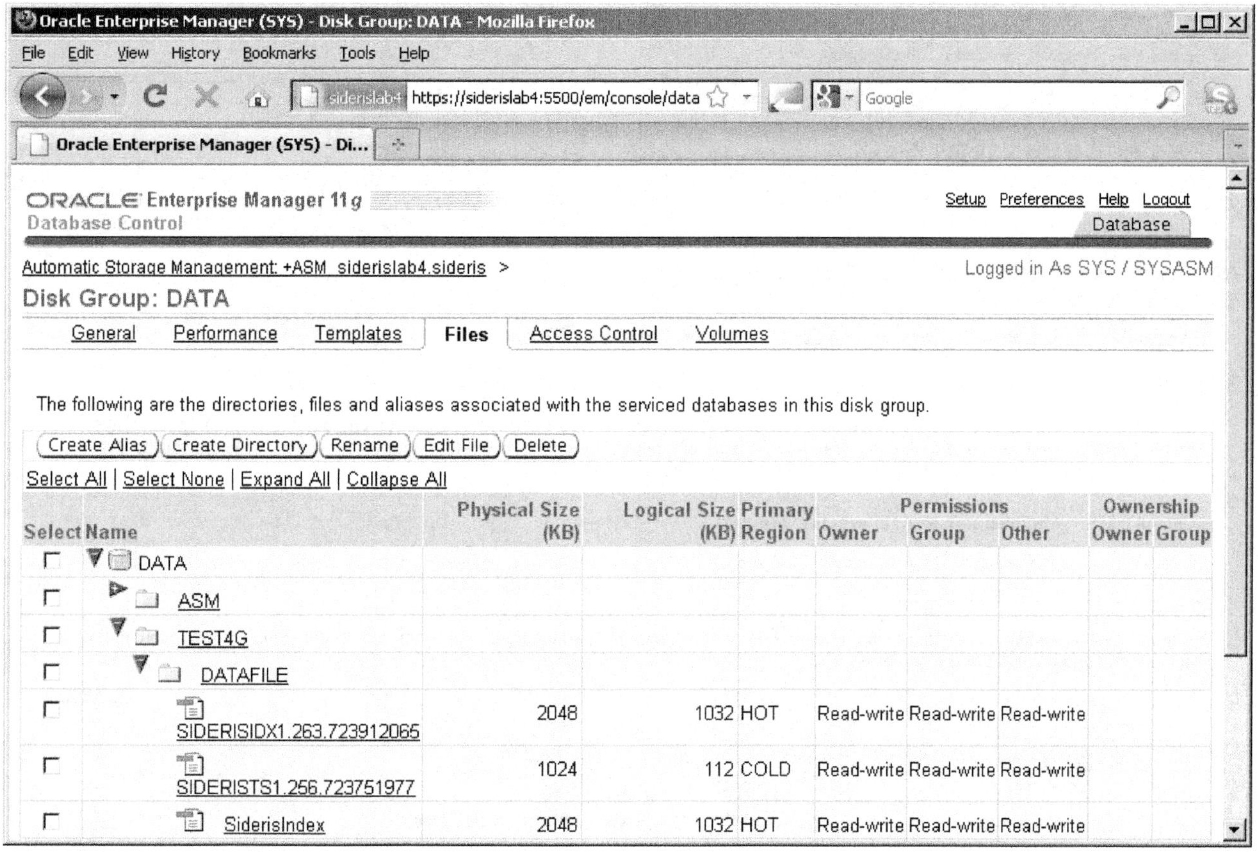

The Files page will list the different file categories or types which can exist within ASM. By expanding a particular node within the hierarchy one can see the individual files for any given type which are stored in the disk group in behalf of a relational database instance. One may continue to drill deeper into the storage hierarchy to obtain further details about the objects.

You can see that in addition to size information, each file indicates its data placement priority and the permissions assigned to SYSDBA users.

Access Control

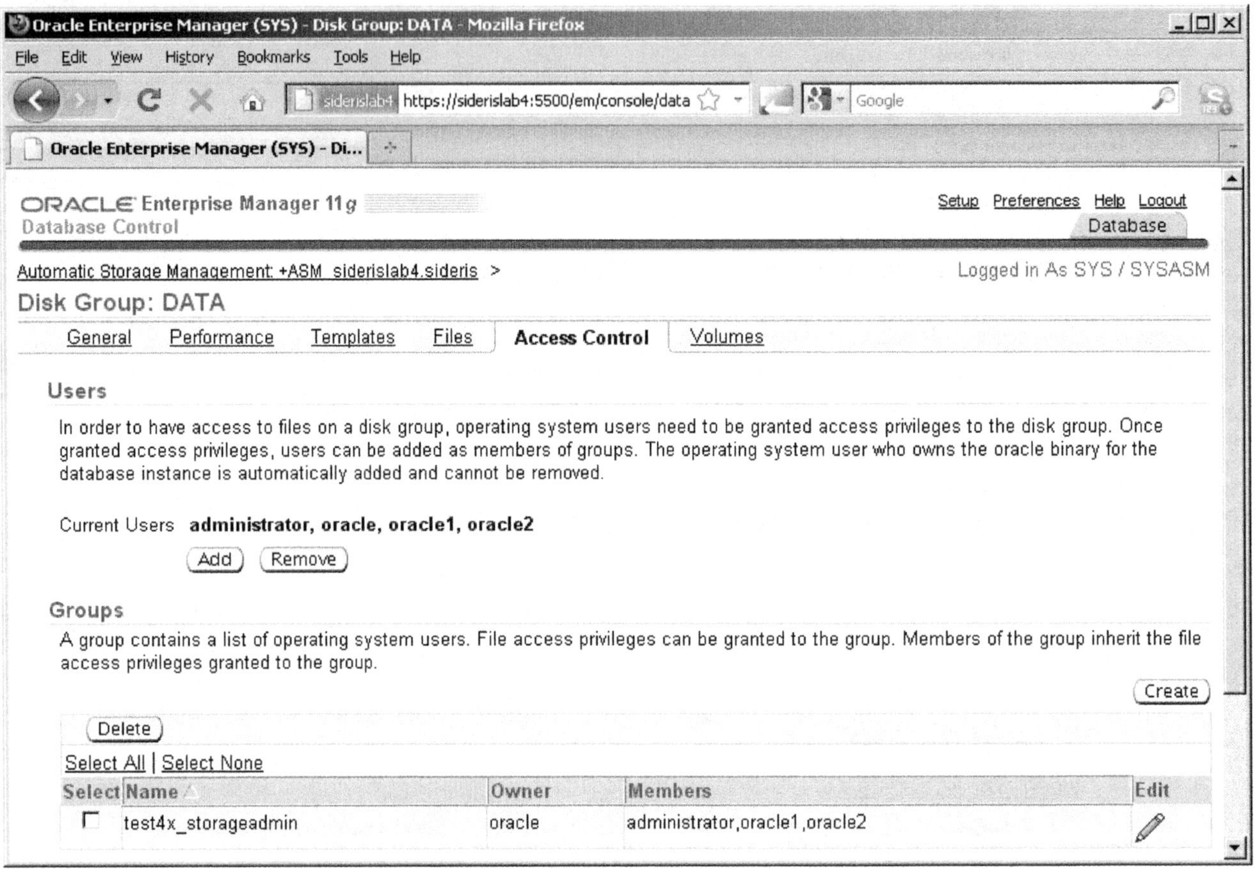

Authorized access control users and user groups associated with the disk group may be managed from this screen. The actual privileges these users will acquire to the disk group is determined by the permission masks associated with the disk group and the individual files.

Managing An Individual Member Disk

The lowest drill-down level within EM is from the Disk Group home page drilling down into the individual member disk pages.

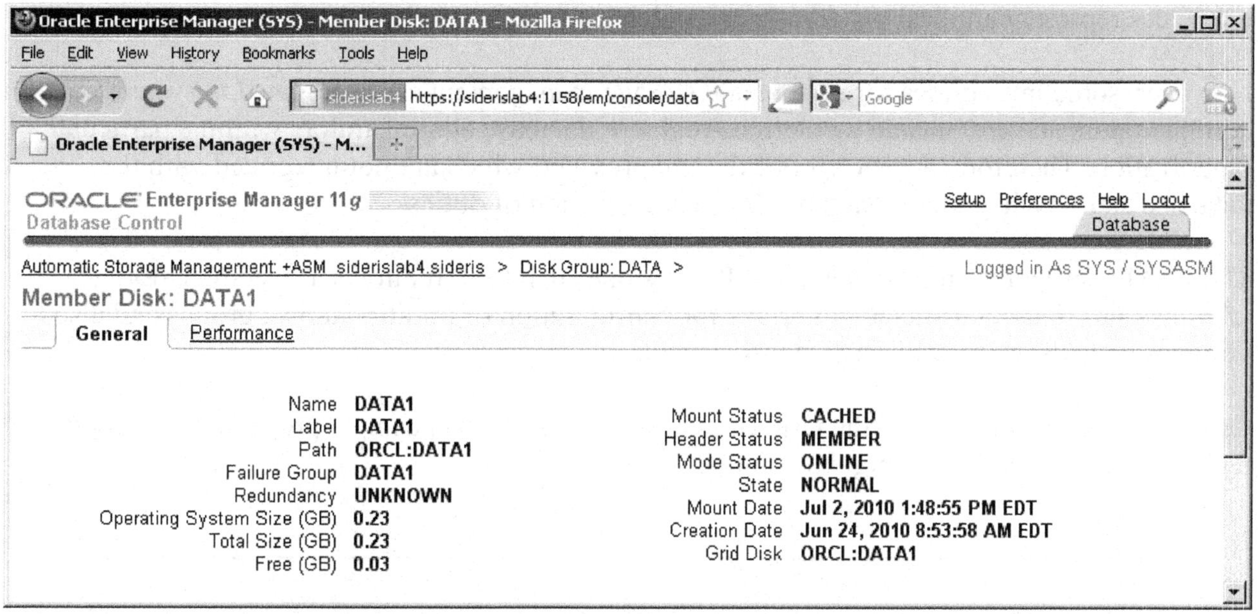

As you can see, in addition to General attributes about the member disk one can use the performance monitors to examine a specific device.

Managing Storage Using ASMCA

The SQL and EM interfaces are the typical working environment for database administrators. When such individuals are also responsible for system and storage management, then these interfaces represent an ideal platform from which to work.

However, sometimes duties for system and storage management are segregated to system administrators and are outside the defined realm of database administrators within a particular organization. Therefore, additional utilities are provided which are not integrated with the database and which are more suitable for such a division of duties.

The ASM Configuration Assistant (ASMCA) is one such tool. It allows a system or storage administrator to use a dedicated interface for configuration of traditional disk groups and also volumes and ASM Cluster File Systems as well.

One launches the utility from the Grid Infrastructure installation using a properly configured terminal session and by issuing the command `asmca`.

Note

This feature is available starting with Oracle 11g R2.

ASMCA Disk Groups

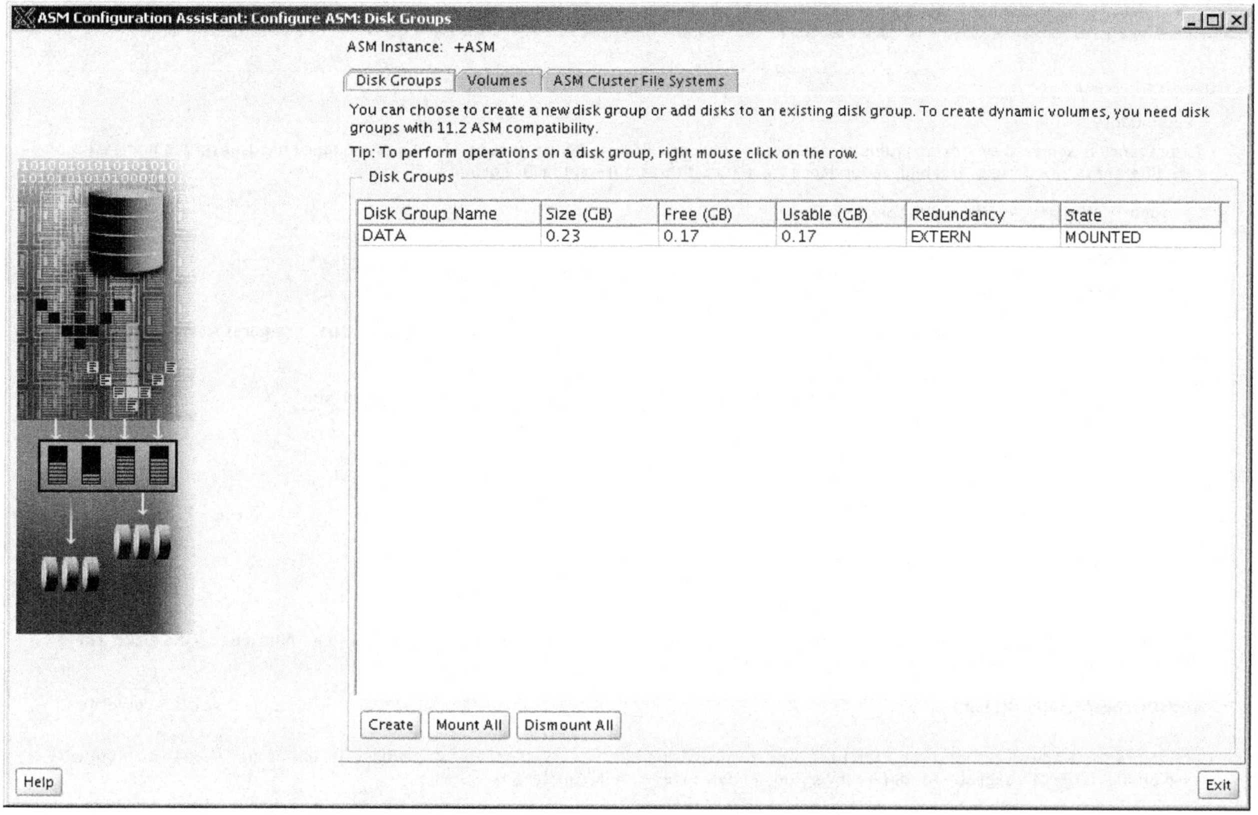

ASMCA presents a Disk Groups page where one may manage disk groups.

- Create – Similar to what was shown earlier in this course, one can discover and create additional disk groups.

- Mount All, Dismount All – once additional disks have been added to the display, these may be mounted and thereby made available to the databases.

Create Disk Group

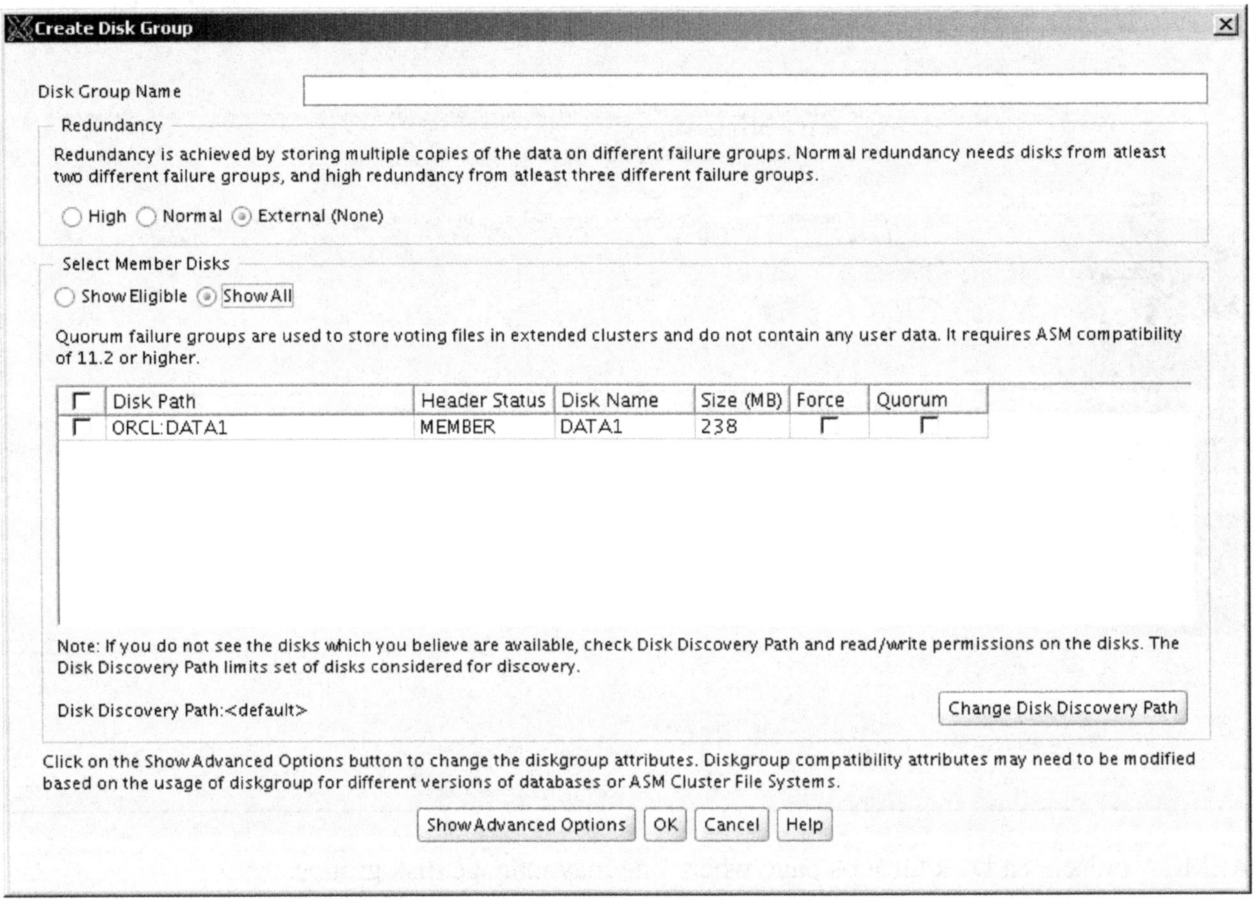

If one clicks on the Create button then the Create Disk Group page is presented, offering similar options as that provided by the Installer when the ASM instance was first created. But from this point one may create additional disk groups from eligible candidate devices.

Show Advanced Options

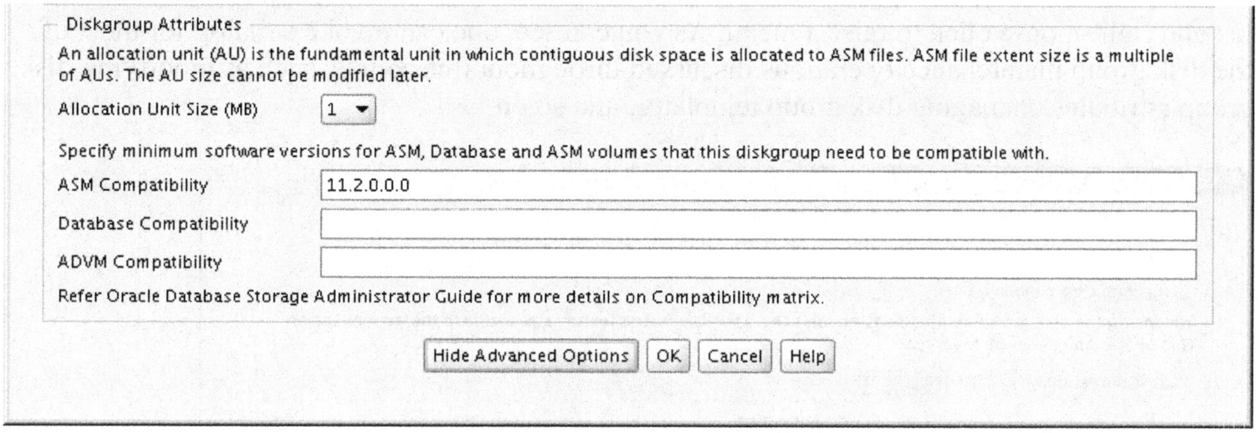

From the Advanced Options portion of the page one can configure the compatibility attributes of the disk group and modify the Allocation Unit size from its initial default of 1 MB.

Manage Existing Disk Groups

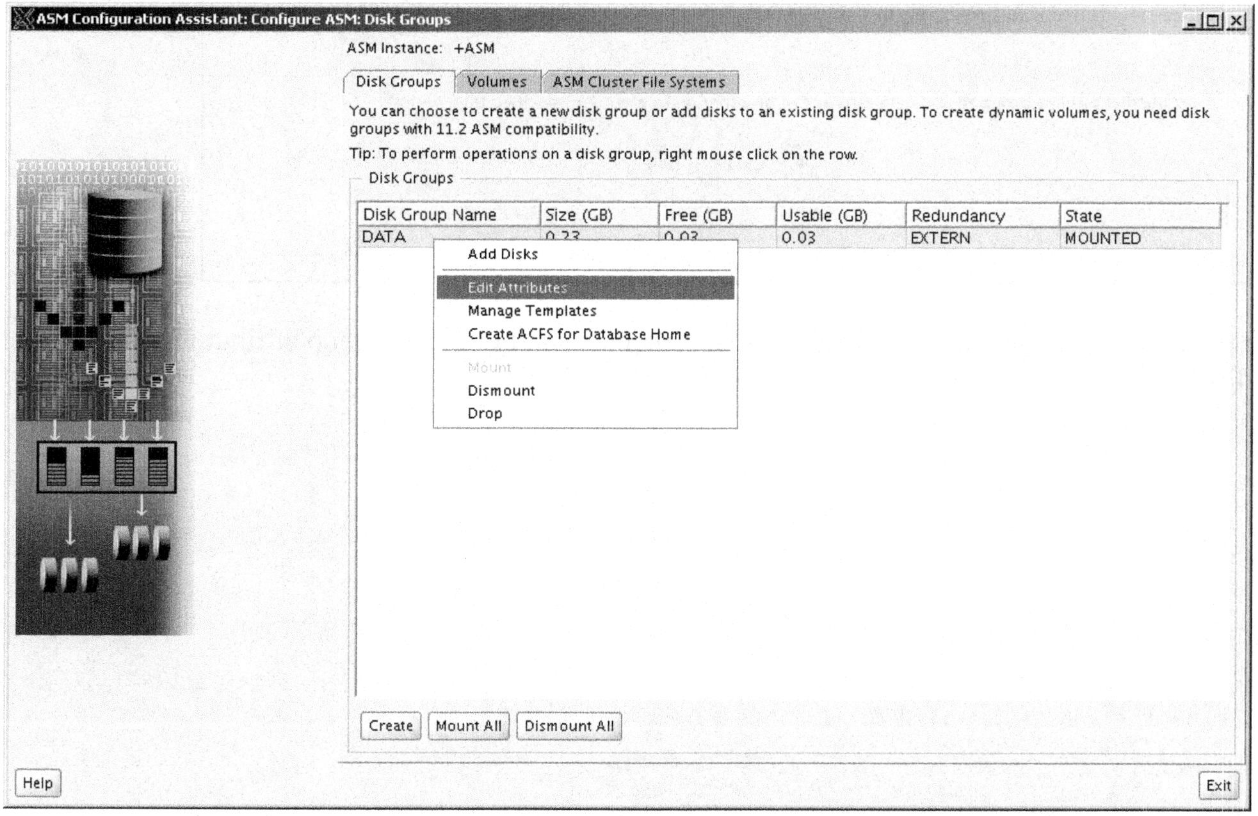

With regard to managing existing disk groups, one can select an individual disk group from the list and right-mouse click to raise a menu. As you can see, one can invoke a dialog for most of the disk group maintenance operations discussed throughout this course, such as modifying disk group attributes, managing disk group templates, and so on.

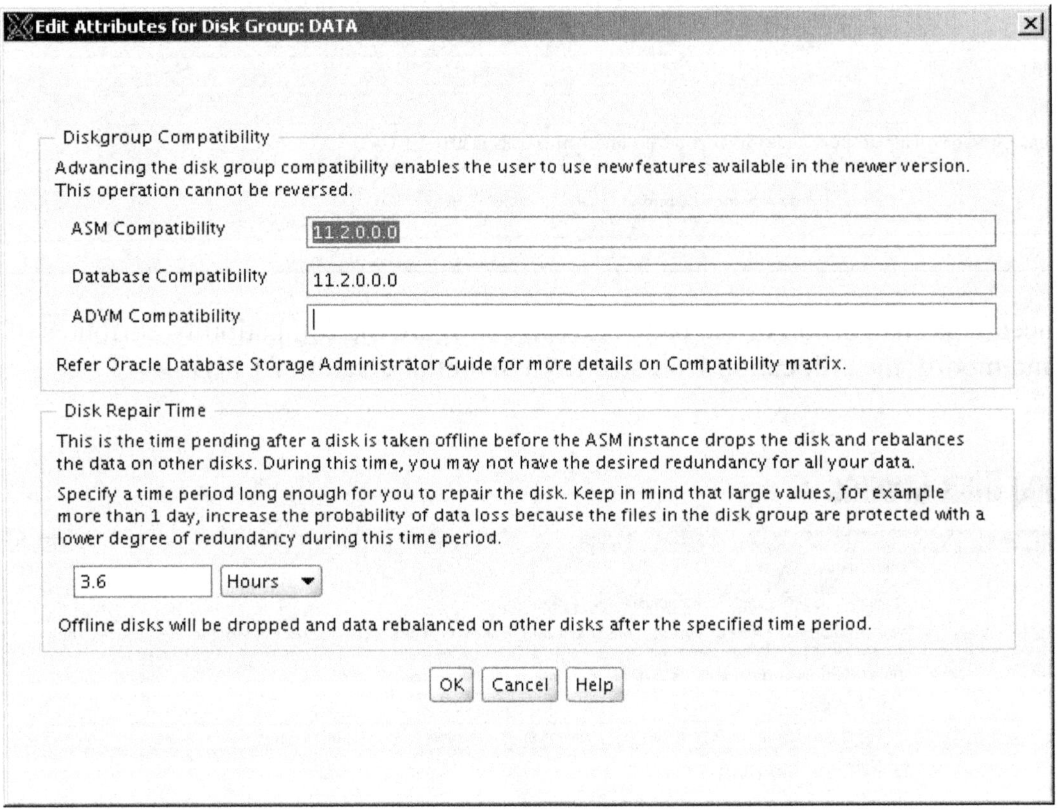

For example, if one chose the Edit Attributes menu item, basic disk group attributes are displayed and may be modified from this screen.

Managing Storage Using ASMCMD

Similar to our discussion of the ASMCA utility, when system administration and storage administration duties are separated from database administration, a more appropriate ASM management interface is required. ASMCMD is a command-line interface to ASM which exists in a form comfortable for UNIX or Linux system administrators. It offers some of the same functions available from SQL, EM and ASMCA. In addition, ASMCMD works at a lower, system level than the other utilities and therefore offers additional options not found elsewhere.

ASMCMD is also unique in that in not only allows management of the disk groups, but also the instance, templates and individual files.

Like all other ASM utilities, one launches ASMCMD from the Grid Infrastructure installation using a properly configured terminal session. The utility is started by issuing the command `asmcmd`.

lsdg

Consider an initial example of a disk group management command within ASMCMD. The List Disk Groups (lsdg) command will list basic metadata for the disk groups. This is similar to what is available from the V$ASM_* views but ASMCMD does not require a connection to the ASM instance or a knowledge of the SQL language.

```
$ asmcmd
ASMCMD> lsdg

State     Type    Rebal  Unbal  Sector  Block       AU  Total_MB  Free_MB
Req_mir_free_MB  Usable_file_MB  Offline_disks  Name

MOUNTED   EXTERN  N      N         512   4096  1048576      1702     1549
0                1549               0  sidDG1/

MOUNTED   EXTERN  N      N         512   4096  1048576      3404      450
0                 450               0  sidDG2/

ASMCMD>
```

md_backup

To cite another example, the md_backup command will create a backup XML file of the metadata for one or more disk groups. This file could be used later as part of a metadata restore operation by means of the md_restore command.

```
ASMCMD> md_backup ASMdgbackup.xml -G DATA

Disk group metadata to be backed up: DATA
Current alias directory path: TEST4X/PARAMETERFILE
Current alias directory path: TEST4G/DATAFILE
Current alias directory path: TEST4X/DATAFILE
Current alias directory path: TEST4G
Current alias directory path: TEST4X
Current alias directory path: ASM/ASMPARAMETERFILE
Current alias directory path: TEST4X/ONLINELOG
Current alias directory path: ASM
Current alias directory path: TEST4X/CONTROLFILE

ASMCMD> exit

[oracle@siderislab4 ~]$ cat ASMdgbackup.xml
@diskgroup_set = (
                   {
                     'ATTRINFO' => {
                                     'TEMPLATE.PARAMETERFILE.MIRROR_REGION' => '0',
                                     'TEMPLATE.TEMPFILE.REDUNDANCY' => '17',
                                     'TEMPLATE.OCRBACKUP.REDUNDANCY' => '17',
                                     'TEMPLATE.TEMPFILE.MIRROR_REGION' => '0',
                                     'TEMPLATE.PARAMETERFILE.REDUNDANCY' => '17'
...

[oracle@siderislab4 ~]$
```

Command Highlights

With this brief explanation in hand, consider some selected excerpts from the many additional instance, disk group and file maintenance commands supported by this utility.

Command	*Category*	*Description*
ls	Disk group	List all mounted disk groups, which is different than the listing of all disk groups shown above with the `lsdg` command.

remap	Disk group	Storage device vendors include *disk-scrubbing* utilities to examine bad spots on the disk platters which are unusable for storage. Once ASM detects such spots it will migrate the extents to clean spots on the platter. The REMAP command will take the initiative to migrate extents from bad spots before these are accessed by ASM and then detected, but will do so as directed by the disk-scrubbing utilities.
cd DiskGroup	Disk group	Change the context to a particular disk group. This context will be used for all subsequent disk group maintenance commands.
iostat	Disk group	Report I/O statistics for read and write operations performed by the disk group since the disk group was mounted.
startup	Instance	Performs a startup of the ASM instance.
shutdown	Instance	Performs a shutdown of the ASM instance.
lstmpl	Template	List templates.
rmtmpl	Template	Remove a template.
lsof	File	List all open files.

Section Review

Remember These Points

- Disk groups may be created after the initial ASM installation.
- Disk group attributes may be managed to control software version compatibility using the compatible.asm and compatible.rdbms attributes.
- Access control privileges allow strict control on what privileges, if any, SYSDBA users will obtain to specific disk groups.
- Intelligent Data Placement allows priority placement of critical files on the storage devices.
- High-capacity 4K sector disks may be efficiently used by appropriately setting the SECTOR_SIZE attribute.
- Templates allow file type standards to be implemented among disk groups.
- The EM and SQL interfaces are ideal storage management work areas for database administrators.
- The ASMCA and ASMCMD interfaces represent alternative interfaces for storage administrators.

Workshop Section
ASM Storage Administration

Exercises

What You Will Do in This Workshop

In this workshop, you will:

- Use the SQL interface to examine metadata for the disk groups.
- Set the compatibility attributes for the disk group to exploit the latest features available.
- Define an access control specification for a disk group and for an existing file.
- Assign a data file to the hot portion of the disk platters.
- Use the EM interface to examine ASM instance and storage attributes.
- Use the ASMCA and ASMCMD interfaces to examine disk group attributes.

STORAGE ADMINISTRATION-1

❑ Configure a terminal session with access to the ASM instance and launch SQL*Plus. Using this interface examine basic metadata for the storage structures, as outlined here:

- Starting from the lowest level, examine basic metadata for individual disks which are currently online.
- Moving up the storage hierarchy, examine disk group attributes such as AU size.

STORAGE ADMINISTRATION-2

❑ Ensure that you will be able to use the latest features of ASM in the disk group. Also, advance the compatibility setting for database instances which will use the disk group. Bear in mind that you will not be able to downgrade these settings once they are made.

STORAGE ADMINISTRATION-3

❑ Implement access control for the disk group and set the privileges as follows:

- Read-write for the owner
- Read-write for the user group

- No privileges for other users

STORAGE ADMINISTRATION-4

❑ Since the access control privileges assigned to the disk group in the previous exercise will only apply to newly created files, select the data file within the disk group and specify the same access control privileges for the file.

STORAGE ADMINISTRATION-5

❑ Imagine that this same data file is a high priority and high access storage object. Specify its placement on the disk platters to be the optimum or hot track area.

STORAGE ADMINISTRATION-6

❑ Launch a browser and make a SYSDBA connection to the database instance. Then, from the database home page, drill-down through the ASM storage hierarchy by following these basic steps:

1. Click on the ASM instance link to view the ASM home page
2. Click on the Disk Groups link to view the Disk Groups listing.
3. Click on the Name link to drill-down into a specific disk group.
4. Click on the Disk link to drill-down to an individual member disk device.

Take the time to peruse each of the screens available at each level of the storage hierarchy. These will provide a good visualization of the concepts and operations discussed in the lecture section and throughout this course.

STORAGE ADMINISTRATION-7

❑ To obtain at least some basic familiarity with the other ASM management interfaces, access the attributes for a disk group using the ASMCA utility.

STORAGE ADMINISTRATION-8

❑ Similarly, to become familiar with the system administrator interface to ASM, access the attributes for a disk group using the ASMCMD utility.

Solutions

STORAGE ADMINISTRATION-1

```
SQL> SELECT group_number, disk_number, mount_status, header_status,
            mode_status, state, redundancy, name, failgroup, path
     FROM v$asm_disk
     WHERE mode_status = 'ONLINE';

GROUP_NUMBER DISK_NUMBER MOUNT_S HEADER_STATU MODE_ST STATE  REDUNDA NAME   FAILGROUP  PATH
------------ ----------- ------- ------------ ------- ------ ------- ------ ---------- ----------
           1           0 CACHED  MEMBER       ONLINE  NORMAL UNKNOWN DATA1  DATA1      ORCL:DATA1
...
```

```
SQL> SELECT name, allocation_unit_size, state, type, offline_disks
     FROM v$asm_diskgroup;

NAME       ALLOCATION_UNIT_SIZE STATE       TYPE   OFFLINE_DISKS
---------- -------------------- ----------- ------ -------------
DATA                    1048576 MOUNTED     EXTERN             0
...
```

STORAGE ADMINISTRATION-2

```
SQL> ALTER DISKGROUP data
       SET ATTRIBUTE 'compatible.asm' = '11.2';
Diskgroup altered.
```

```
SQL> ALTER DISKGROUP data
       SET ATTRIBUTE 'compatible.rdbms' = '11.2';
Diskgroup altered.
```

STORAGE ADMINISTRATION-3

```
SQL> ALTER DISKGROUP data
        SET ATTRIBUTE 'access_control.enabled' = 'true';
Diskgroup altered.

SQL> ALTER DISKGROUP data
        SET ATTRIBUTE 'access_control.umask' = '002';
Diskgroup altered.
```

STORAGE ADMINISTRATION-4

```
SQL> ALTER DISKGROUP data
        SET PERMISSION OWNER=Read write, GROUP=Read write, OTHER=Read only
        FOR FILE '+DATA/TEST4G/DATAFILE/SIDERISTS1.256.723751977';
Diskgroup altered.
```

STORAGE ADMINISTRATION-5

```
SQL> ALTER DISKGROUP data
       MODIFY FILE
       '+DATA/test4g/datafile/sideristsl.256.723751977'
       ATTRIBUTE (HOT);
Diskgroup altered.
```

STORAGE ADMINISTRATION-6

No specific exercise solution required. Please follow the exercise instructions.

STORAGE ADMINISTRATION-7

From a terminal session properly configured for ASM access, perform these steps:

1. Enter the command `asmca`.
2. Click on the Disk Groups tab.
3. Click on an individual disk group and then click the right-mouse button.
4. Select the Edit Attributes menu item.

Exit the utility when you have finished.

STORAGE ADMINISTRATION-8

From a terminal session perform these steps:

1. Enter the command `asmcmd`.
2. Enter the command `lsdg` to list the disk groups and their attributes.

References

1. Discussion on disk drive mechanisms – see Microsoft Technet computer professionals reference.

2. Discussion on high-capacity 4K sector disk drives – see Western Digital Corporation web site and product publications.